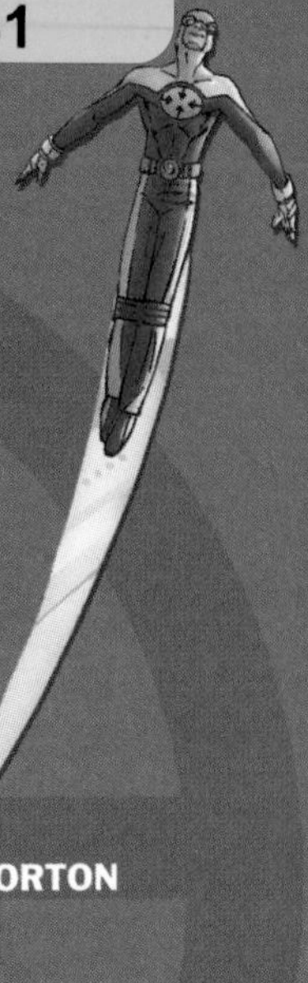

WRITER: **SEAN MCKEEVER**
PENCILS: **MIKE NORTON**
INKS: **JONATHAN GLAPION**
COLORS: **GURU EFX**
LETTERS: **VIRTUAL CALLIGRAPHY'S**
CORY PETIT WITH RUS WOOTON
ASSISTANT EDITOR: **NATHAN COSBY**
EDITOR: **MACKENZIE CADENHEAD**
CONSULTING EDITOR: **MARK PANICCIA**

GRAVITY CREATED BY **SEAN MCKEEVER & MIKE NORTON**

COLLECTION EDITOR: **JENNIFER GRÜNWALD**
ASSISTANT EDITOR: **MICHAEL SHORT**
SENIOR EDITOR, SPECIAL PROJECTS: **JEFF YOUNGQUIST**
DIRECTOR OF SALES: **DAVID GABRIEL**
BOOK DESIGNER: **JHONSON ETENG**
CREATIVE DIRECTOR: **TOM MARVELLI**

EDITOR IN CHIEF: **JOE QUESADA**
PUBLISHER: **DAN BUCKLEY**

GRAVITY
BIG-CITY SUPER HERO

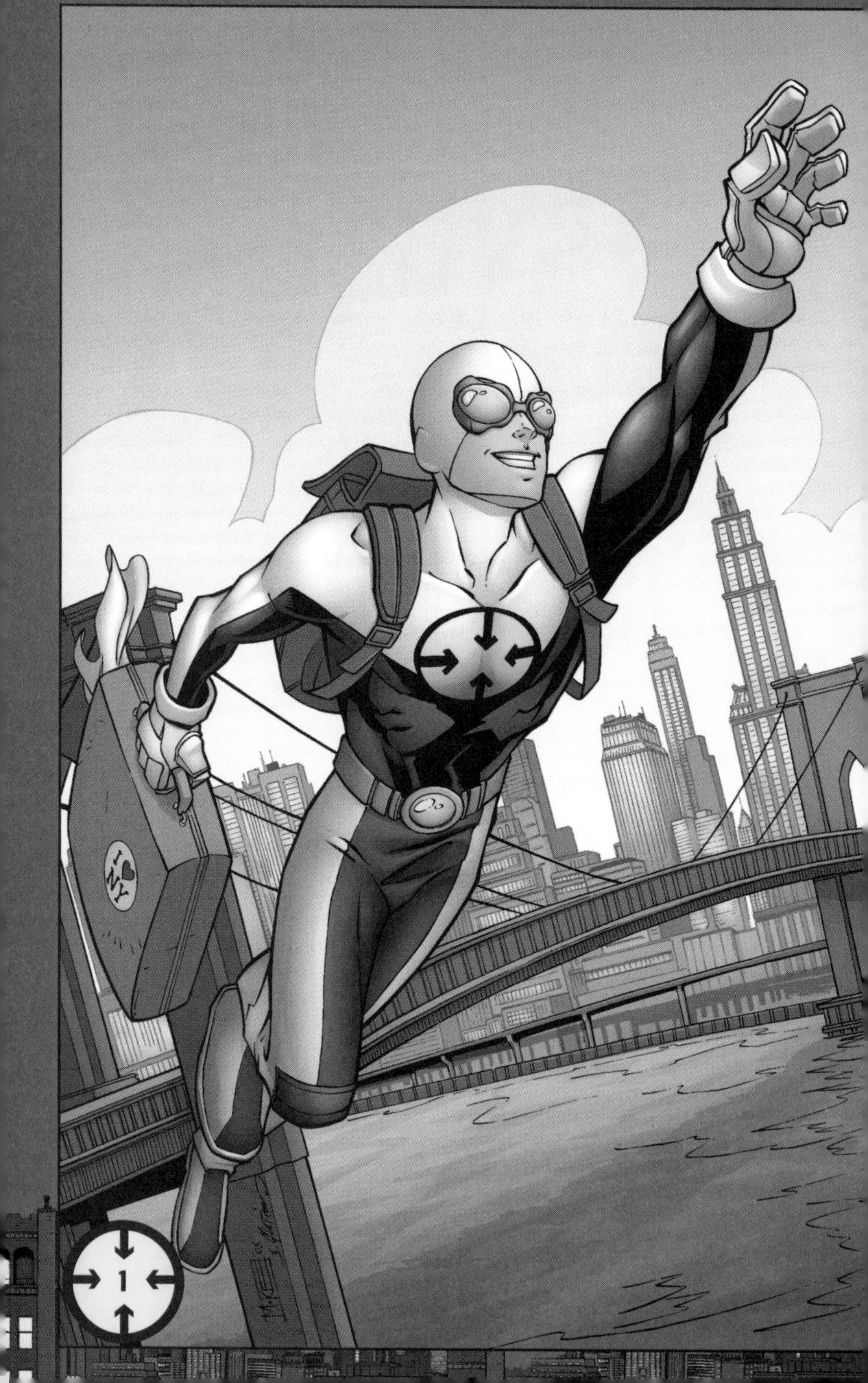
I ♥ NY
1

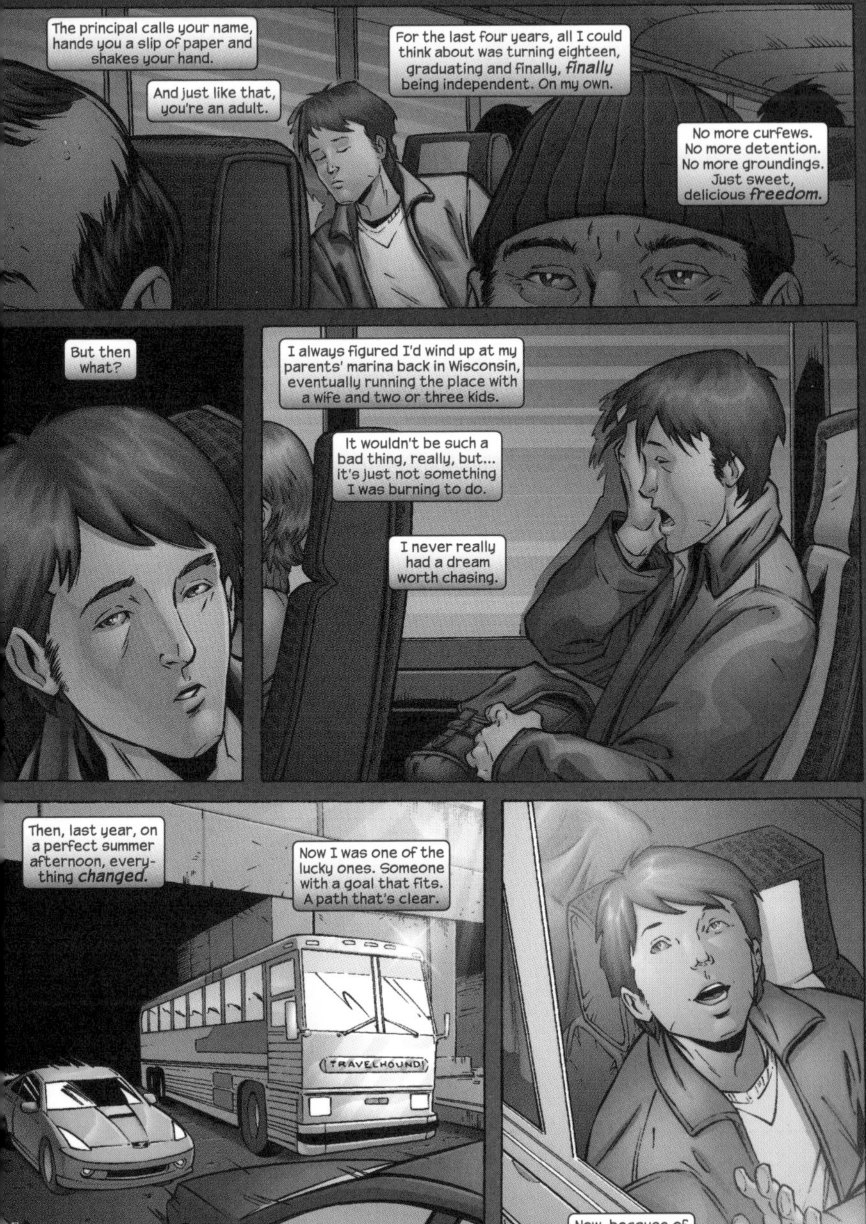
The principal calls your name, hands you a slip of paper and shakes your hand.
And just like that, you're an adult.
For the last four years, all I could think about was turning eighteen, graduating and finally, *finally* being independent. On my own.
No more curfews. No more detention. No more groundings. Just sweet, delicious *freedom.*
But then what?
I always figured I'd wind up at my parents' marina back in Wisconsin, eventually running the place with a wife and two or three kids.
It wouldn't be such a bad thing, really, but... it's just not something I was burning to do.
I never really had a dream worth chasing.
Then, last year, on a perfect summer afternoon, every-thing *changed.*
Now I was one of the lucky ones. Someone with a goal that fits. A path that's clear.
TRAVELHOUND
Now, because of The Accident...

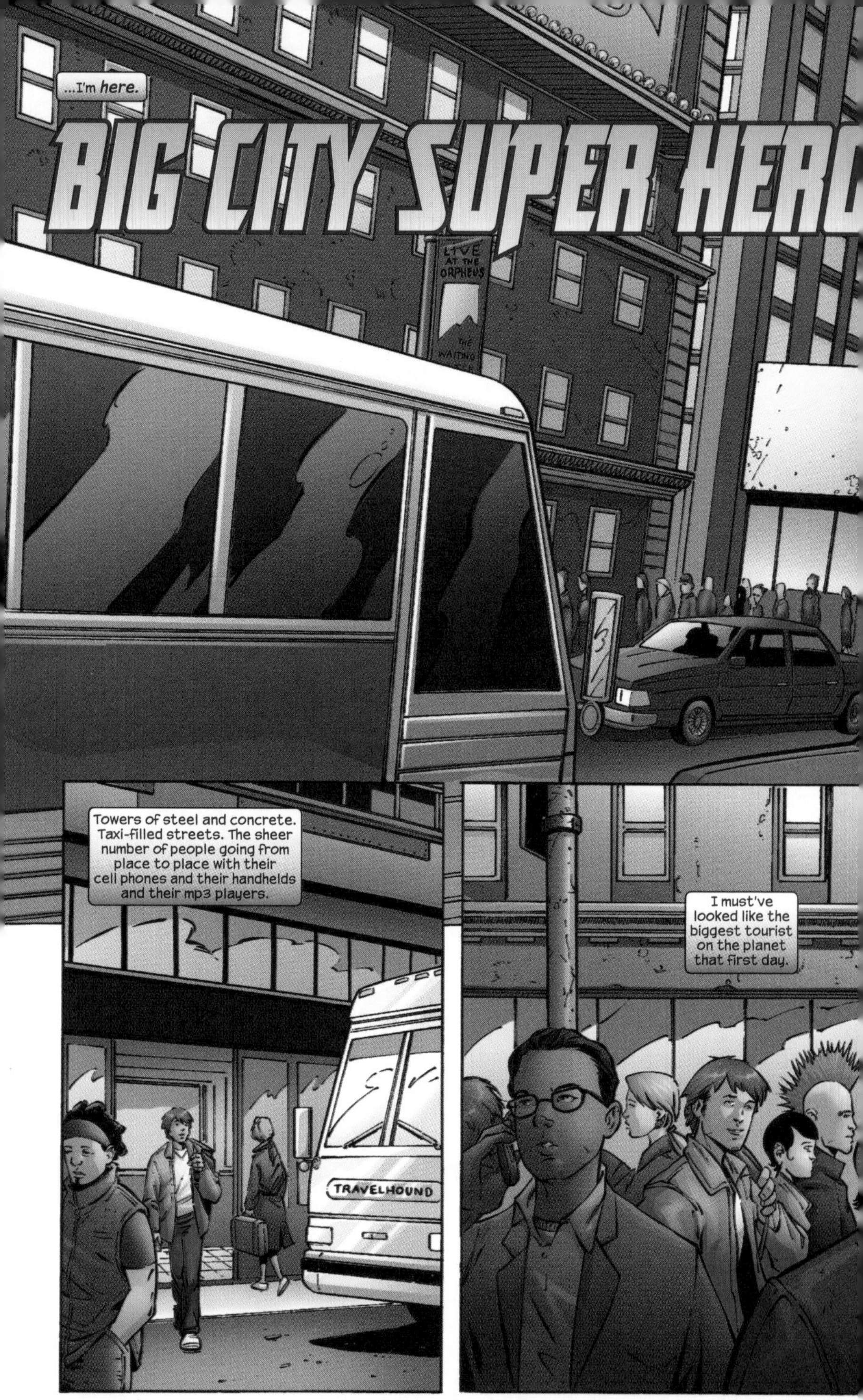
...I'm here.
BIG CITY SUPER HERO
LIVE AT THE ORPHEUS
THE WAITING
Towers of steel and concrete. Taxi-filled streets. The sheer number of people going from place to place with their cell phones and their handhelds and their mp3 players.
TRAVELHOUND
I must've looked like the biggest tourist on the planet that first day.

BLOWOUT
ALE CHEAP!
CHEAP!
CHEAP!

ACCESSORIES or Stock

IT AL CAMERA

EAKER
HEAP!

The rural Wisconsin
boy with his mouth
gaping. Eyes wide.

THE
PRODUCERS
the new
BROOK
musical

CUPC
JOE!

Witnessing things
he never *imagined*
he'd ever see.

HOT

SODA
CHIPS

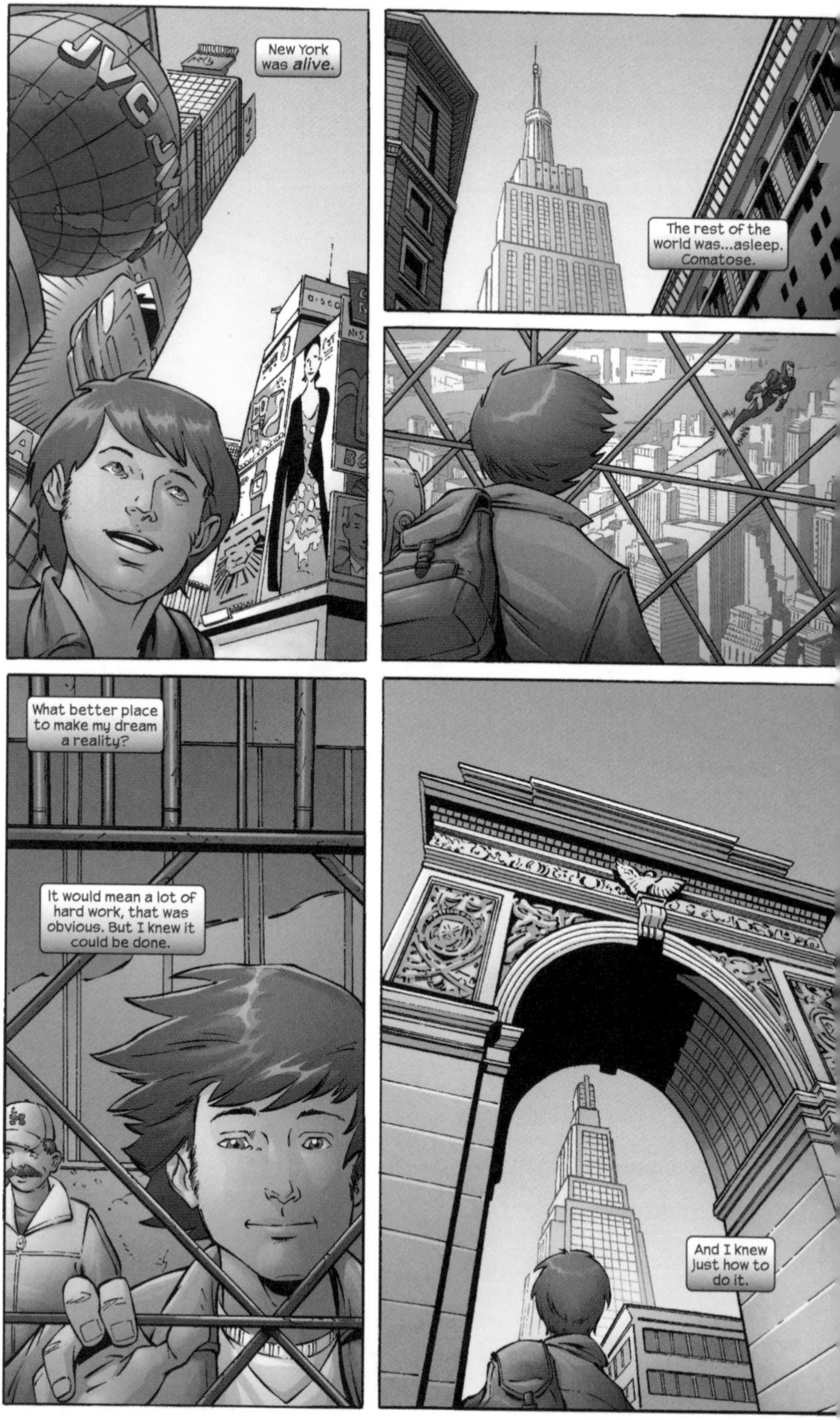
New York was *alive*.
JVC
The rest of the world was...asleep. Comatose.
What better place to make my dream a reality?
It would mean a lot of hard work, that was obvious. But I knew it could be done.
And I knew just how to do it.

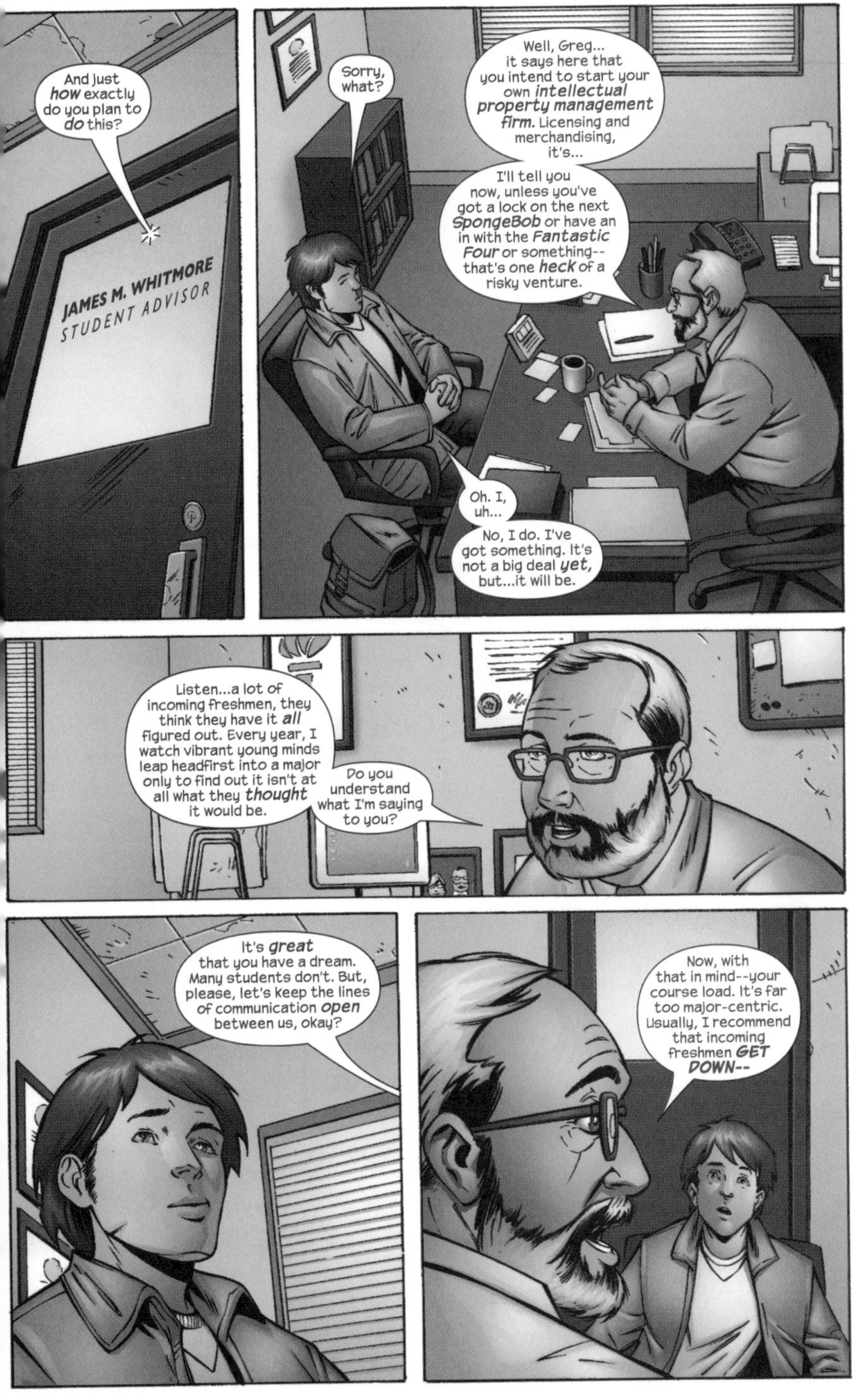

And just *how* exactly do you plan to *do* this?
JAMES M. WHITMORE
STUDENT ADVISOR
Sorry, what?
Well, Greg... it says here that you intend to start your own *intellectual property management firm.* Licensing and merchandising, it's...
I'll tell you now, unless you've got a lock on the next *SpongeBob* or have an in with the *Fantastic Four* or something--that's one *heck* of a risky venture.
Oh. I, uh...
No, I do. I've got something. It's not a big deal *yet,* but...it will be.
Listen...a lot of incoming freshmen, they think they have it *all* figured out. Every year, I watch vibrant young minds leap headfirst into a major only to find out it isn't at all what they *thought* it would be.
Do you understand what I'm saying to you?
It's *great* that you have a dream. Many students don't. But, please, let's keep the lines of communication *open* between us, okay?
Now, with that in mind--your course load. It's far too major-centric. Usually, I recommend that incoming freshmen *GET DOWN--*

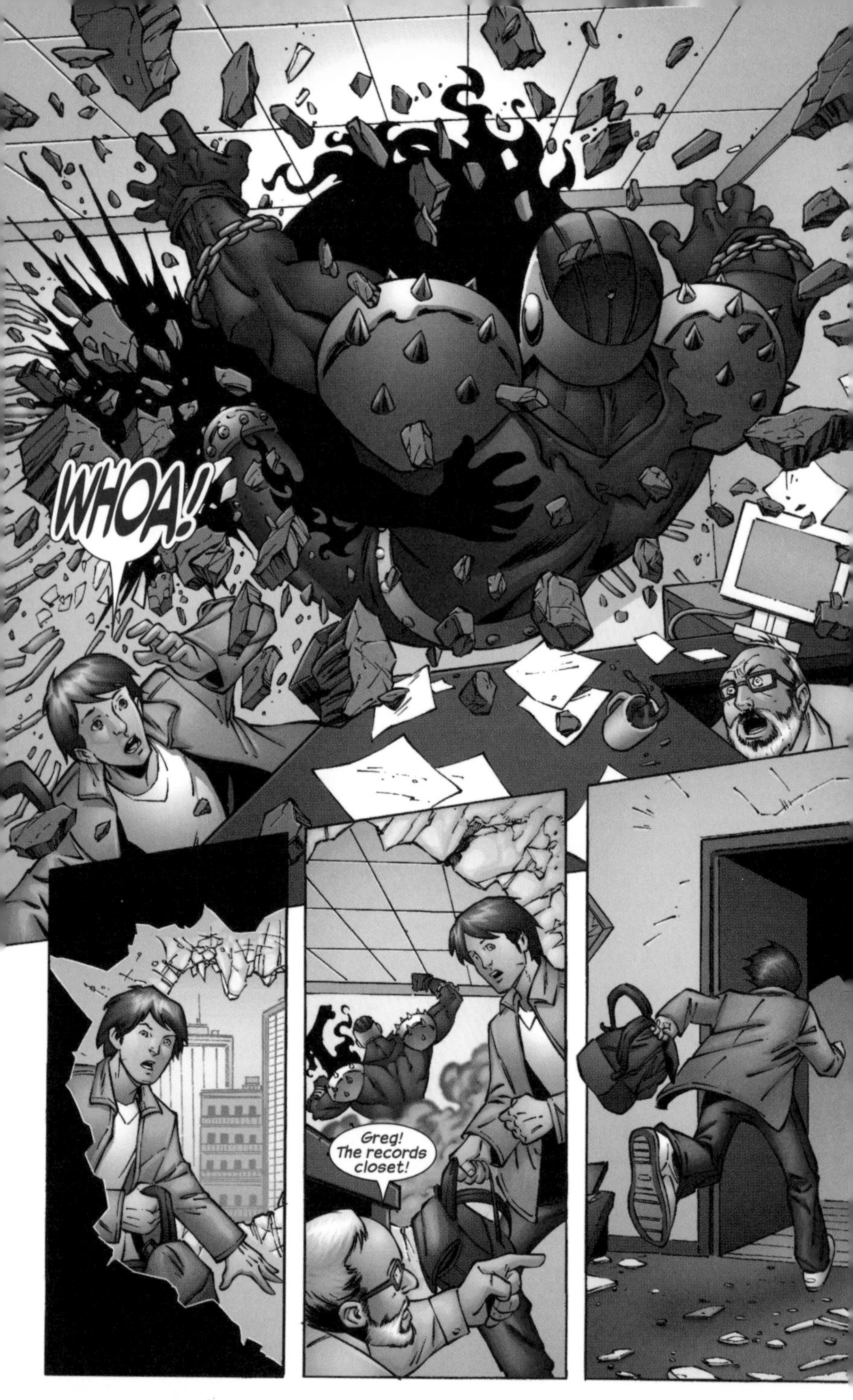
WHOA!
Greg! The records closet!

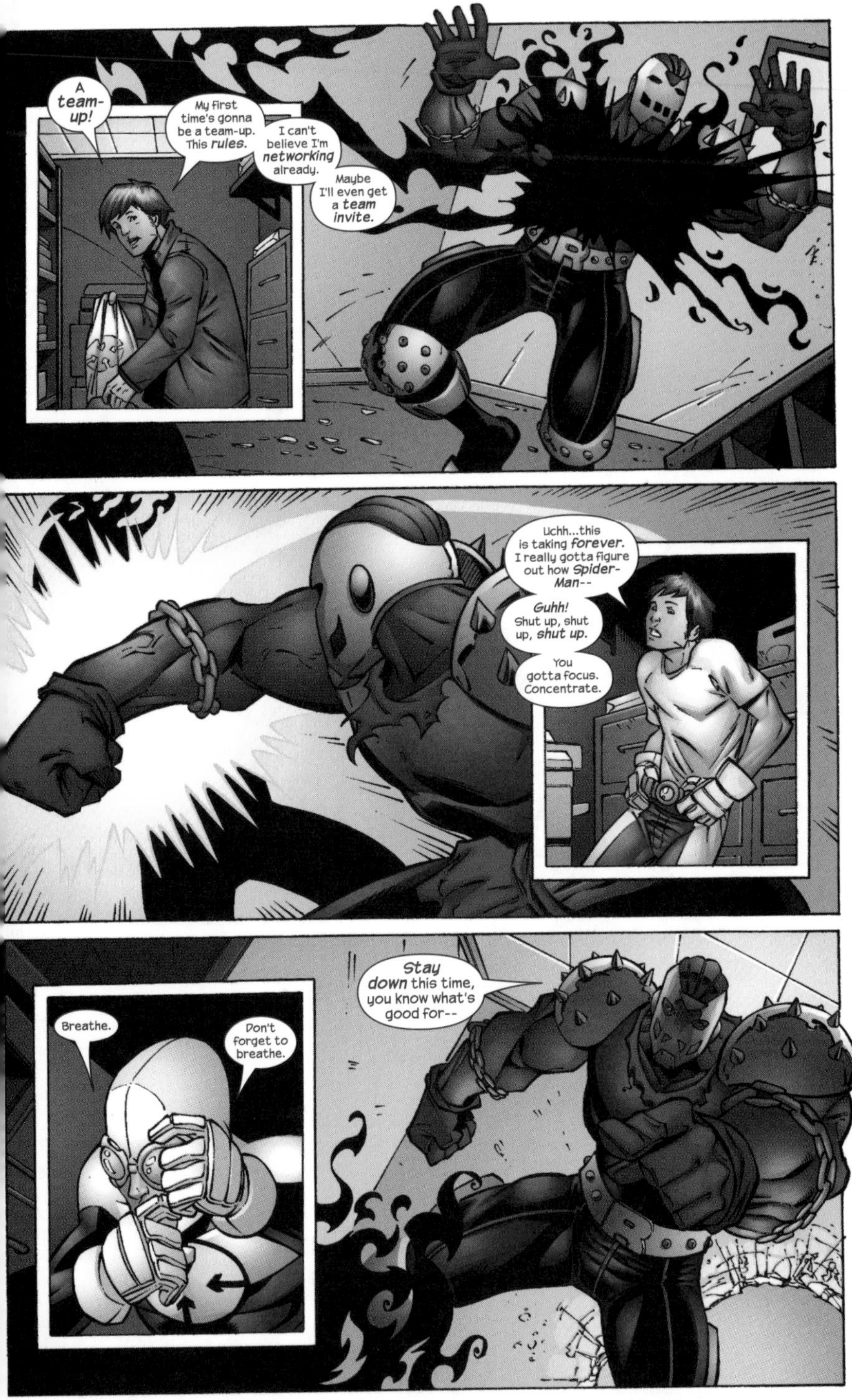

A *team-up!*
My first time's gonna be a team-up. This *rules.*
I can't believe I'm *networking* already.
Maybe I'll even get a *team invite.*
Uchh...this is taking *forever.* I really gotta figure out how *Spider-Man--*
Guhh! Shut up, shut up, *shut up.*
You gotta focus. Concentrate.
Breathe.
Don't forget to breathe.
Stay down this time, you know what's good for--

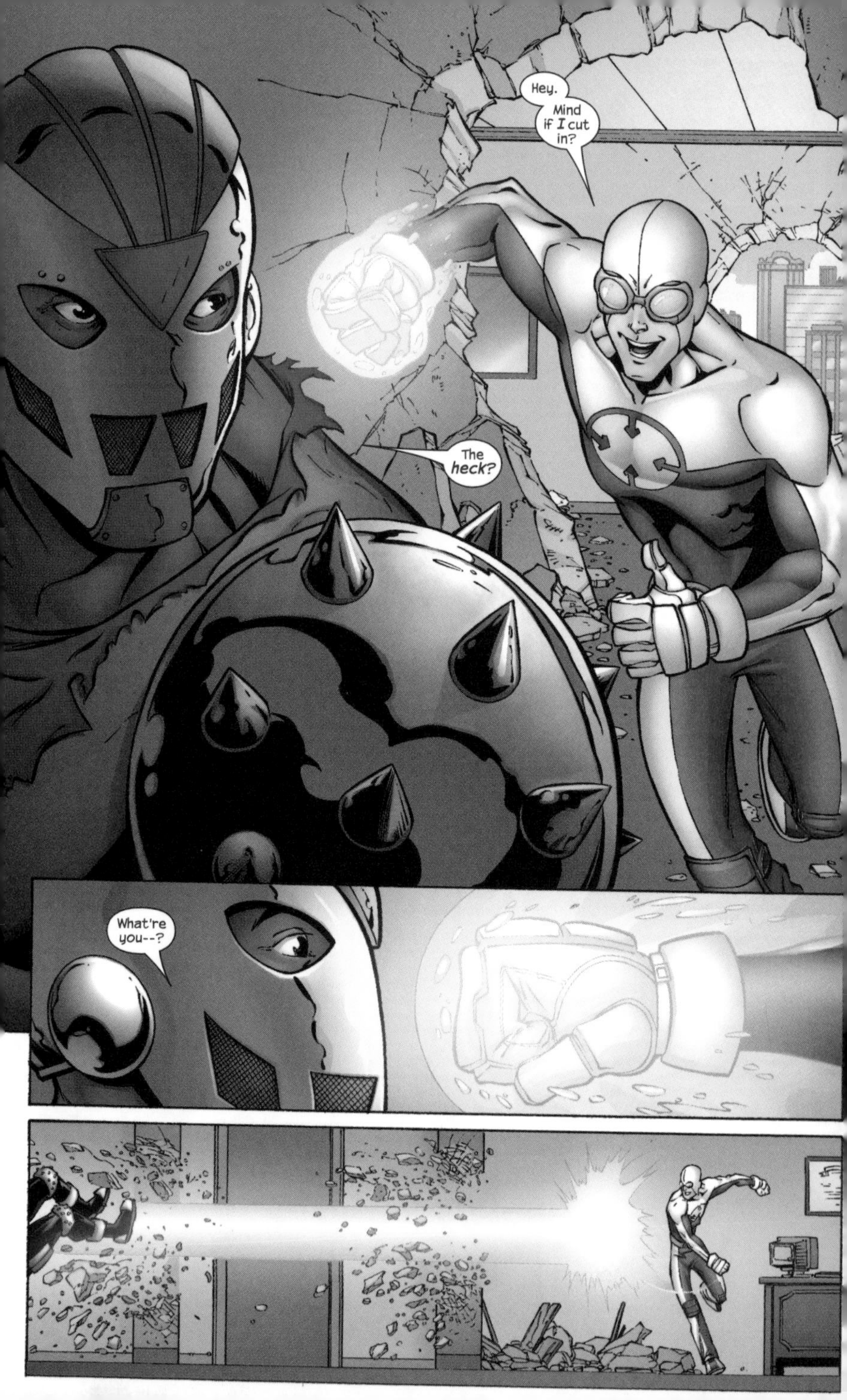
Hey.
Mind if I cut in?
The heck?
What're you--?

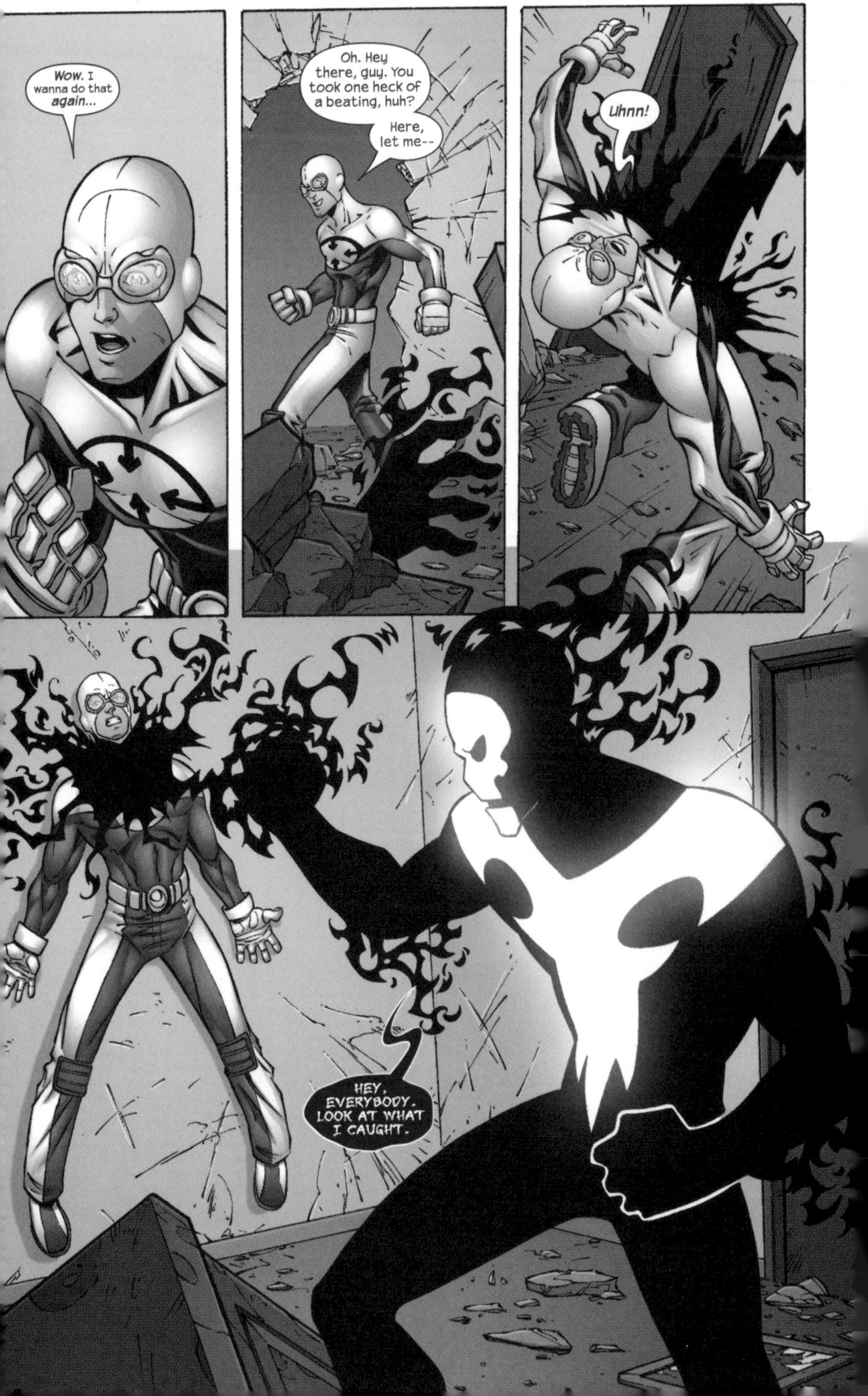
Wow. I wanna do that again...
Oh. Hey there, guy. You took one heck of a beating, huh?
Here, let me--
Uhnn!
HEY, EVERYBODY. LOOK AT WHAT I CAUGHT.

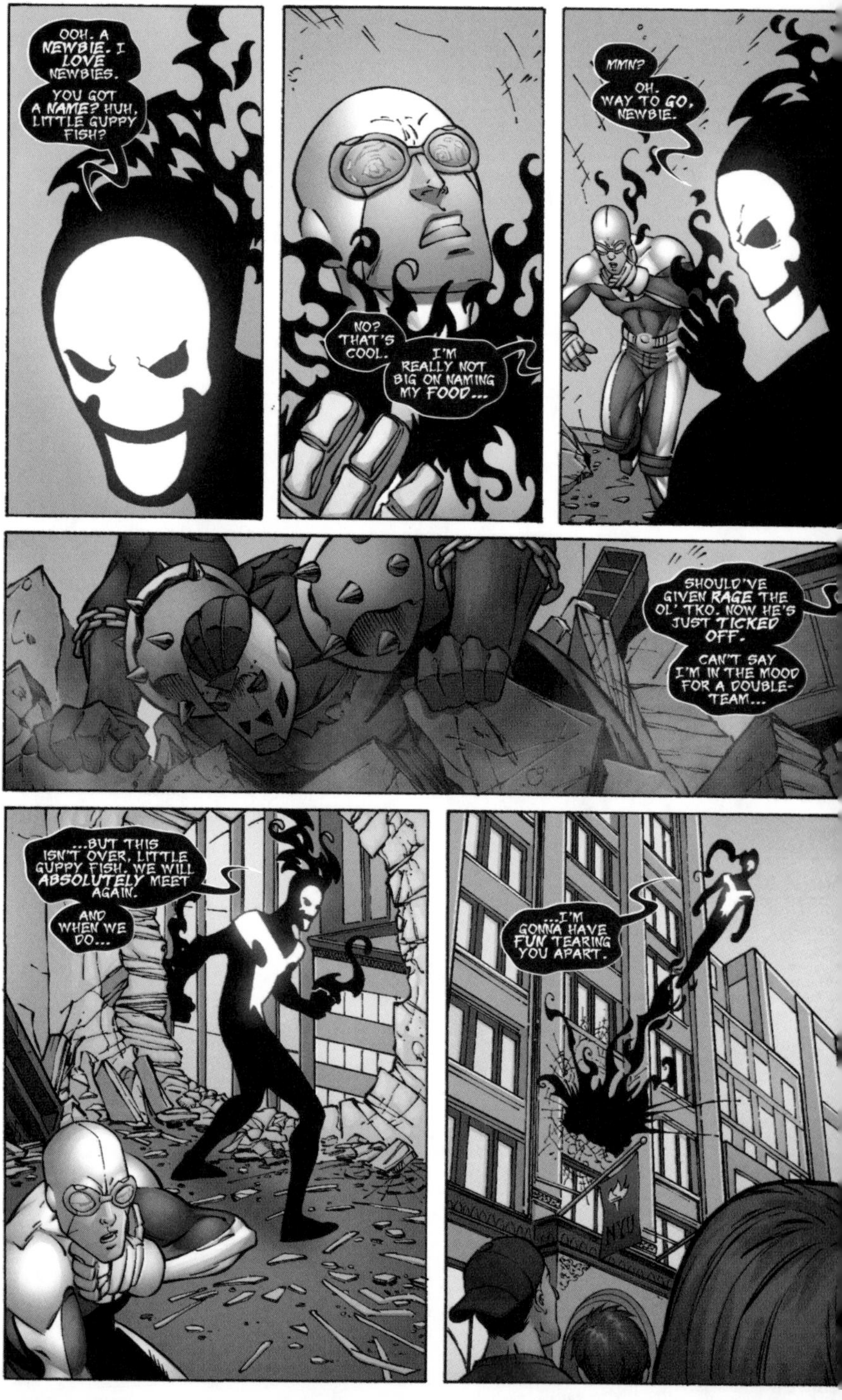
OOH. A NEWBIE. I LOVE NEWBIES.
YOU GOT A NAME? HUH, LITTLE GUPPY FISH?
NO? THAT'S COOL.
I'M REALLY NOT BIG ON NAMING MY FOOD...
MMN?
OH. WAY TO GO, NEWBIE.
SHOULD'VE GIVEN RAGE THE OL' TKO. NOW HE'S JUST TICKED OFF.
CAN'T SAY I'M IN THE MOOD FOR A DOUBLE-TEAM...
...BUT THIS ISN'T OVER, LITTLE GUPPY FISH. WE WILL ABSOLUTELY MEET AGAIN.
AND WHEN WE DO...
...I'M GONNA HAVE FUN TEARING YOU APART.
NYU

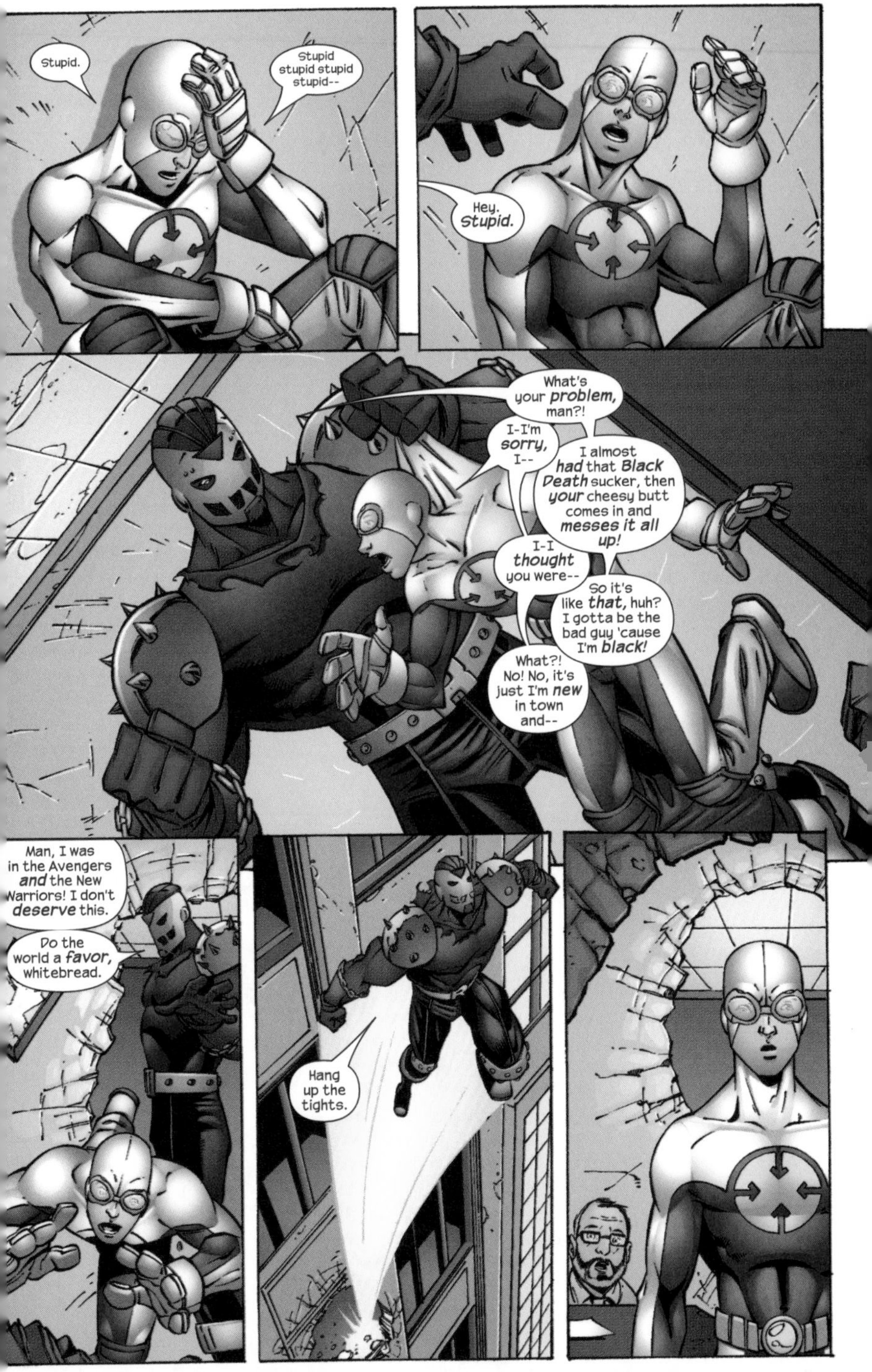
Stupid.
Stupid stupid stupid stupid--
Hey. Stupid.
What's your problem, man?!
I-I'm sorry, I--
I almost had that Black Death sucker, then your cheesy butt comes in and messes it all up!
I-I thought you were--
So it's like that, huh? I gotta be the bad guy 'cause I'm black!
What?! No! No, it's just I'm new in town and--
Man, I was in the Avengers and the New Warriors! I don't deserve this.
Do the world a favor, whitebread.
Hang up the tights.

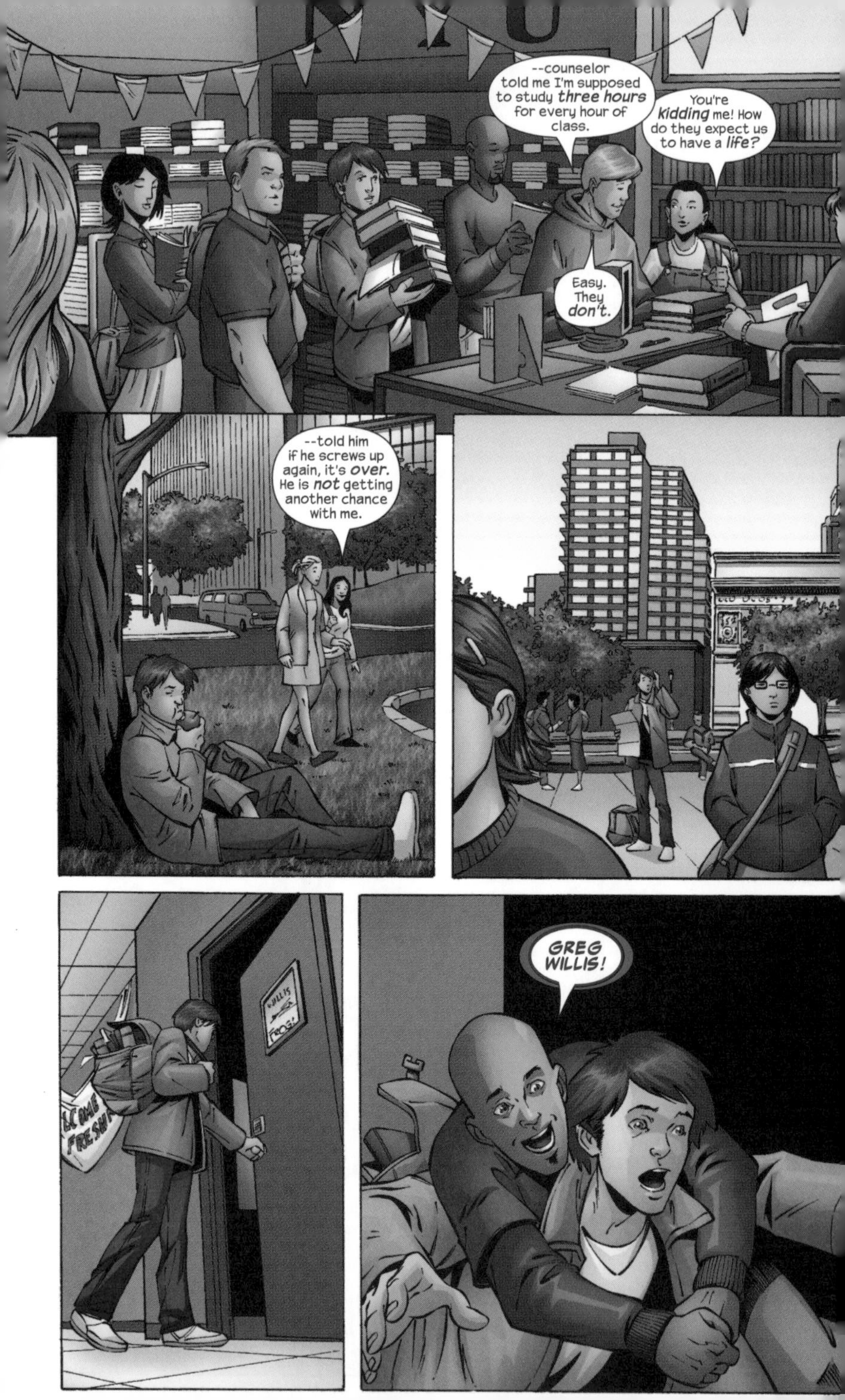
--counselor told me I'm supposed to study three hours for every hour of class.
You're kidding me! How do they expect us to have a life?
Easy. They don't.
--told him if he screws up again, it's over. He is not getting another chance with me.
GREG WILLIS!

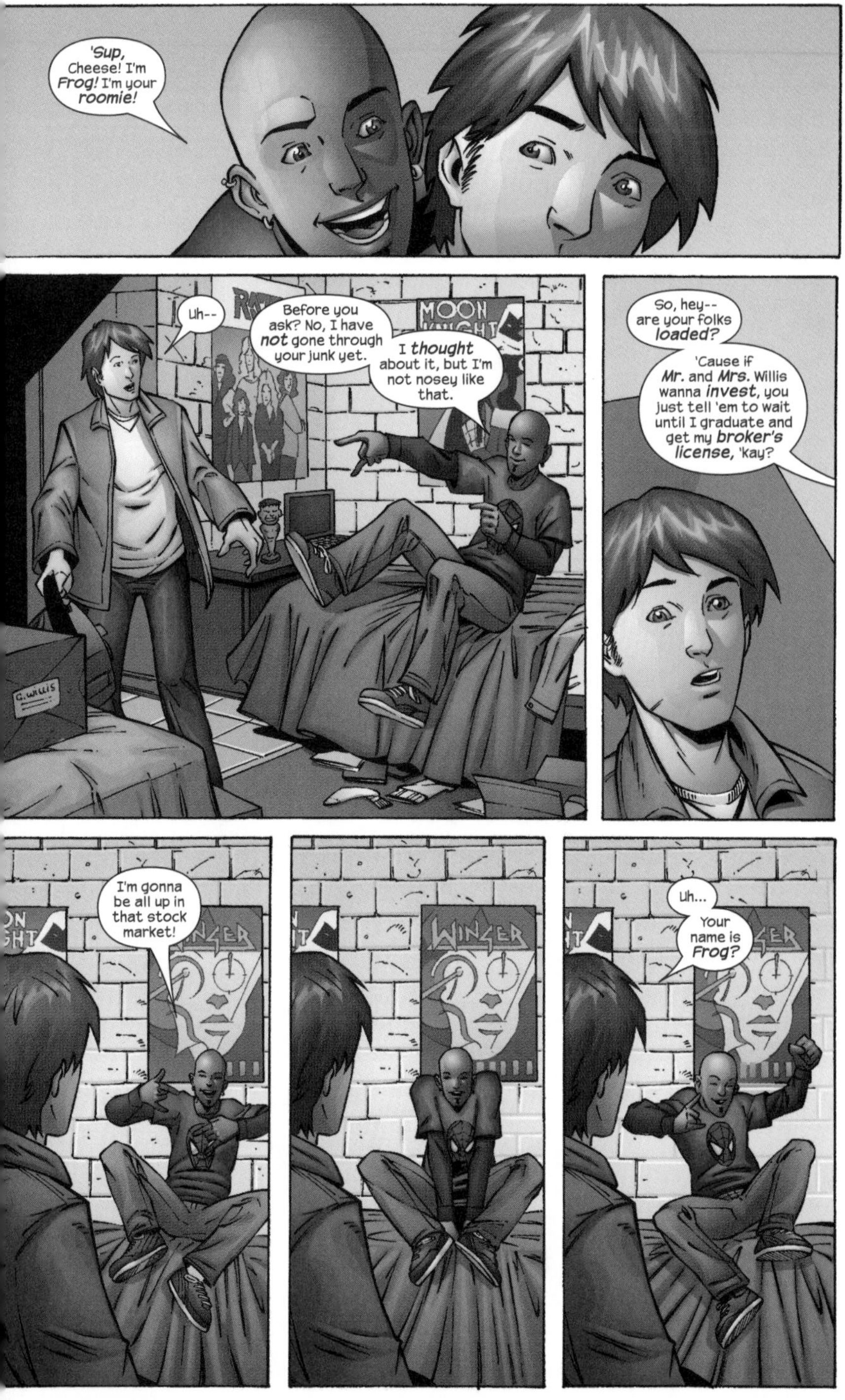
'Sup, Cheese! I'm Frog! I'm your roomie!
Uh--
Before you ask? No, I have not gone through your junk yet.
I thought about it, but I'm not nosey like that.
RATT
MOON KNIGHT
G. WILLIS
So, hey-- are your folks loaded?
'Cause if Mr. and Mrs. Willis wanna invest, you just tell 'em to wait until I graduate and get my broker's license, 'kay?
I'm gonna be all up in that stock market!
WINGER
Uh...
Your name is Frog?

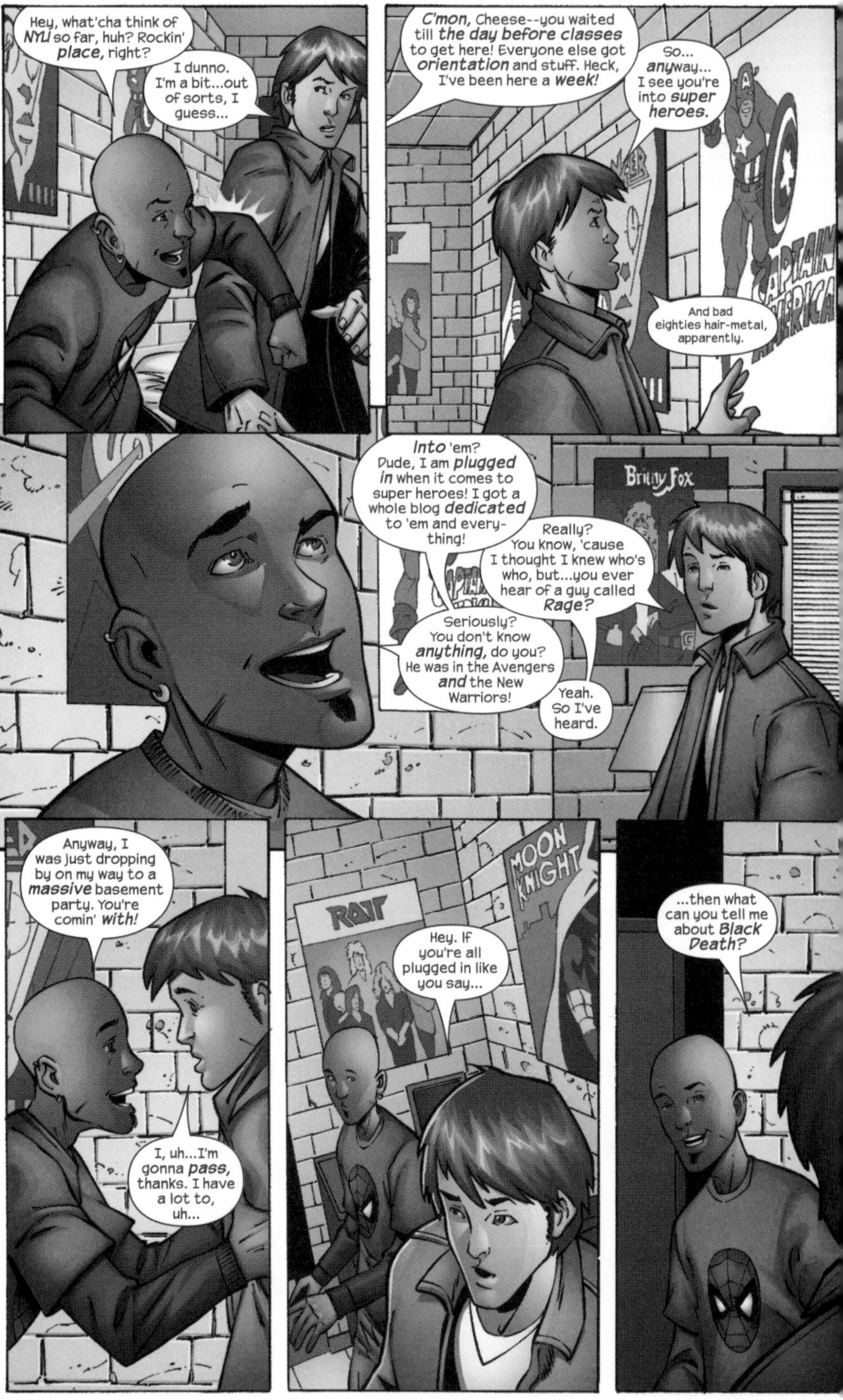

Hey, what'cha think of NYU so far, huh? Rockin' place, right?
I dunno. I'm a bit...out of sorts, I guess...
C'mon, Cheese--you waited till the day before classes to get here! Everyone else got orientation and stuff. Heck, I've been here a week!
So... anyway... I see you're into super heroes.
CAPTAIN AMERICA
And bad eighties hair-metal, apparently.
Into 'em? Dude, I am plugged in when it comes to super heroes! I got a whole blog dedicated to 'em and every-thing!
Britny Fox
Really? You know, 'cause I thought I knew who's who, but...you ever hear of a guy called Rage?
Seriously? You don't know anything, do you? He was in the Avengers and the New Warriors!
Yeah. So I've heard.
Anyway, I was just dropping by on my way to a massive basement party. You're comin' with!
I, uh...I'm gonna pass, thanks. I have a lot to, uh...
RATT
MOON KNIGHT
Hey. If you're all plugged in like you say...
...then what can you tell me about Black Death?

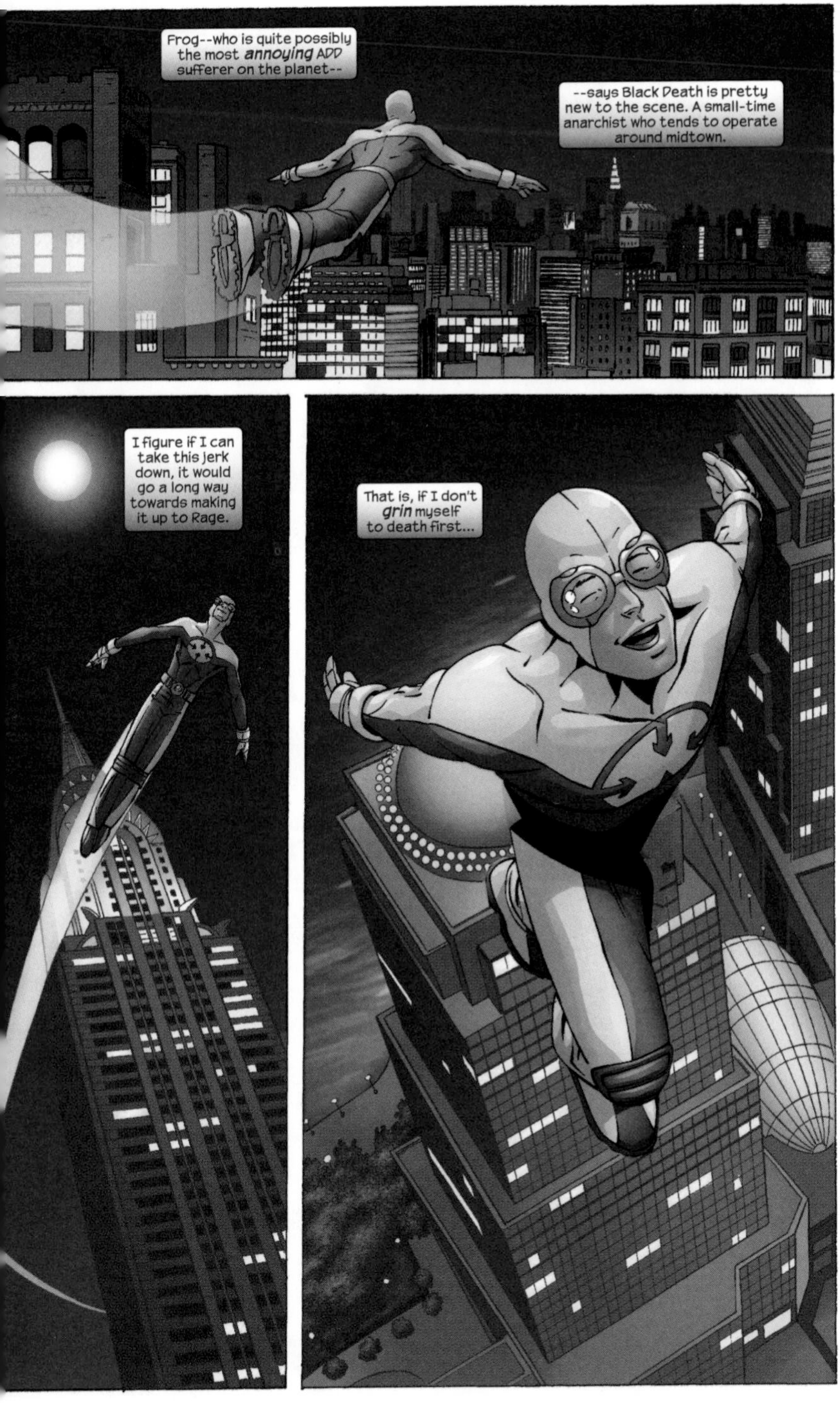

Frog--who is quite possibly the most *annoying* ADD sufferer on the planet--
--says Black Death is pretty new to the scene. A small-time anarchist who tends to operate around midtown.
I figure if I can take this jerk down, it would go a long way towards making it up to Rage.
That is, if I don't *grin* myself to death first...

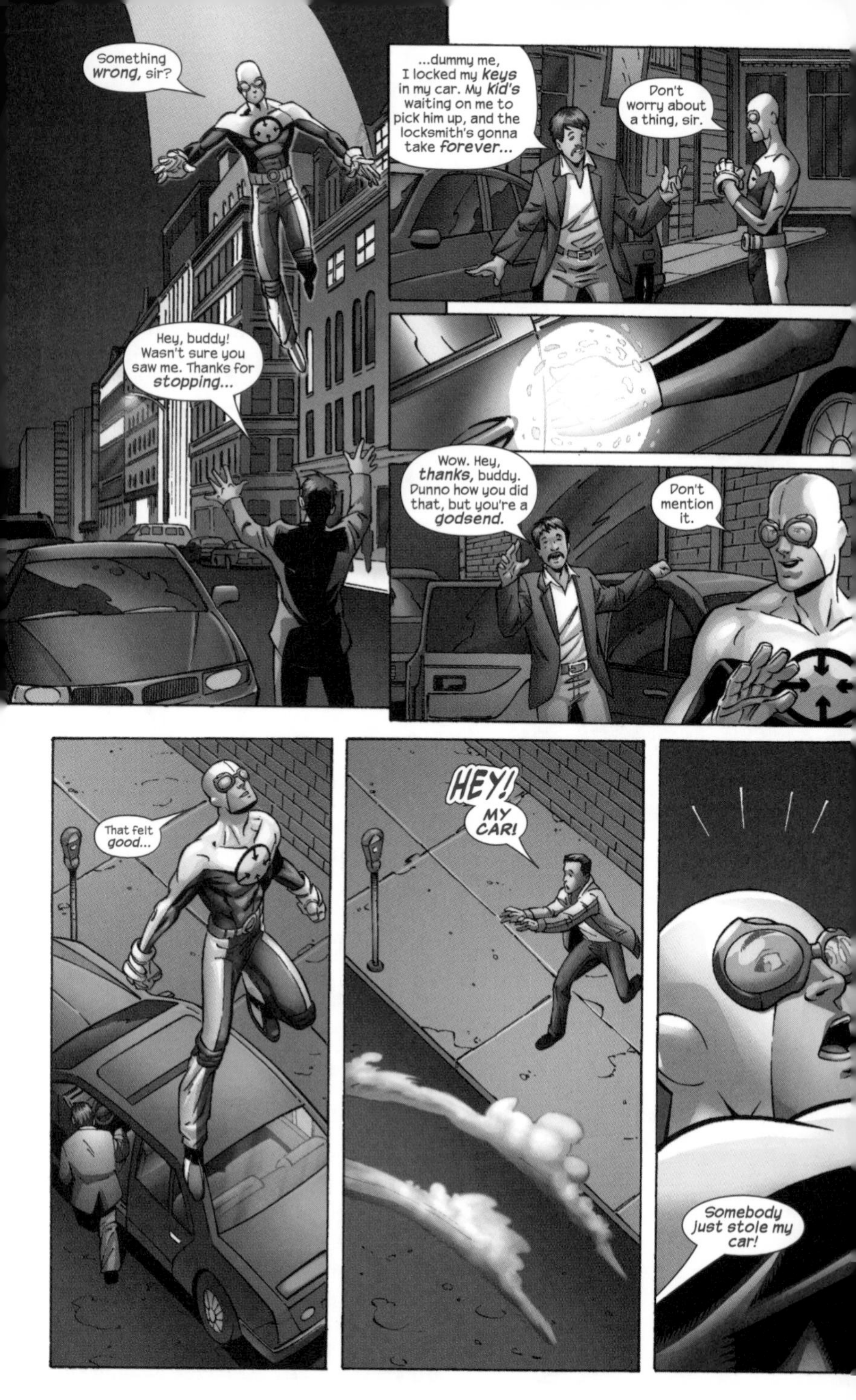
Something wrong, sir?
Hey, buddy! Wasn't sure you saw me. Thanks for stopping...
...dummy me, I locked my keys in my car. My kid's waiting on me to pick him up, and the locksmith's gonna take forever...
Don't worry about a thing, sir.
Wow. Hey, thanks, buddy. Dunno how you did that, but you're a godsend.
Don't mention it.
That felt good...
HEY! MY CAR!
Somebody just stole my car!

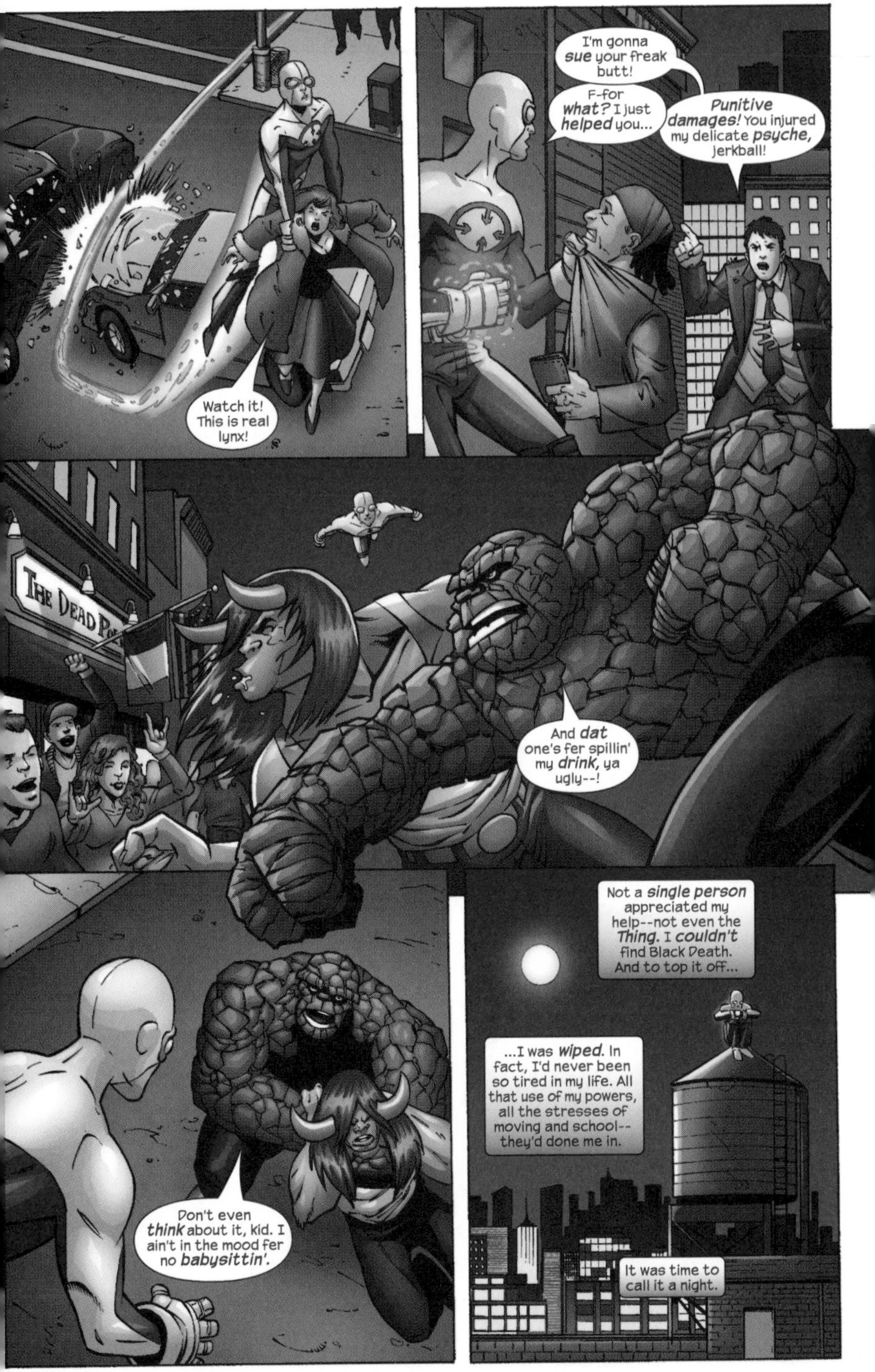
Watch it! This is real lynx!
I'm gonna sue your freak butt!
F-for what? I just helped you...
Punitive damages! You injured my delicate psyche, jerkball!
THE DEAD PO
And dat one's fer spillin' my drink, ya ugly--!
Don't even think about it, kid. I ain't in the mood fer no babysittin'.
Not a single person appreciated my help--not even the Thing. I couldn't find Black Death. And to top it off...
...I was wiped. In fact, I'd never been so tired in my life. All that use of my powers, all the stresses of moving and school--they'd done me in.
It was time to call it a night.

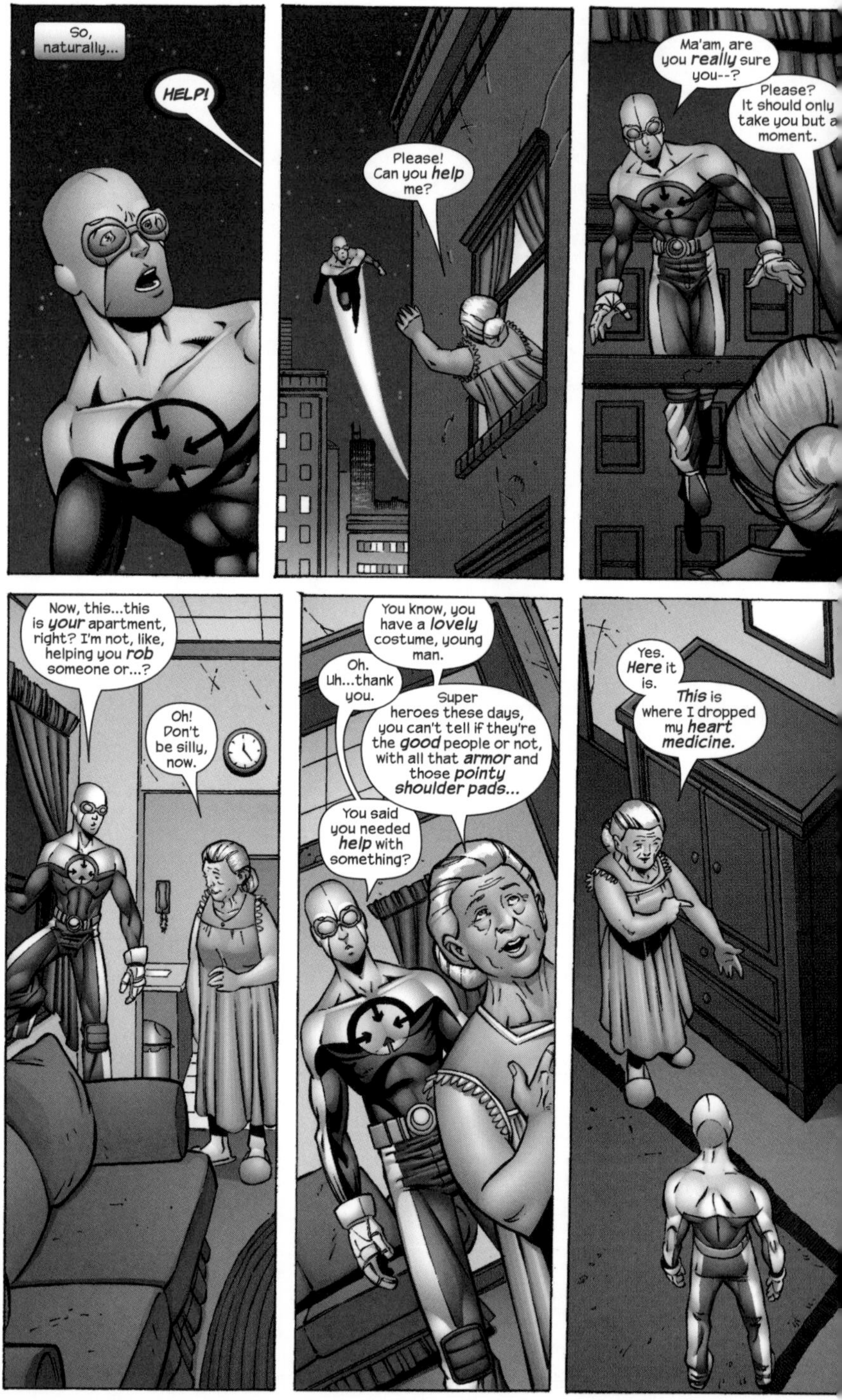

So, naturally...
HELP!
Please! Can you help me?
Ma'am, are you really sure you--?
Please? It should only take you but a moment.
Now, this...this is your apartment, right? I'm not, like, helping you rob someone or...?
Oh! Don't be silly, now.
You know, you have a lovely costume, young man.
Oh. Uh...thank you.
Super heroes these days, you can't tell if they're the good people or not, with all that armor and those pointy shoulder pads...
You said you needed help with something?
Yes. Here it is.
This is where I dropped my heart medicine.

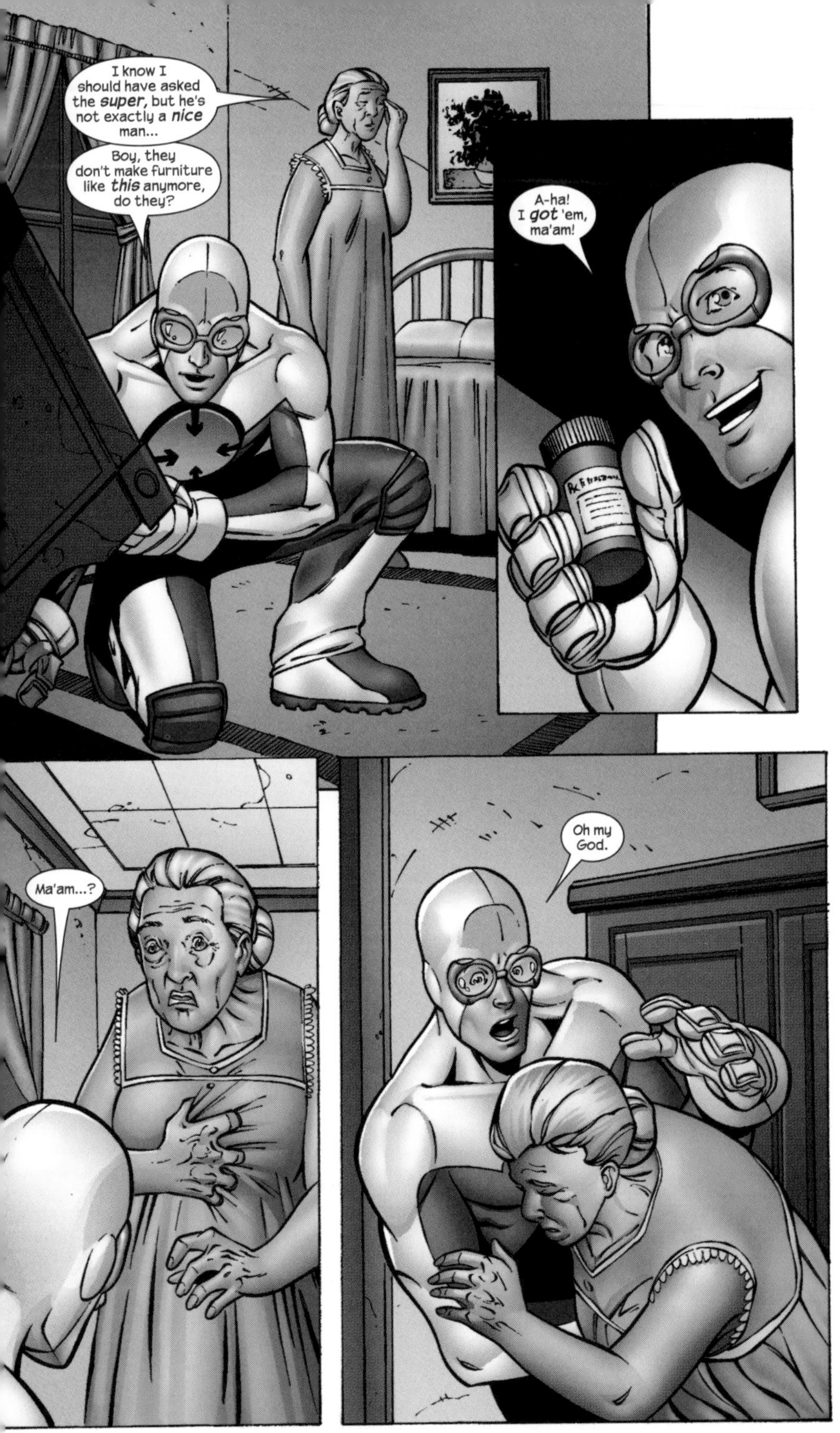
I know I should have asked the *super*, but he's not exactly a *nice* man...
Boy, they don't make furniture like *this* anymore, do they?
A-ha! I *got* 'em, ma'am!
Ma'am...?
Oh my God.

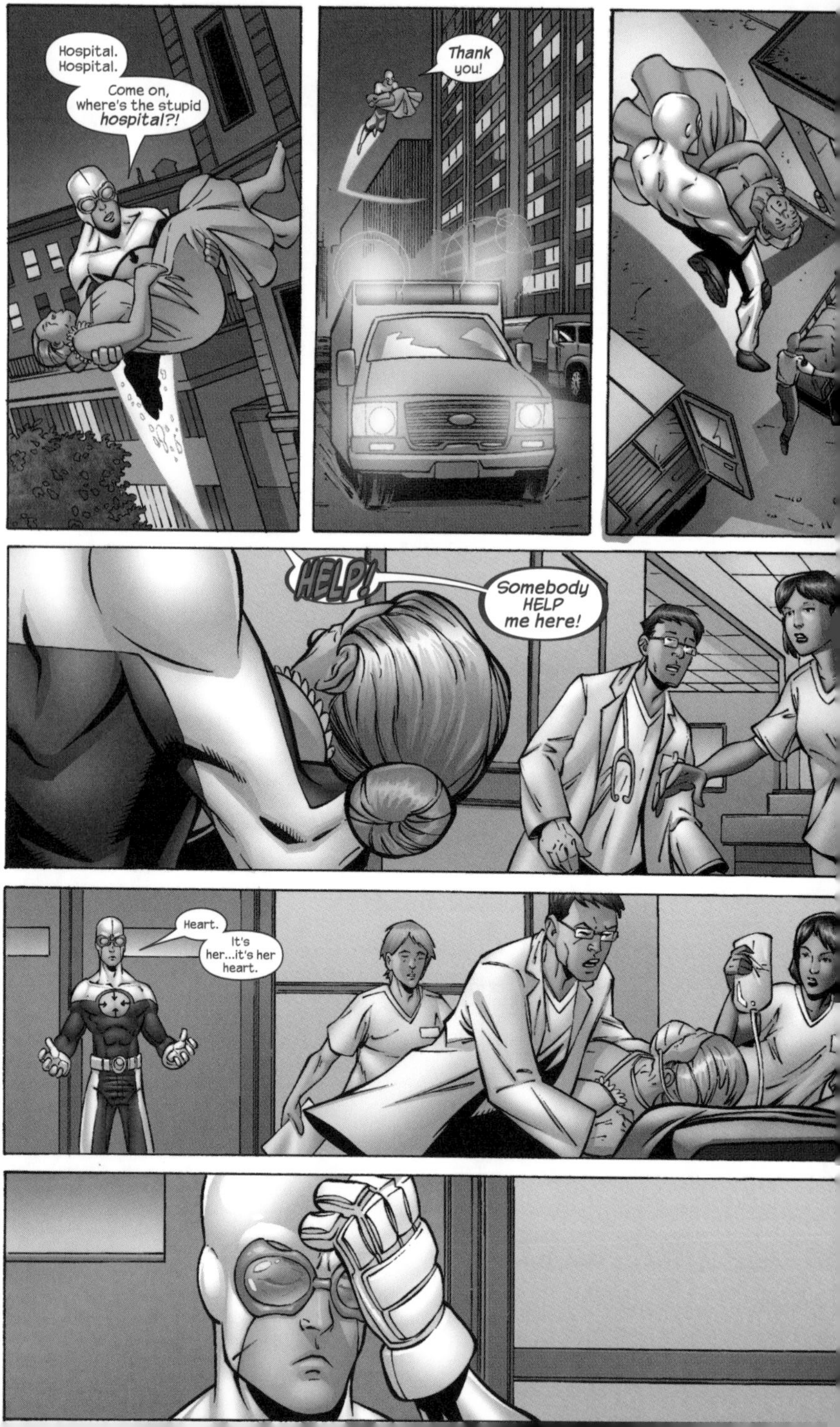
Hospital.
Hospital.
Come on, where's the stupid hospital?!
Thank you!
HELP!
Somebody HELP me here!
Heart.
It's her...it's her heart.

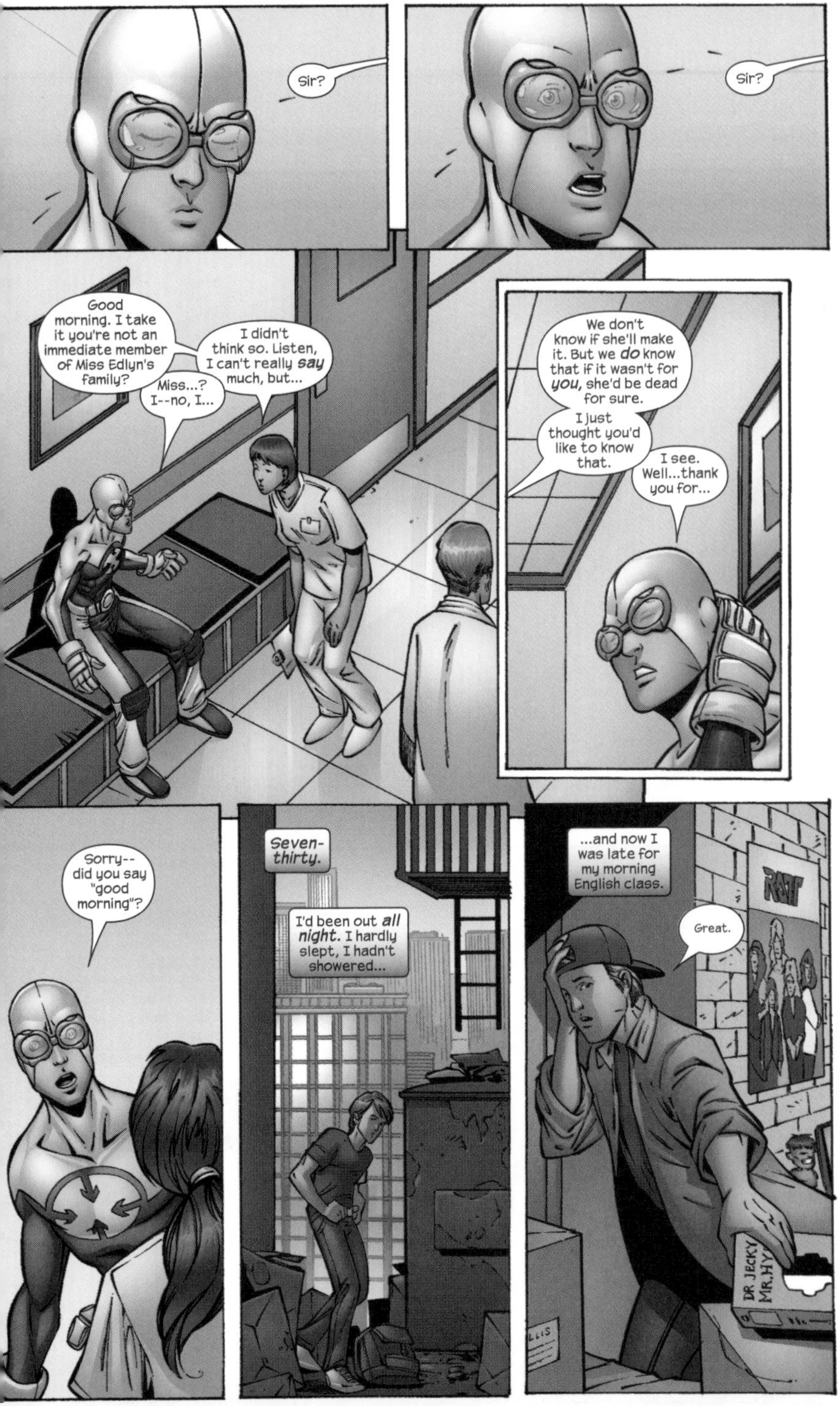
Sir?
Sir?
Good morning. I take it you're not an immediate member of Miss Edlyn's family?
Miss...? I--no, I...
I didn't think so. Listen, I can't really *say* much, but...
We don't know if she'll make it. But we *do* know that if it wasn't for *you,* she'd be dead for sure.
I just thought you'd like to know that.
I see. Well...thank you for...
Sorry--did you say "good morning"?
Seven-thirty.
I'd been out *all night.* I hardly slept, I hadn't showered...
...and now I was late for my morning English class.
Great.
DR. JECKY
MR.HY

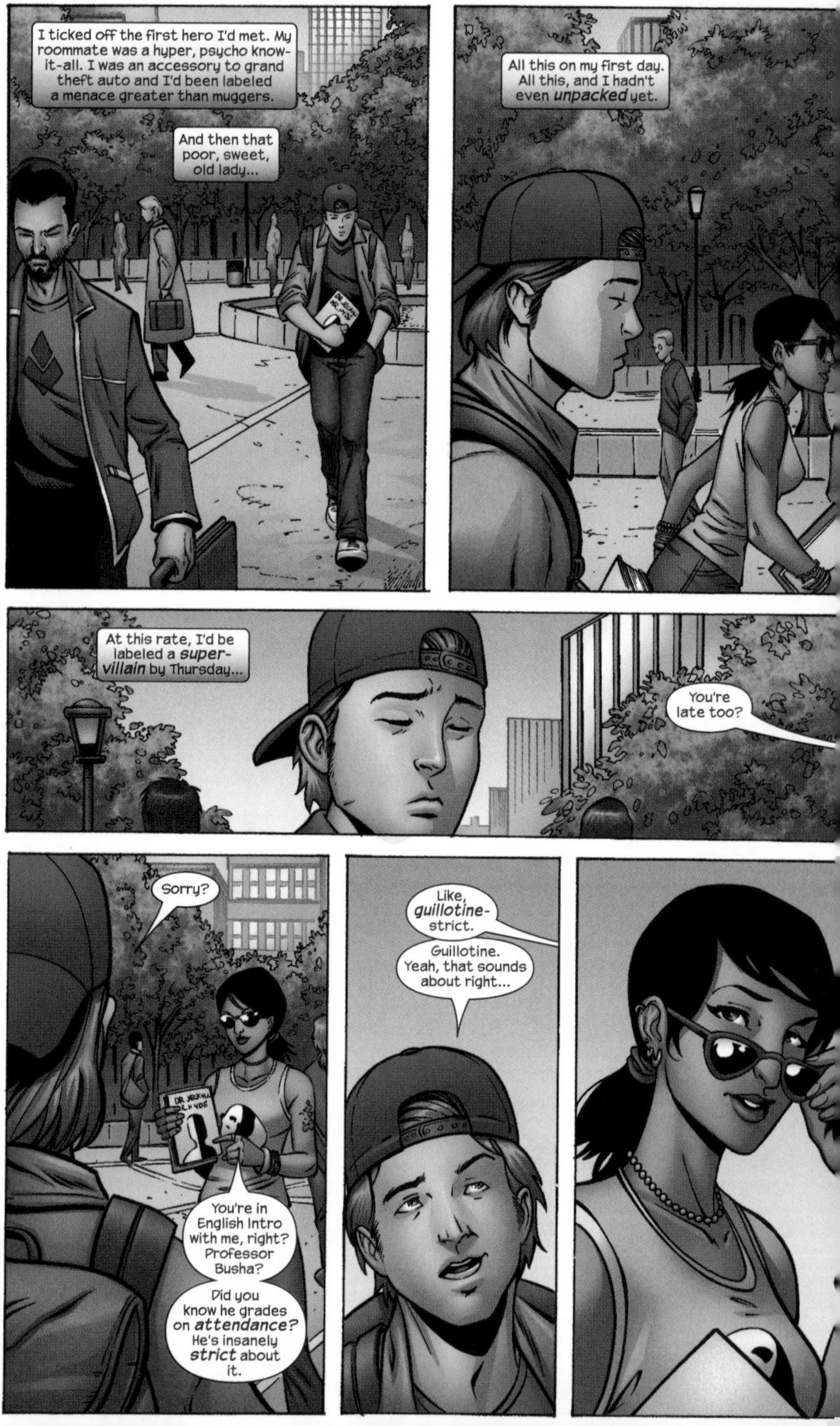
I ticked off the first hero I'd met. My roommate was a hyper, psycho know-it-all. I was an accessory to grand theft auto and I'd been labeled a menace greater than muggers.
And then that poor, sweet, old lady...
All this on my first day. All this, and I hadn't even *unpacked* yet.
At this rate, I'd be labeled a *super-villain* by Thursday...
You're late too?
Sorry?
You're in English Intro with me, right? Professor Busha?
Did you know he grades on *attendance?* He's insanely *strict* about it.
Like, *guillotine*-strict.
Guillotine. Yeah, that sounds about right...

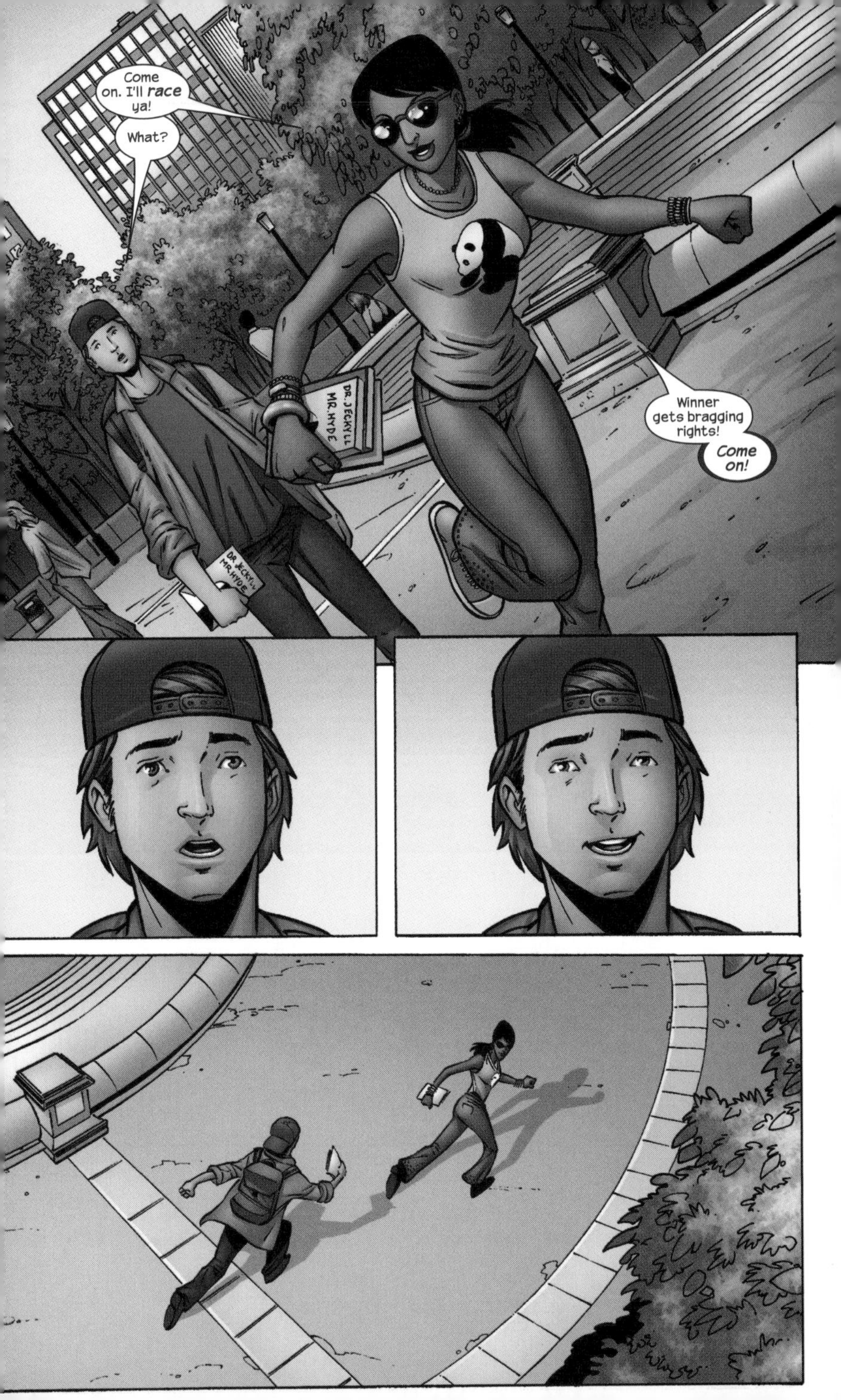

Come on. I'll *race* ya!
What?
DR. JECKYLL MR. HYDE
DR. JECKYLL MR. HYDE
Winner gets bragging rights!
Come on!

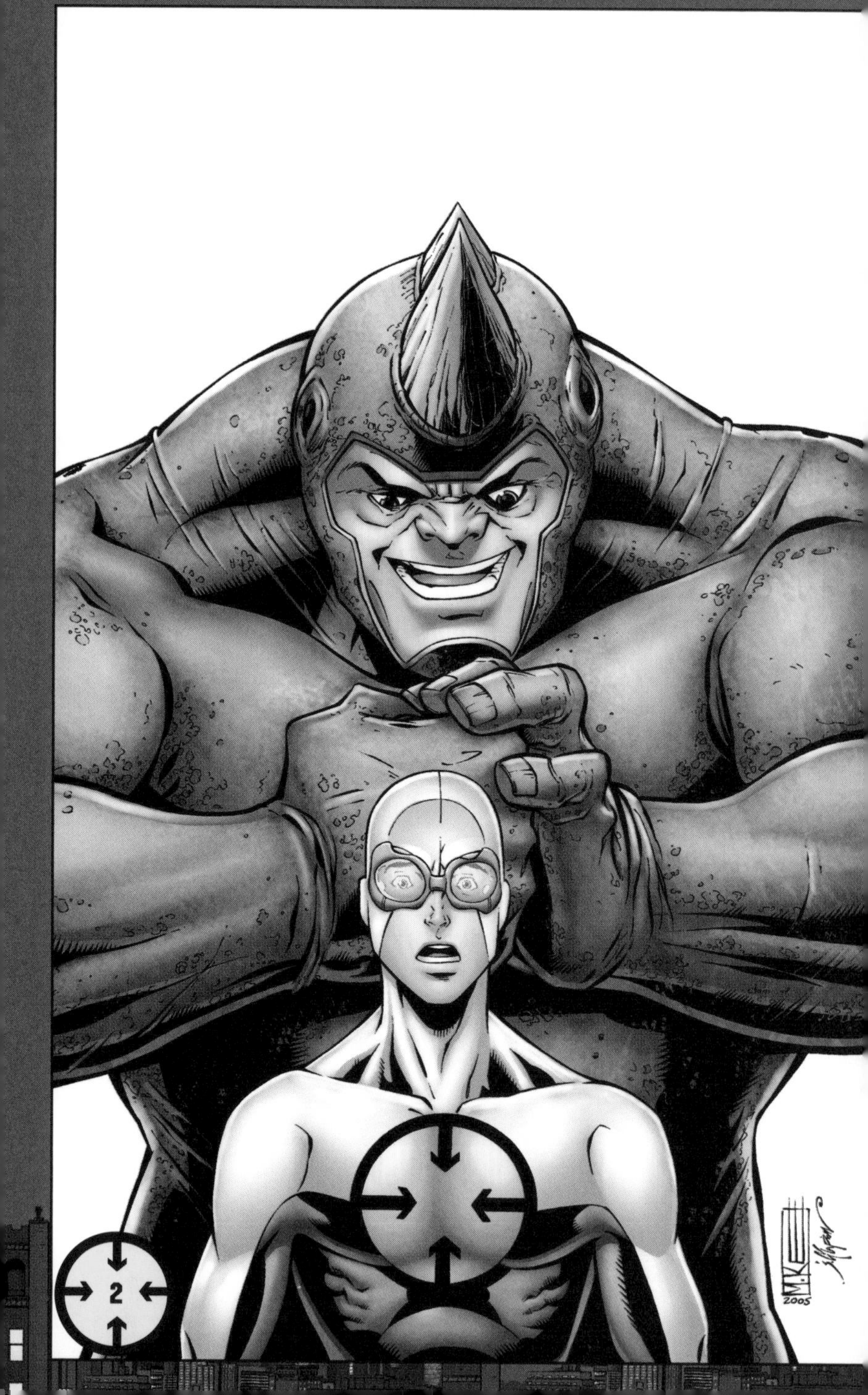
2
2005

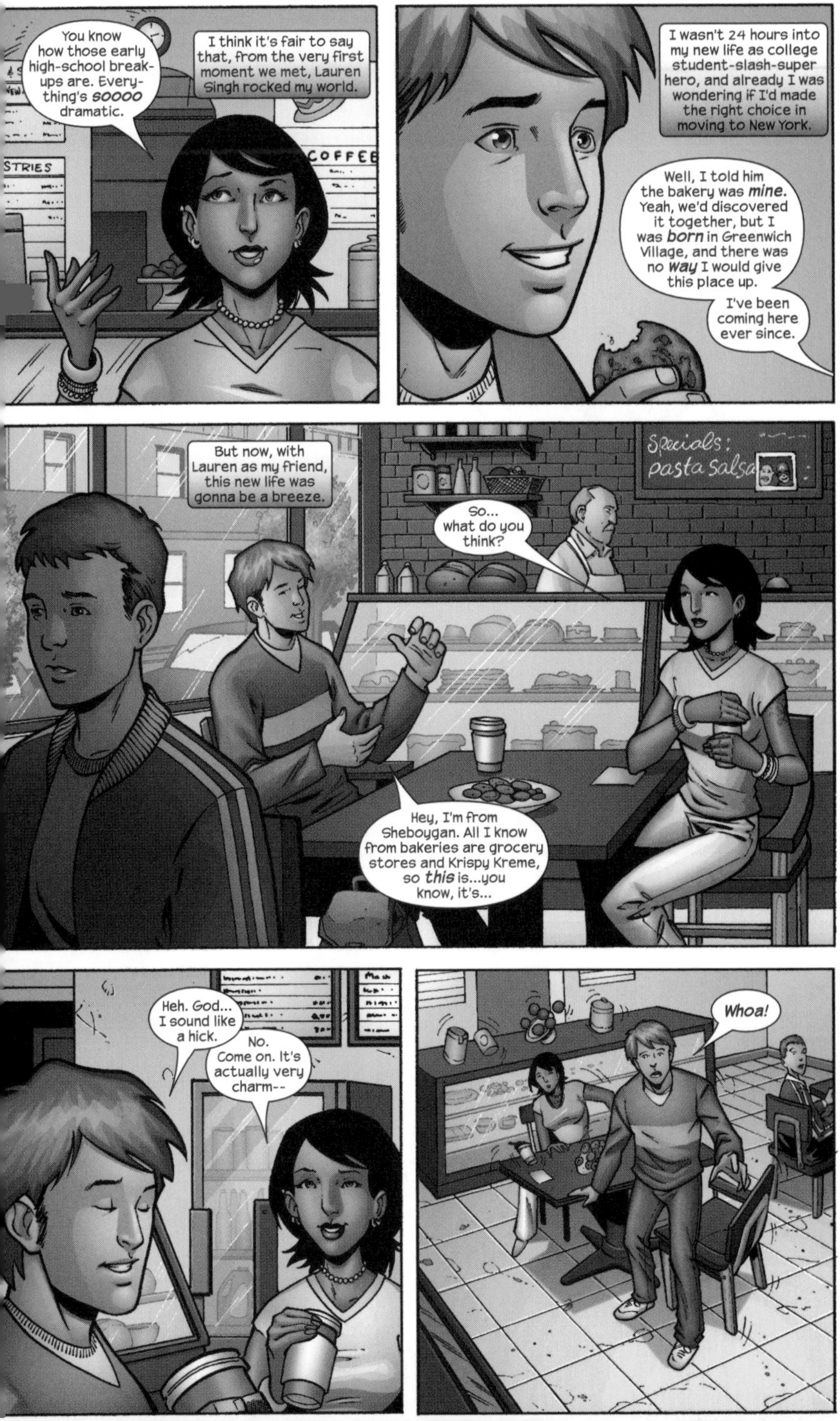
You know how those early high-school break-ups are. Every-thing's *soooo* dramatic.
I think it's fair to say that, from the very first moment we met, Lauren Singh rocked my world.
COFFEE
STRIES
I wasn't 24 hours into my new life as college student-slash-super hero, and already I was wondering if I'd made the right choice in moving to New York.
Well, I told him the bakery was *mine.* Yeah, we'd discovered it together, but I was *born* in Greenwich Village, and there was no *way* I would give this place up.
I've been coming here ever since.
But now, with Lauren as my friend, this new life was gonna be a breeze.
Specials: pasta salsa
So... what do you think?
Hey, I'm from Sheboygan. All I know from bakeries are grocery stores and Krispy Kreme, so *this* is...you know, it's...
Heh. God... I sound like a hick.
No. Come on. It's actually very charm--
Whoa!

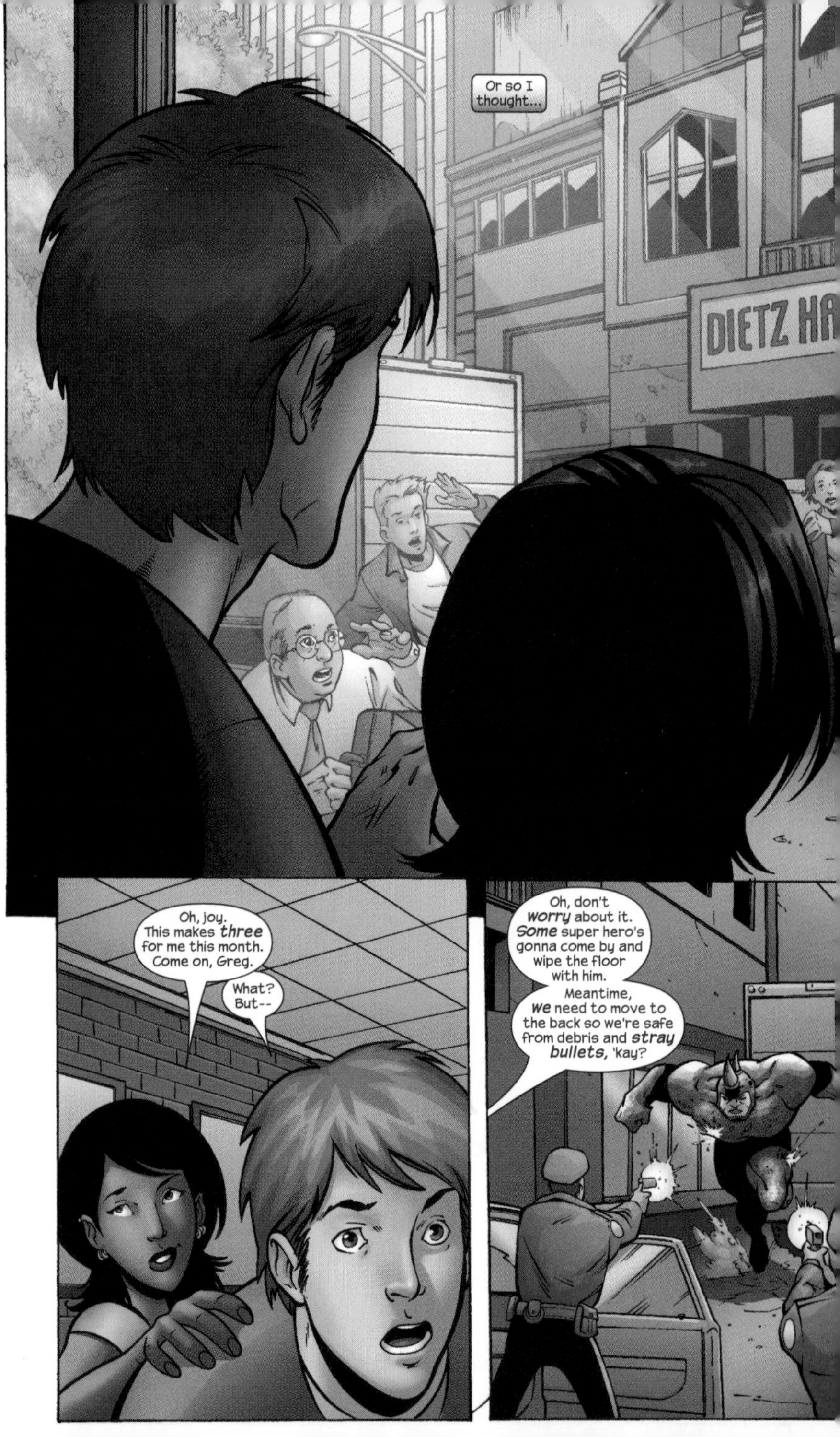
Or so I thought...
DIETZ HA
Oh, joy. This makes three for me this month. Come on, Greg.
What? But--
Oh, don't worry about it. Some super hero's gonna come by and wipe the floor with him.
Meantime, we need to move to the back so we're safe from debris and stray bullets, 'kay?

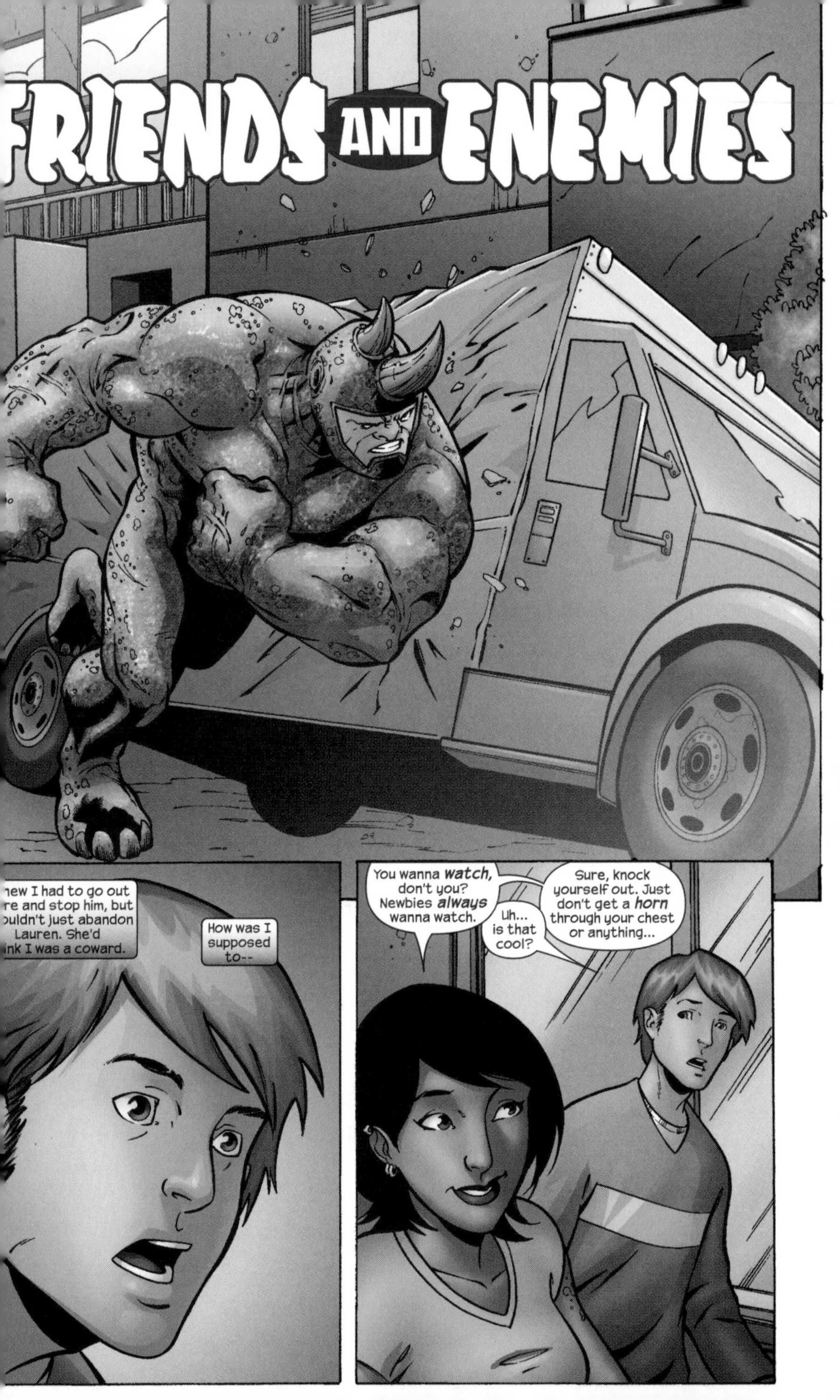

FRIENDS AND ENEMIES
new I had to go out re and stop him, but ouldn't just abandon Lauren. She'd ink I was a coward.
How was I supposed to--
You wanna *watch,* don't you? Newbies *always* wanna watch.
Uh... is that cool?
Sure, knock yourself out. Just don't get a *horn* through your chest or anything...

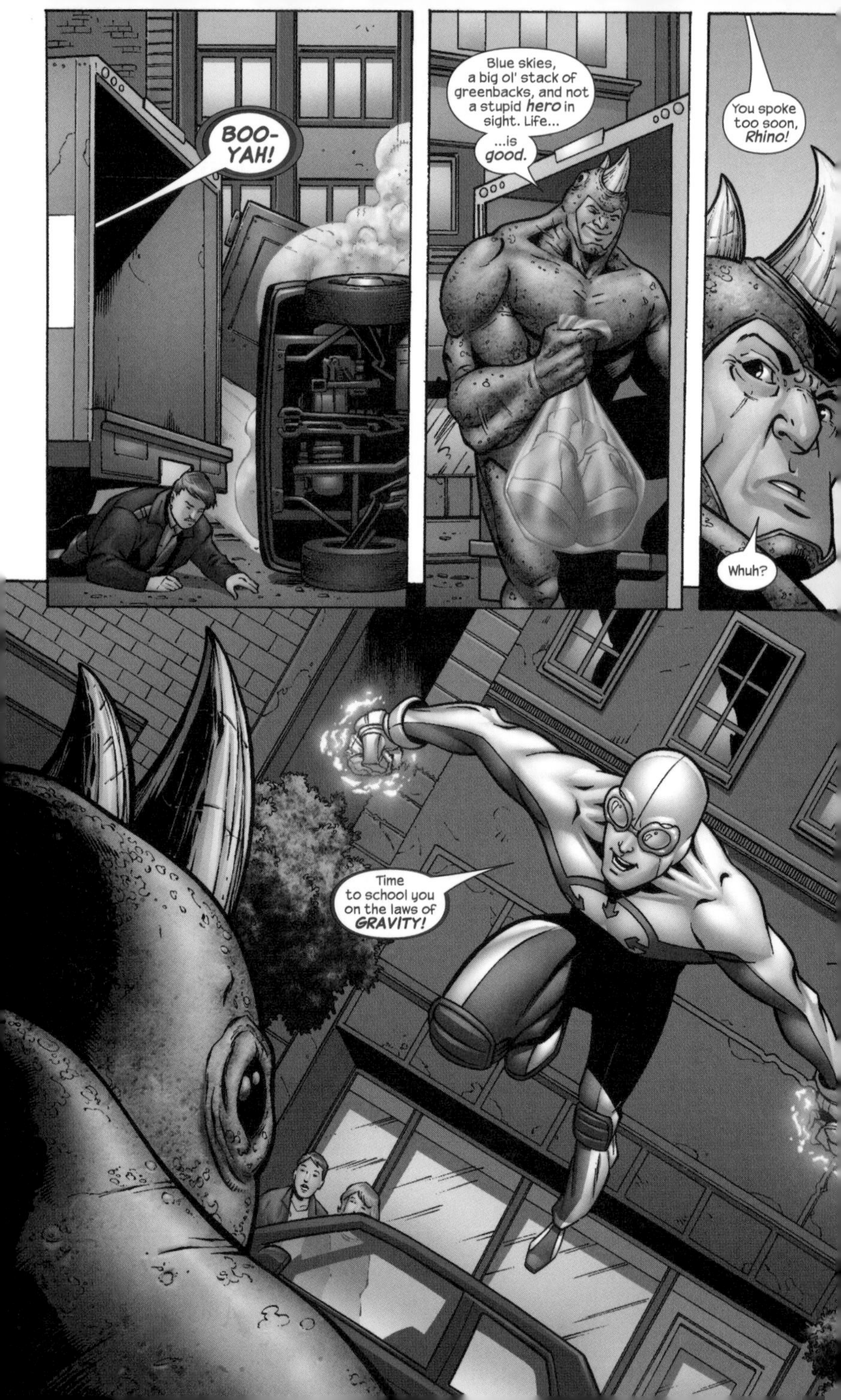
BOO-YAH!
Blue skies, a big ol' stack of greenbacks, and not a stupid *hero* in sight. Life...
...is *good.*
You spoke too soon, *Rhino!*
Whuh?
Time to school you on the laws of **GRAVITY!**

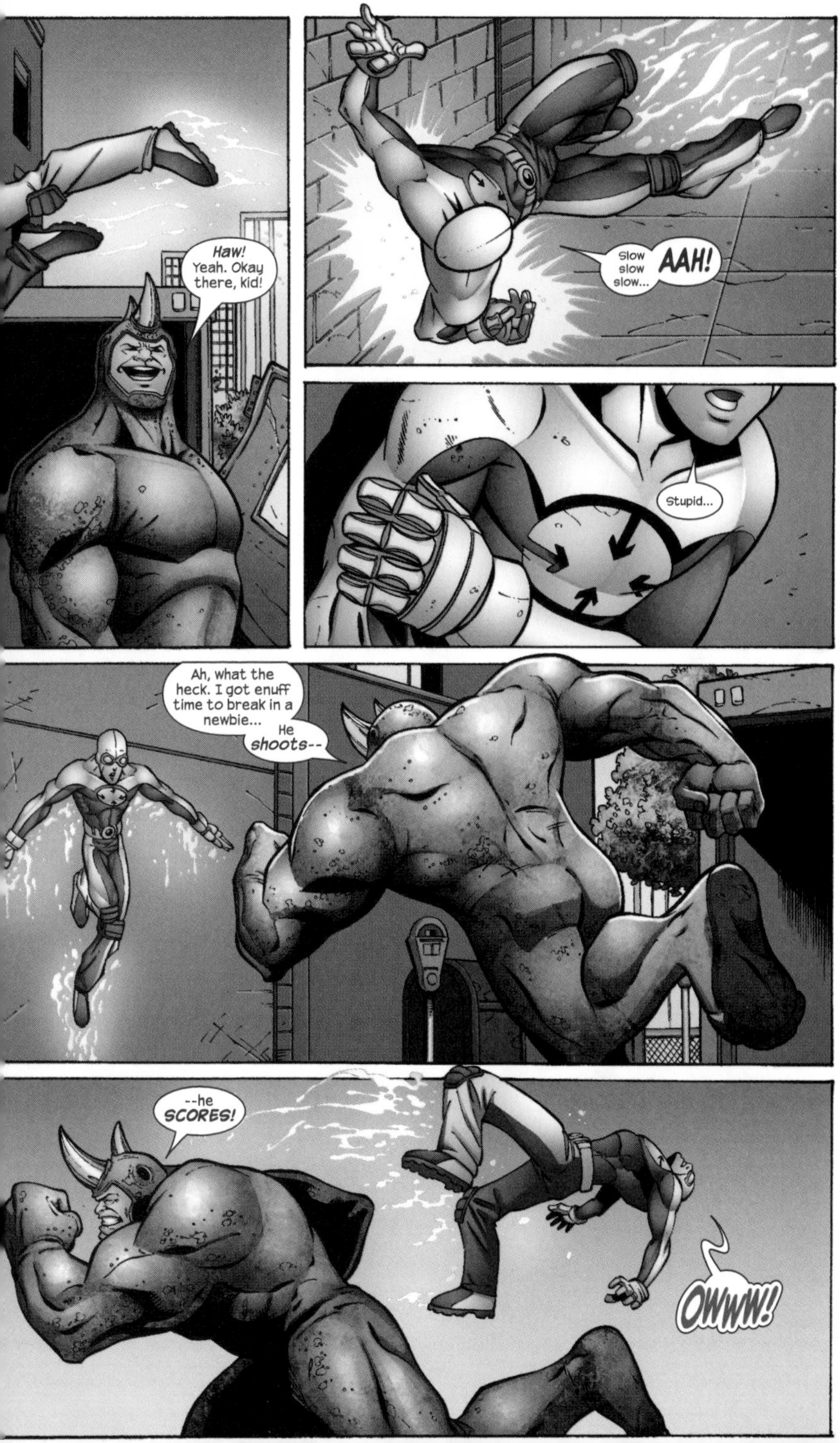

Haw! Yeah. Okay there, kid!
Slow slow slow...
AAH!
Stupid...
Ah, what the heck. I got enuff time to break in a newbie...
He shoots--
--he SCORES!
OWWW!

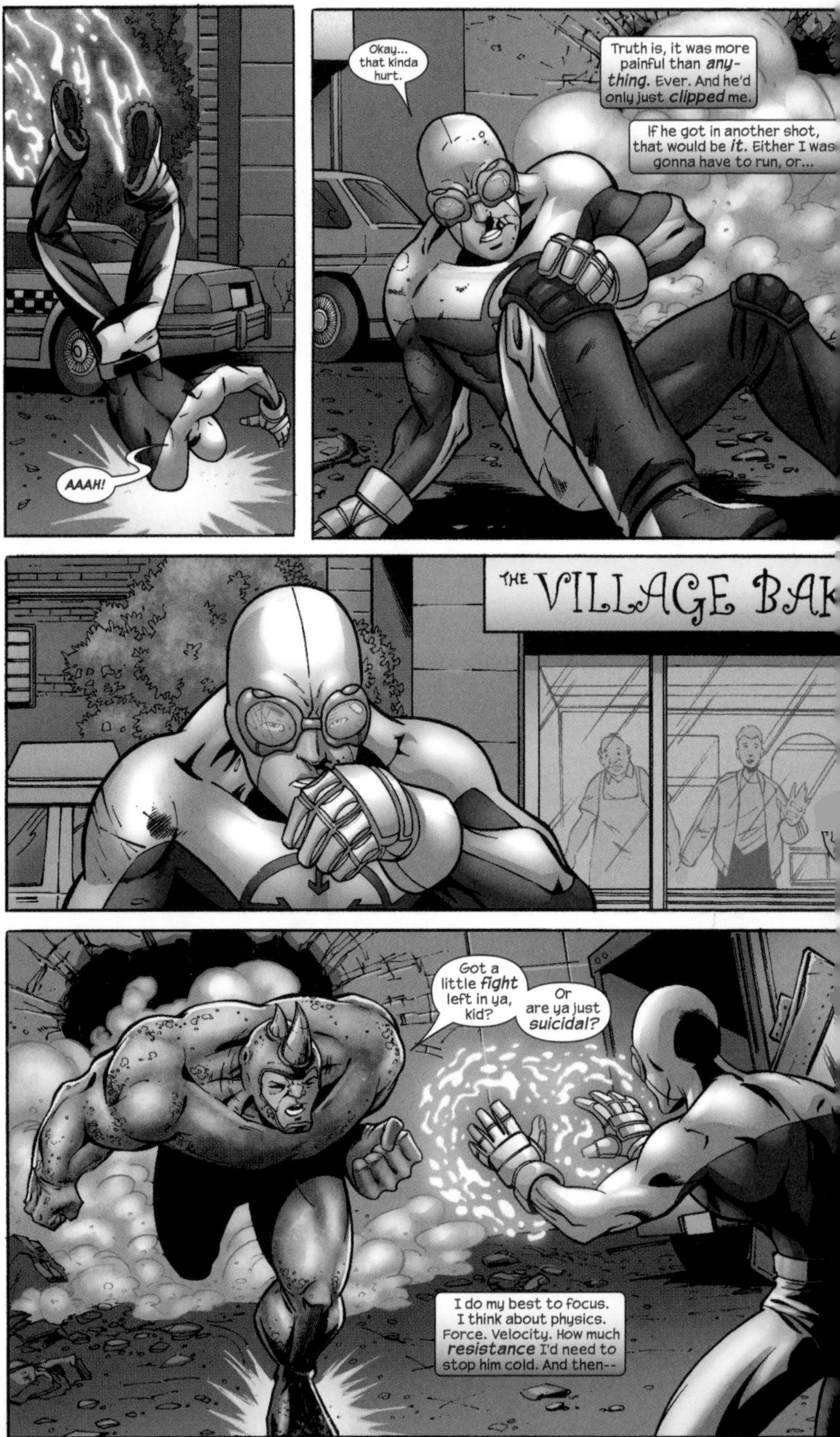
AAAH!
Okay... that kinda hurt.
Truth is, it was more painful than *any-thing.* Ever. And he'd only just *clipped* me.
If he got in another shot, that would be *it.* Either I was gonna have to run, or...
THE VILLAGE BAK
Got a little *fight* left in ya, kid?
Or are ya just *suicidal?*
I do my best to focus. I think about physics. Force. Velocity. How much *resistance* I'd need to stop him cold. And then--

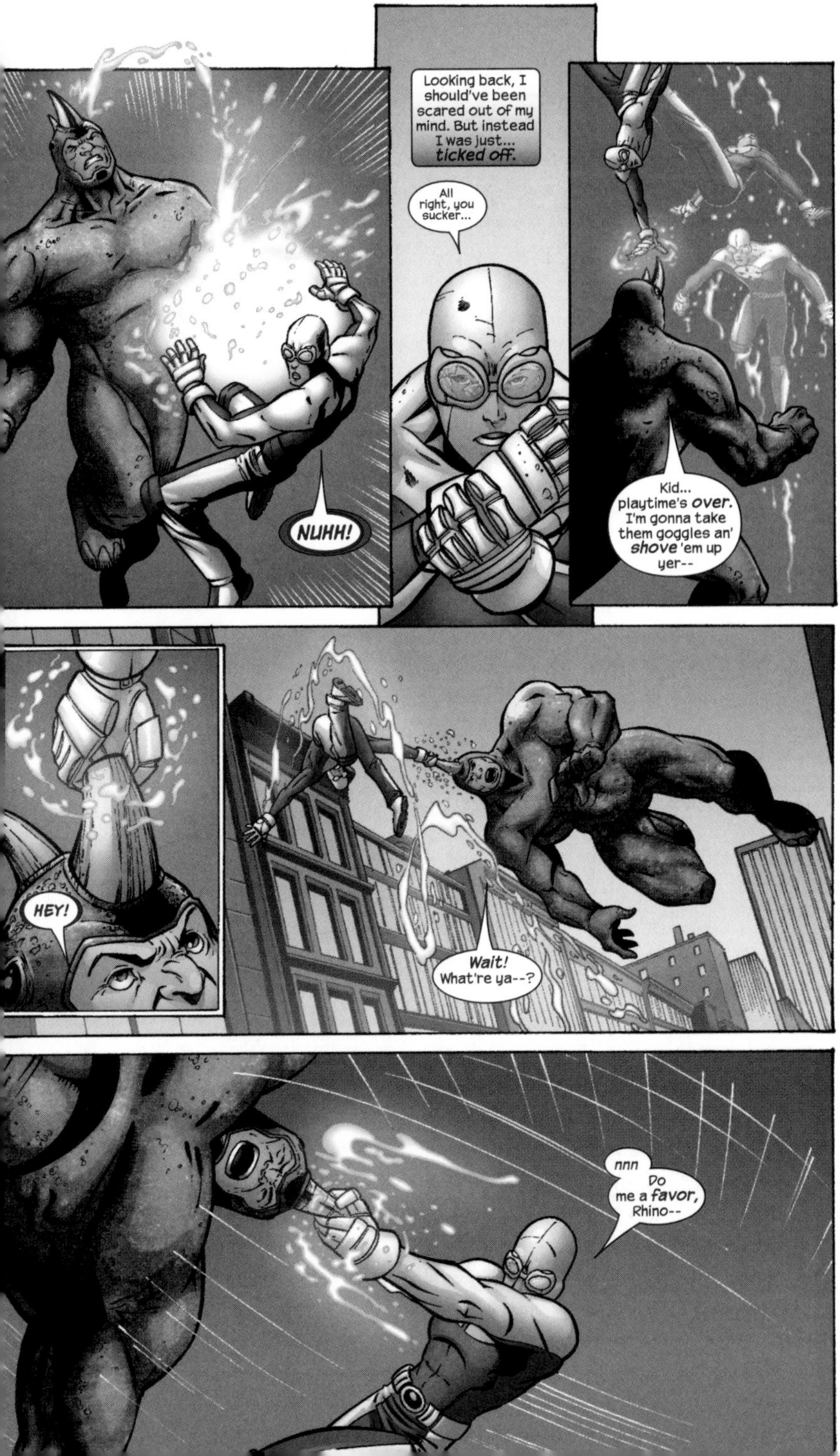
NUHH!
Looking back, I should've been scared out of my mind. But instead I was just... *ticked off*.
All right, you sucker...
Kid... playtime's *over*. I'm gonna take them goggles an' *shove* 'em up yer--
HEY!
Wait! What're ya--?
nnn
Do me a *favor*, Rhino--

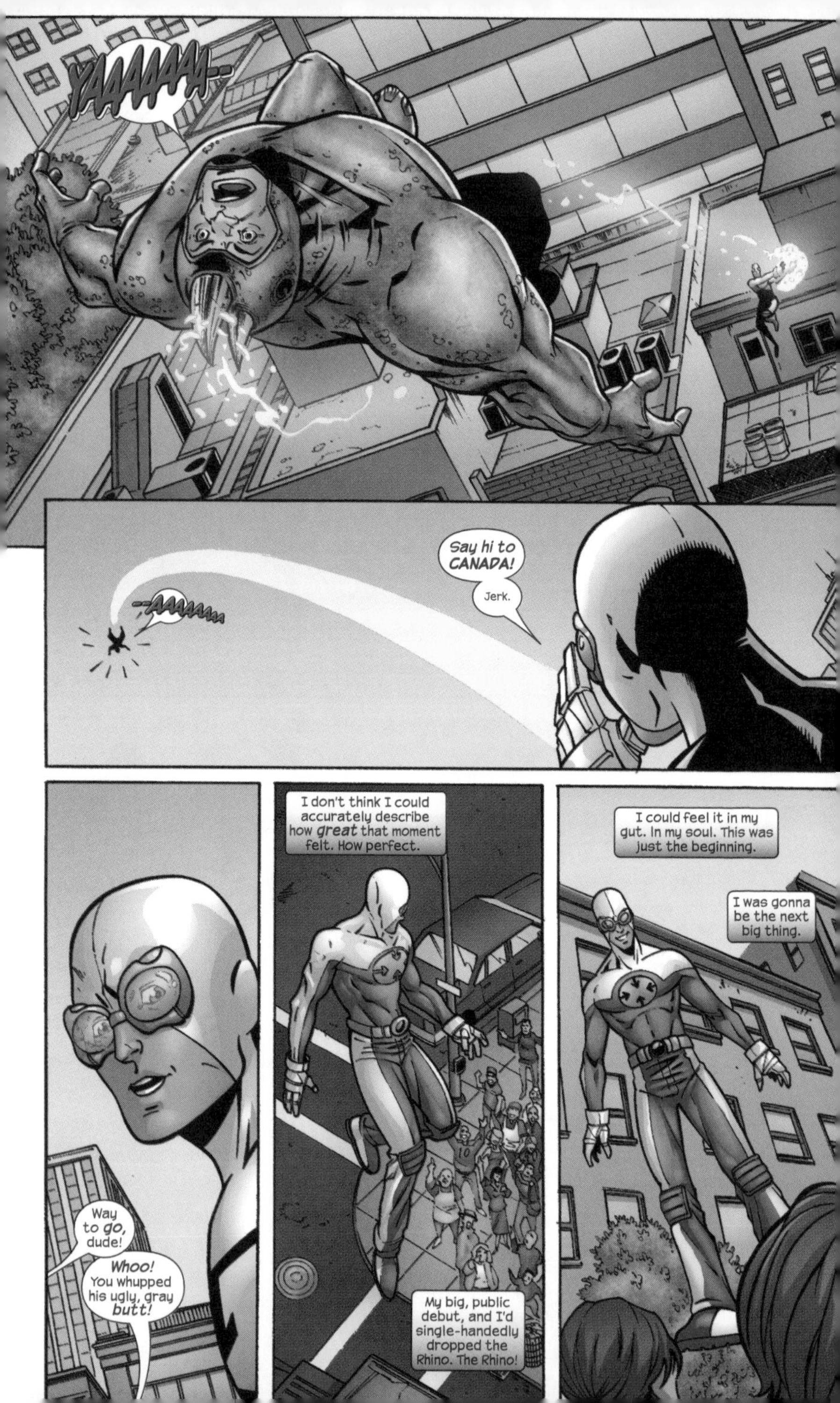
YAAAAAAA--
Say hi to CANADA!
Jerk.
--AAAAAAAA
Way to go, dude!
Whoo! You whupped his ugly, gray butt!
I don't think I could accurately describe how great that moment felt. How perfect.
My big, public debut, and I'd single-handedly dropped the Rhino. The Rhino!
I could feel it in my gut. In my soul. This was just the beginning.
I was gonna be the next big thing.

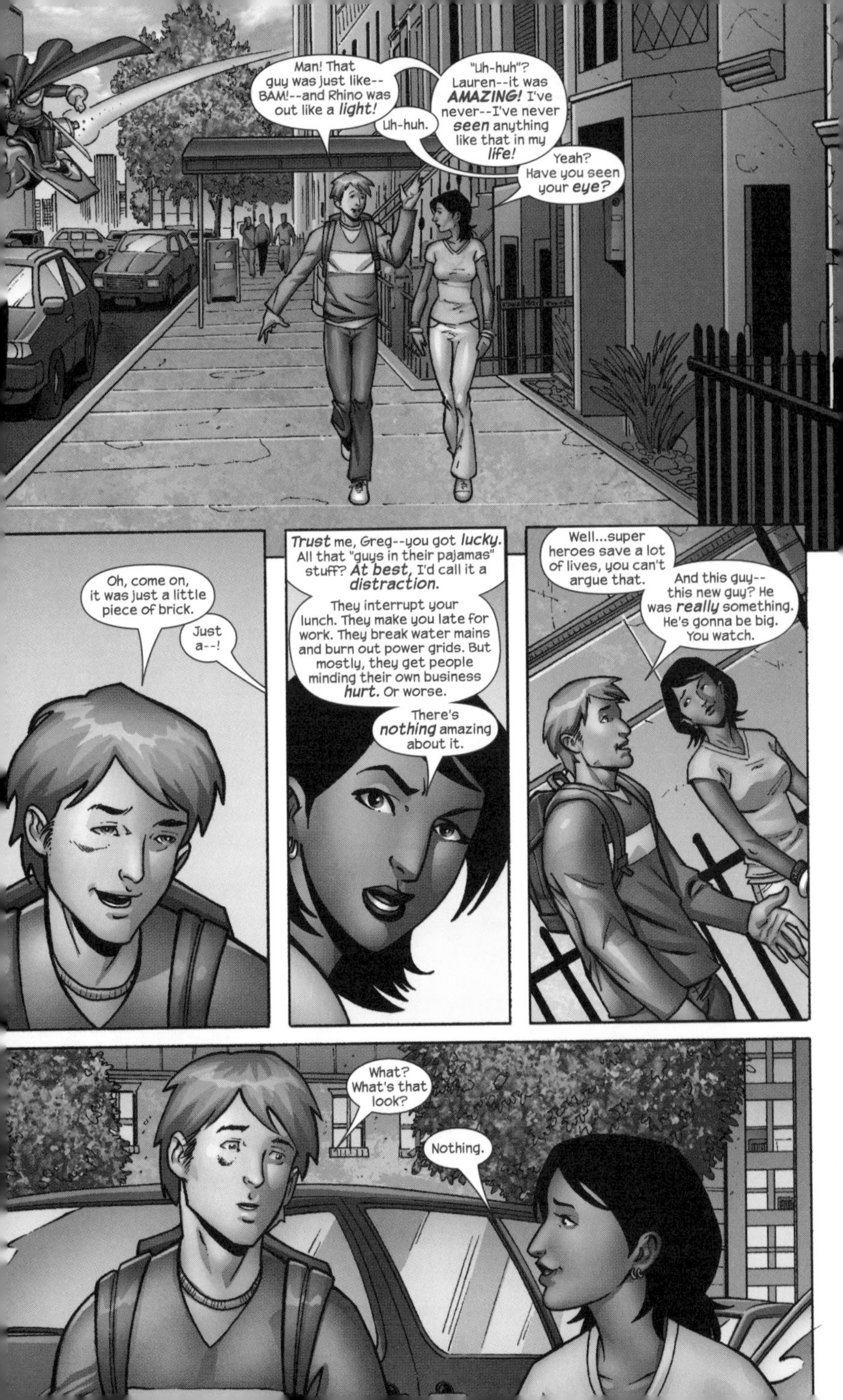

Man! That guy was just like--BAM!--and Rhino was out like a *light!*
Uh-huh.
"Uh-huh"? Lauren--it was **AMAZING!** I've never--I've never ***seen*** anything like that in my *life!*
Yeah? Have you seen your ***eye?***
Oh, come on, it was just a little piece of brick.
Just a--!
Trust me, Greg--you got ***lucky.*** All that "guys in their pajamas" stuff? ***At best,*** I'd call it a ***distraction.***
They interrupt your lunch. They make you late for work. They break water mains and burn out power grids. But mostly, they get people minding their own business ***hurt.*** Or worse.
There's ***nothing*** amazing about it.
Well...super heroes save a lot of lives, you can't argue that.
And this guy--this new guy? He was ***really*** something. He's gonna be big. You watch.
What? What's that look?
Nothing.

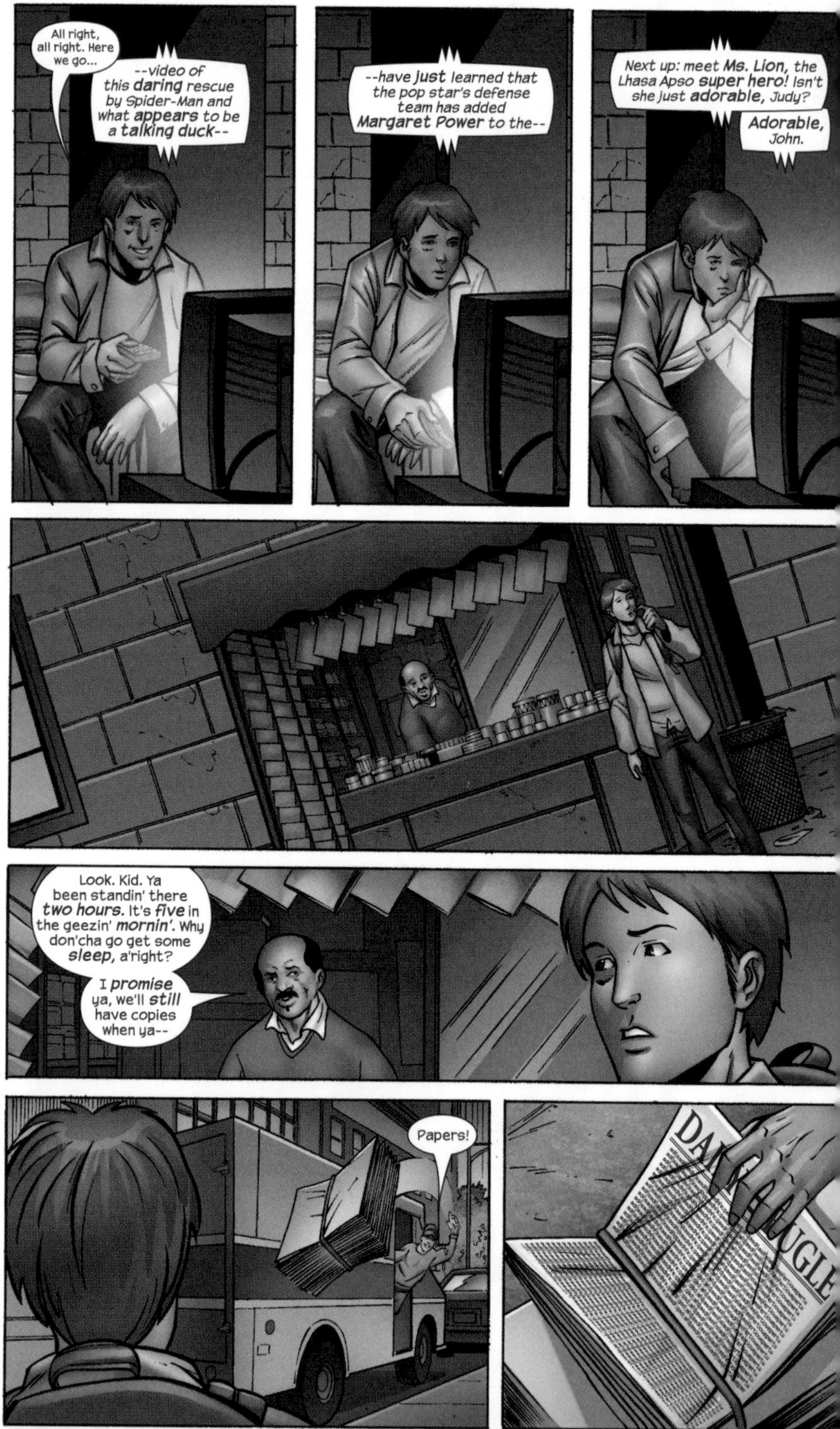
All right, all right. Here we go...
--video of this daring rescue by Spider-Man and what appears to be a talking duck--
--have just learned that the pop star's defense team has added Margaret Power to the--
Next up: meet Ms. Lion, the Lhasa Apso super hero! Isn't she just adorable, Judy?
Adorable, John.
Look. Kid. Ya been standin' there two hours. It's five in the geezin' mornin'. Why don'cha go get some sleep, a'right?
I promise ya, we'll still have copies when ya--
Papers!

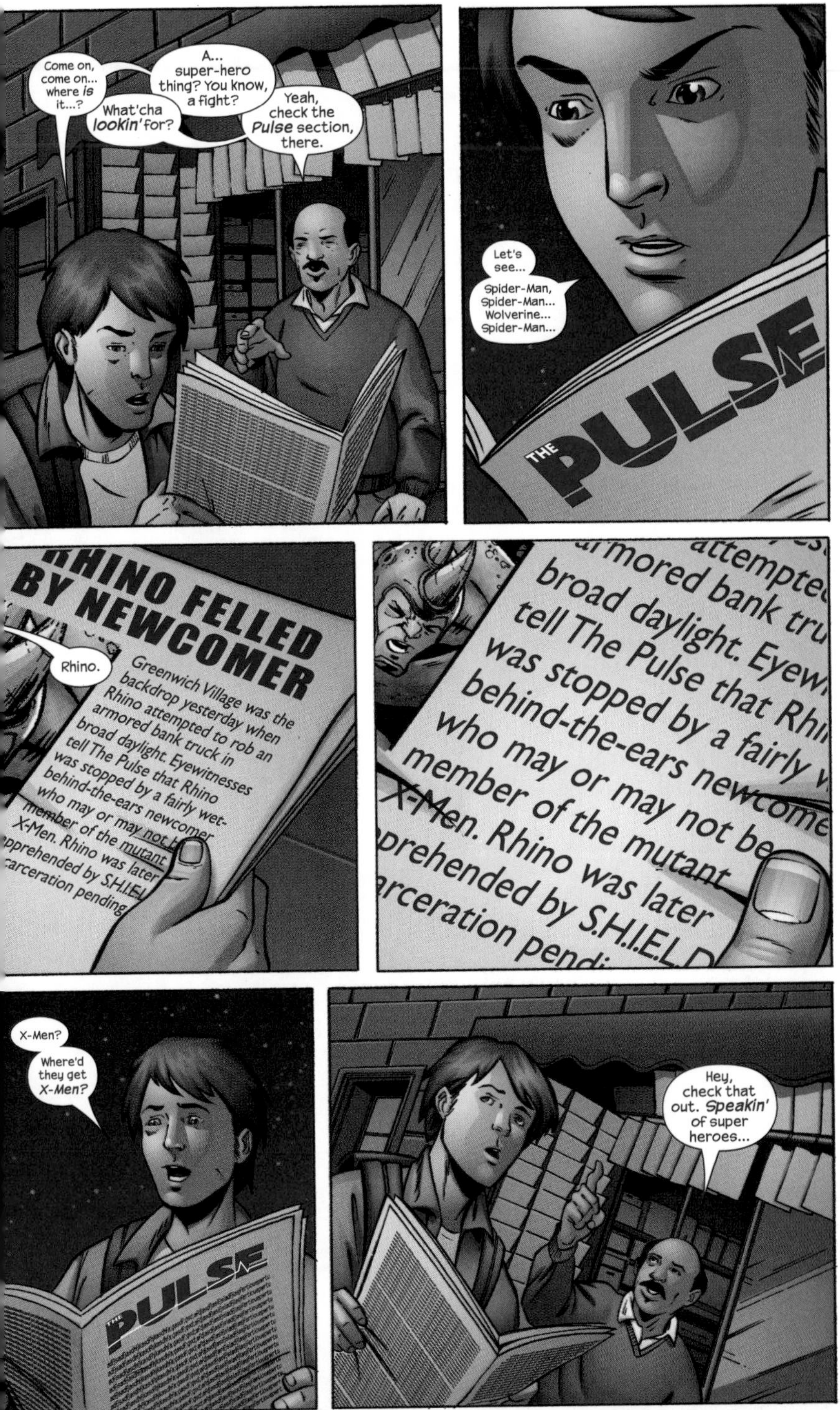

Come on, come on... where *is* it...?
What'cha *lookin'* for?
A... super-hero thing? You know, a fight?
Yeah, check the *Pulse* section, there.
Let's see...
Spider-Man, Spider-Man... Wolverine... Spider-Man...
THE PULSE
RHINO FELLED BY NEWCOMER
Rhino.
Greenwich Village was the backdrop yesterday when Rhino attempted to rob an armored bank truck in broad daylight. Eyewitnesses tell The Pulse that Rhino was stopped by a fairly wet-behind-the-ears newcomer who may or may not b member of the mutant X-Men. Rhino was later pprehended by S.H.I.E.L arceration pending
rmored bank tru
broad daylight. Eyew
tell The Pulse that Rhi
was stopped by a fairly
behind-the-ears newcome
who may or may not be
member of the mutant
X-Men. Rhino was later
prehended by S.H.I.E.L.D
rceration pendi
X-Men?
Where'd they get *X-Men*?
THE PULSE
Hey, check that out. *Speakin'* of super heroes...

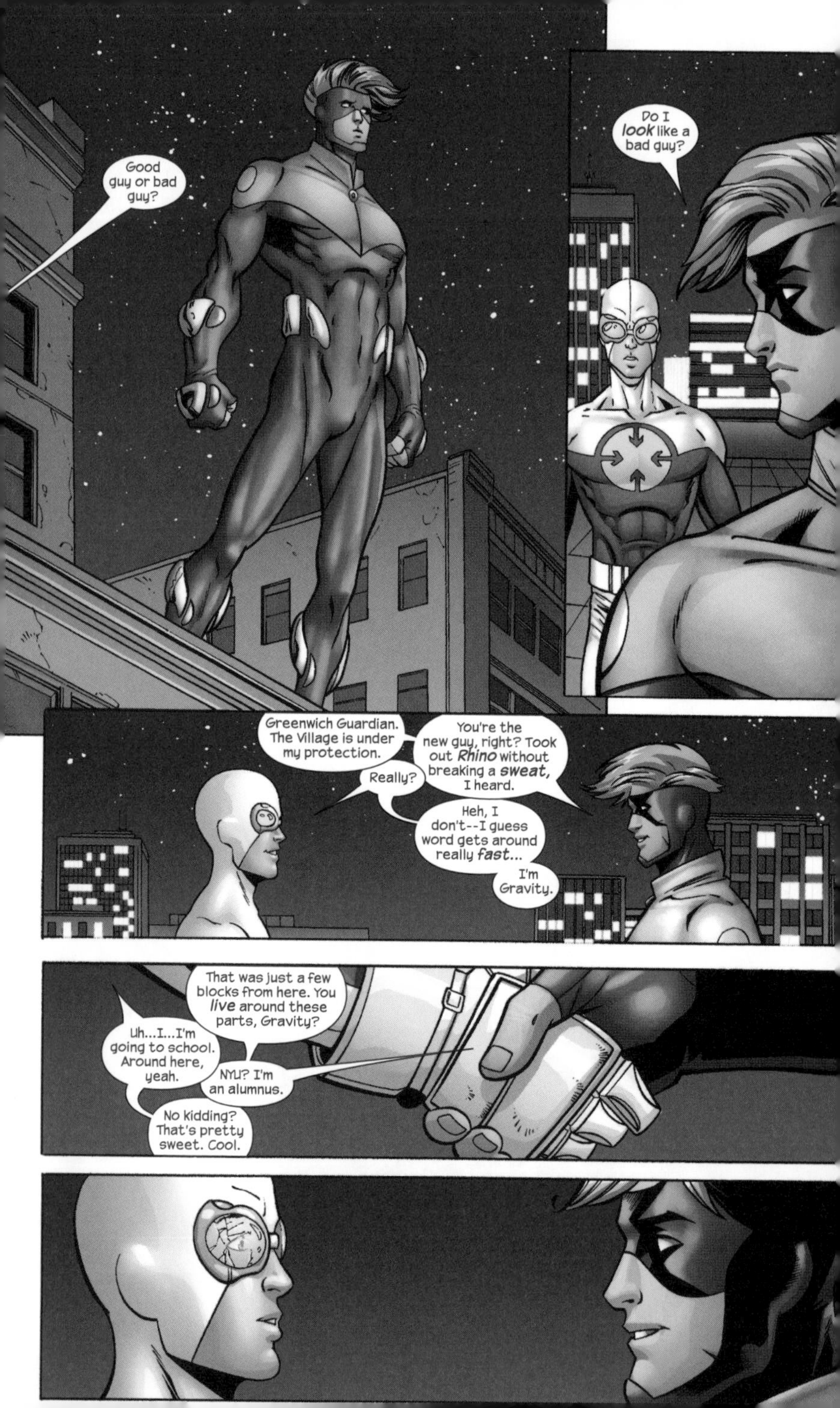
Good guy or bad guy?
Do I *look* like a bad guy?
Greenwich Guardian. The Village is under my protection.
You're the new guy, right? Took out *Rhino* without breaking a *sweat*, I heard.
Really?
Heh, I don't--I guess word gets around really *fast*...
I'm Gravity.
That was just a few blocks from here. You *live* around these parts, Gravity?
Uh...I...I'm going to school. Around here, yeah.
NYU? I'm an alumnus.
No kidding? That's pretty sweet. Cool.

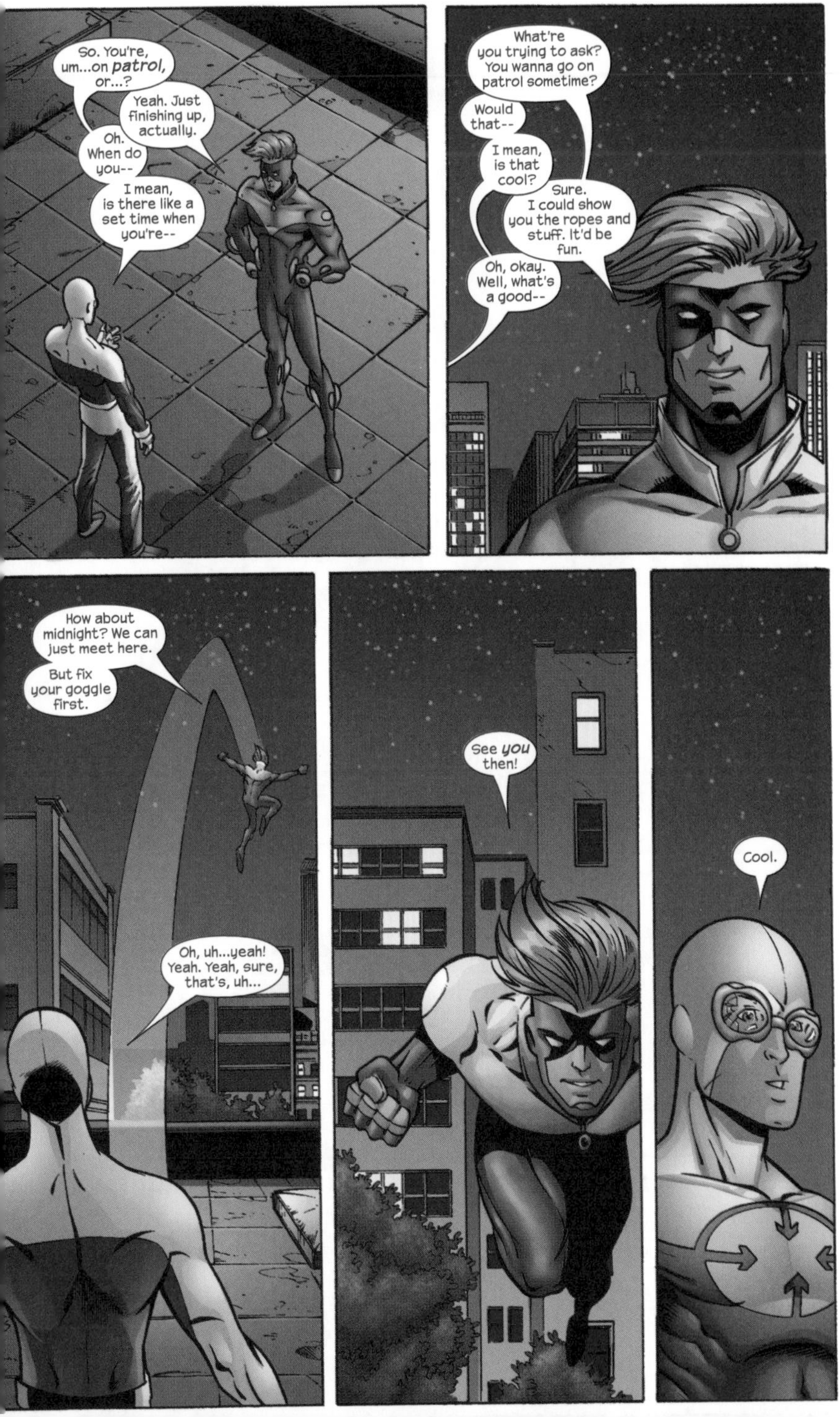

So. You're, um...on *patrol*, or...?
Yeah. Just finishing up, actually.
Oh. When do you--
I mean, is there like a set time when you're--
What're you trying to ask? You wanna go on patrol sometime?
Would that--
I mean, is that cool?
Sure. I could show you the ropes and stuff. It'd be fun.
Oh, okay. Well, what's a good--
How about midnight? We can just meet here.
But fix your goggle first.
Oh, uh...yeah! Yeah. Yeah, sure, that's, uh...
See *you* then!
Cool.

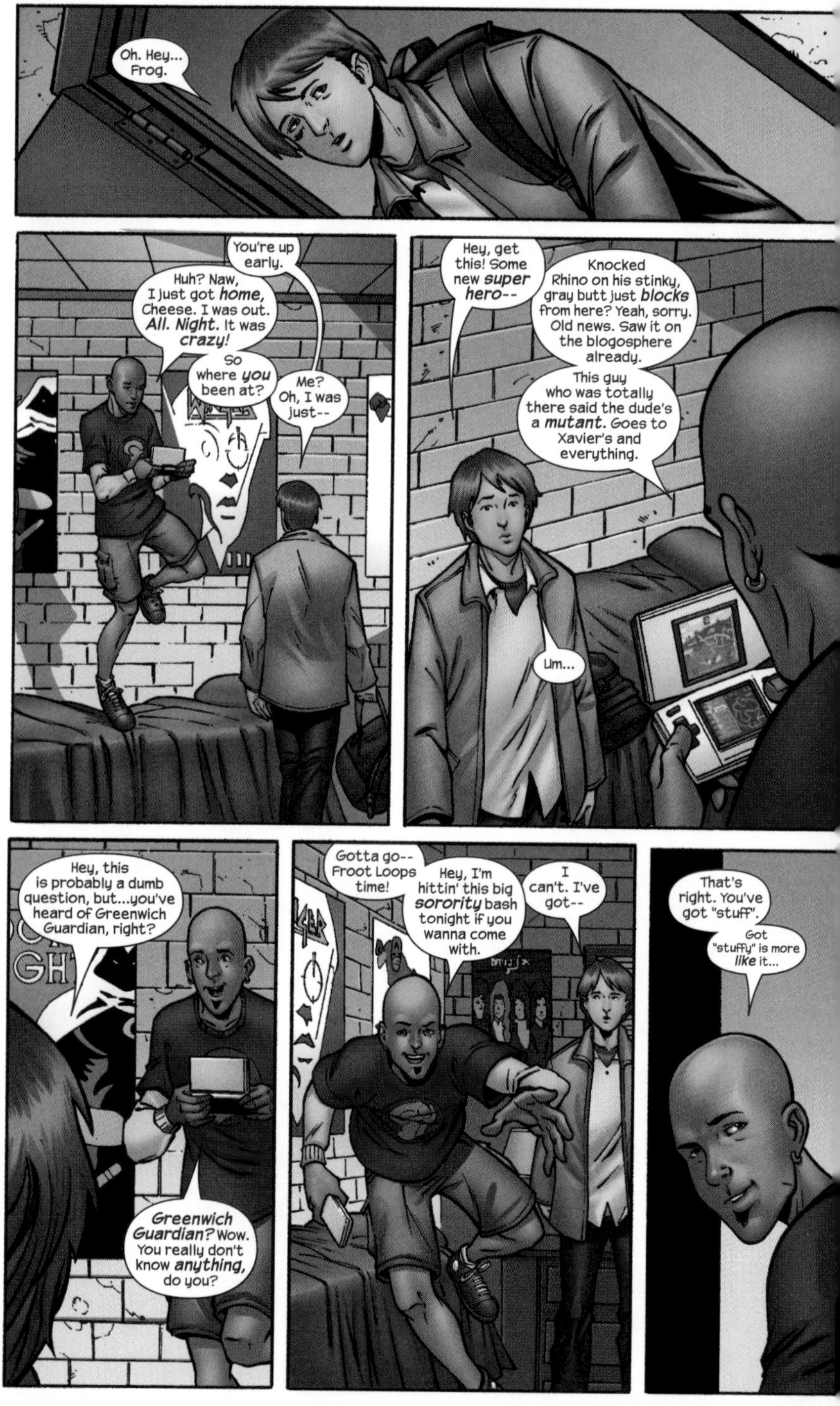

Oh. Hey... Frog.
You're up early.
Huh? Naw, I just got *home,* Cheese. I was out. *All. Night.* It was *crazy!*
So where *you* been at?
Me? Oh, I was just--
Hey, get this! Some new *super hero*--
Knocked Rhino on his stinky, gray butt just *blocks* from here? Yeah, sorry. Old news. Saw it on the blogosphere already.
This guy who was totally there said the dude's a *mutant.* Goes to Xavier's and everything.
Um...
Hey, this is probably a dumb question, but...you've heard of Greenwich Guardian, right?
Greenwich Guardian? Wow. You really don't know *anything,* do you?
Gotta go-- Froot Loops time!
Hey, I'm hittin' this big *sorority* bash tonight if you wanna come with.
I can't. I've got--
That's right. You've got "stuff".
Got "stuffy" is more *like* it...

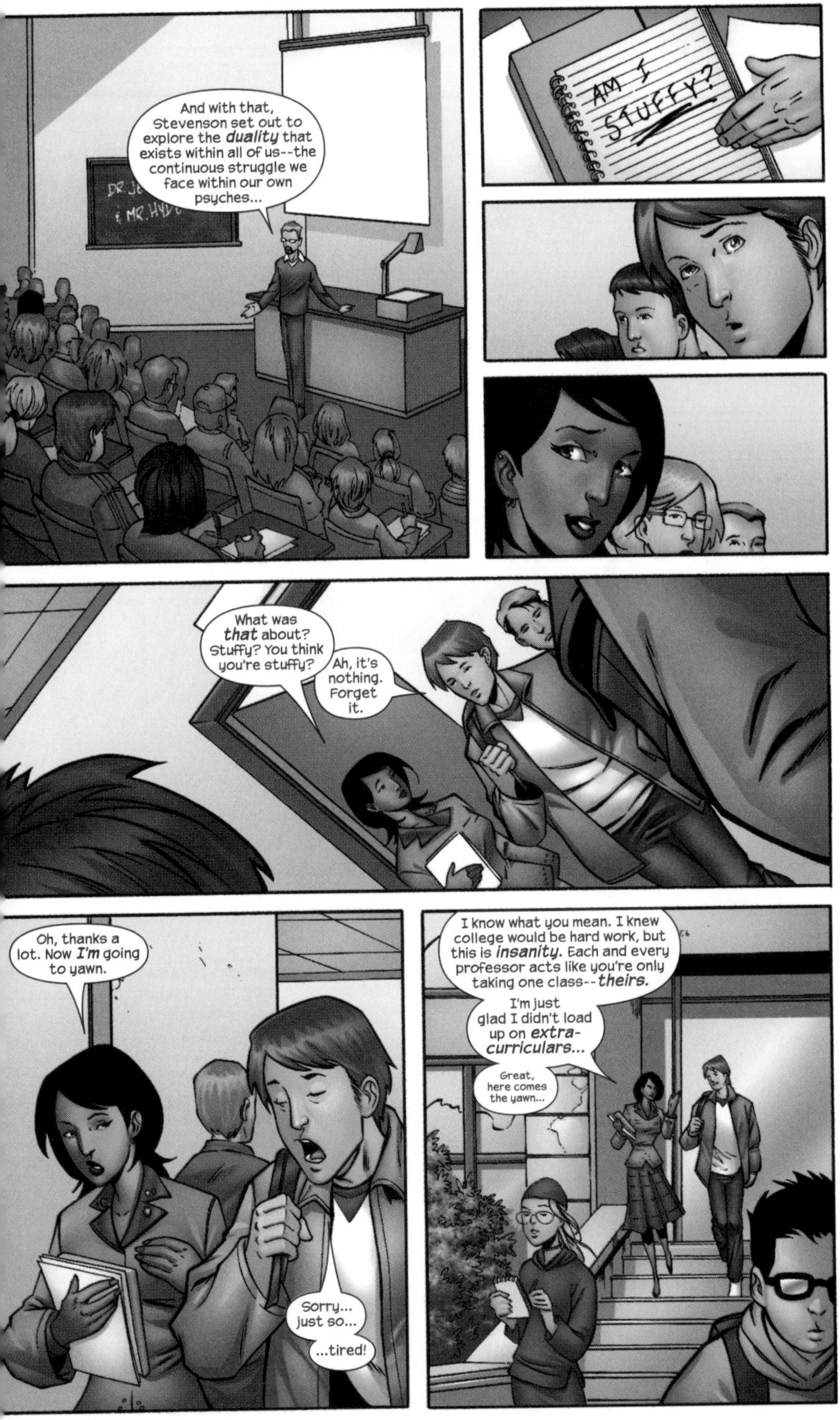

And with that, Stevenson set out to explore the *duality* that exists within all of us--the continuous struggle we face within our own psyches...
DR. JE
& MR. HYD
AM I STUFFY?
What was *that* about? Stuffy? You think you're stuffy?
Ah, it's nothing. Forget it.
Oh, thanks a lot. Now *I'm* going to yawn.
Sorry... just so...
...tired!
I know what you mean. I knew college would be hard work, but this is *insanity.* Each and every professor acts like you're only taking one class--*theirs.*
I'm just glad I didn't load up on *extra-curriculars...*
Great, here comes the yawn...

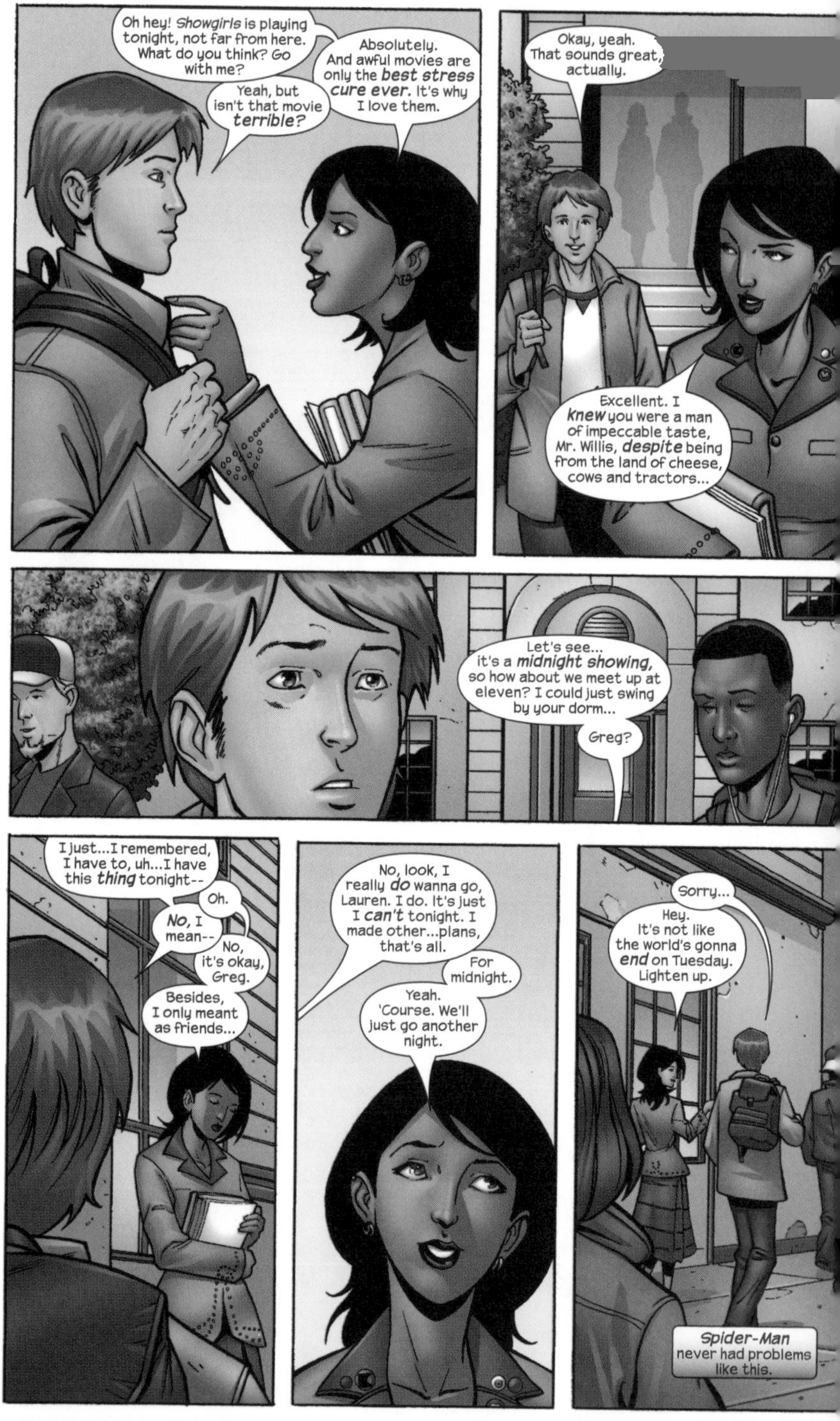

Oh hey! *Showgirls* is playing tonight, not far from here. What do you think? Go with me?
Yeah, but isn't that movie *terrible?*
Absolutely. And awful movies are only the **best stress cure ever.** It's why I love them.
Okay, yeah. That sounds great, actually.
Excellent. I *knew* you were a man of impeccable taste, Mr. Willis, *despite* being from the land of cheese, cows and tractors...
Let's see... it's a *midnight showing,* so how about we meet up at eleven? I could just swing by your dorm...
Greg?
I just...I remembered, I have to, uh...I have this *thing* tonight--
Oh.
No, I mean--
No, it's okay, Greg.
Besides, I only meant as friends...
No, look, I really *do* wanna go, Lauren. I do. It's just I *can't* tonight. I made other...plans, that's all.
For midnight.
Yeah. 'Course. We'll just go another night.
Sorry...
Hey. It's not like the world's gonna *end* on Tuesday. Lighten up.
Spider-Man never had problems like this.

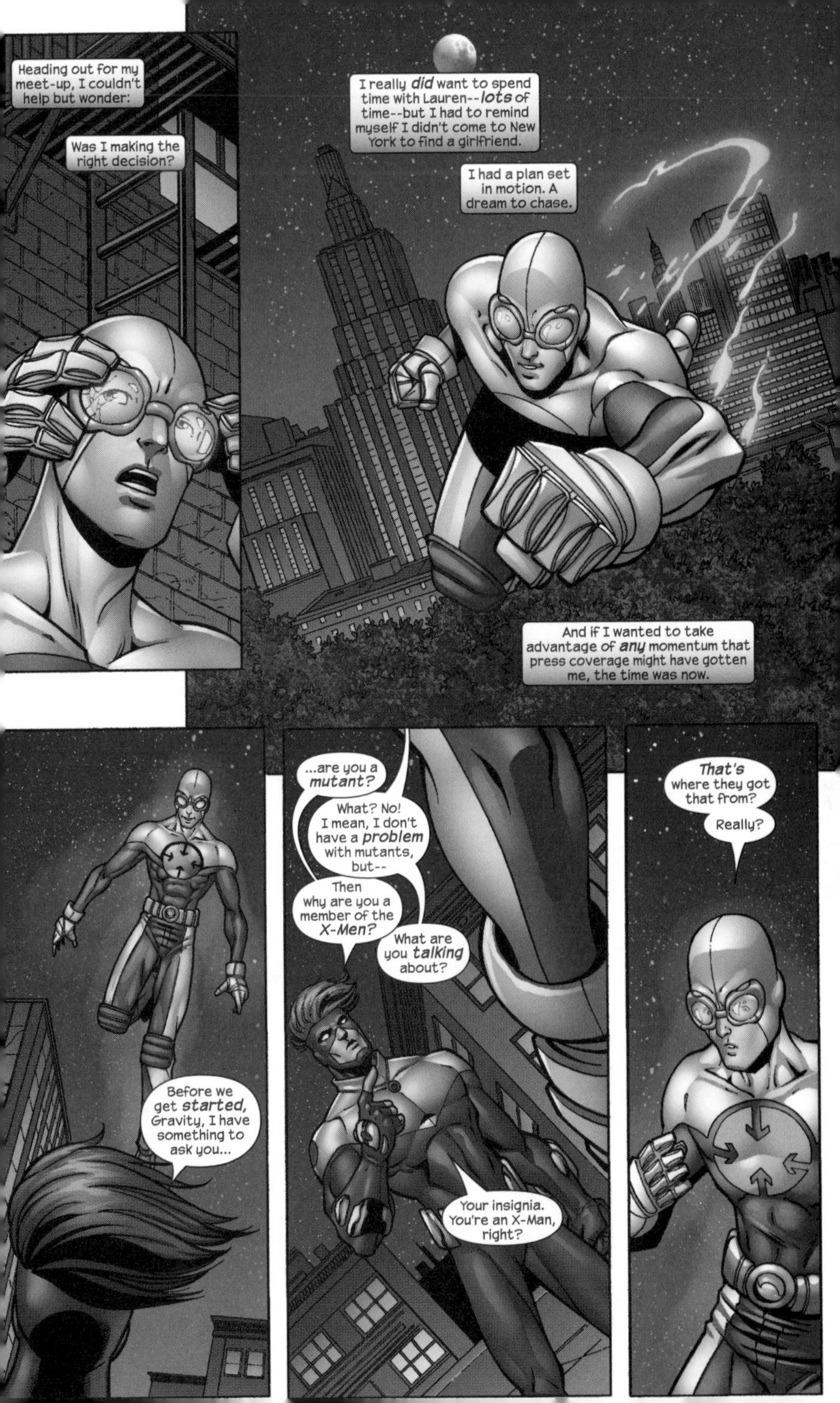

Heading out for my meet-up, I couldn't help but wonder:
Was I making the right decision?
I really did want to spend time with Lauren--lots of time--but I had to remind myself I didn't come to New York to find a girlfriend.
I had a plan set in motion. A dream to chase.
And if I wanted to take advantage of any momentum that press coverage might have gotten me, the time was now.
Before we get started, Gravity, I have something to ask you...
...are you a mutant?
What? No! I mean, I don't have a problem with mutants, but--
Then why are you a member of the X-Men?
What are you talking about?
Your insignia. You're an X-Man, right?
That's where they got that from?
Really?

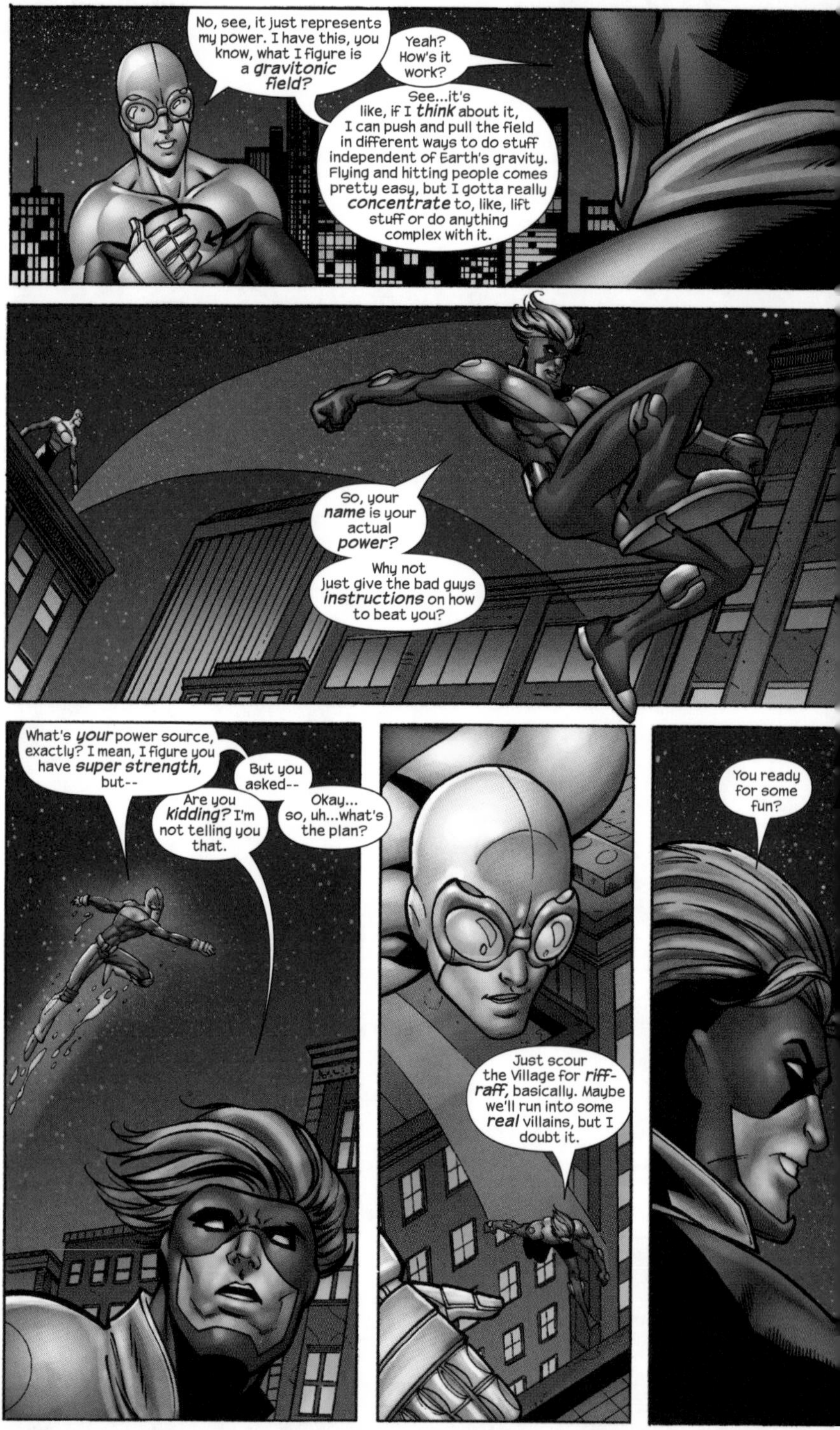
No, see, it just represents my power. I have this, you know, what I figure is a gravitonic field?
Yeah? How's it work?
See...it's like, if I think about it, I can push and pull the field in different ways to do stuff independent of Earth's gravity. Flying and hitting people comes pretty easy, but I gotta really concentrate to, like, lift stuff or do anything complex with it.
So, your name is your actual power?
Why not just give the bad guys instructions on how to beat you?
What's your power source, exactly? I mean, I figure you have super strength, but--
But you asked--
Are you kidding? I'm not telling you that.
Okay... so, uh...what's the plan?
Just scour the Village for riff-raff, basically. Maybe we'll run into some real villains, but I doubt it.
You ready for some fun?

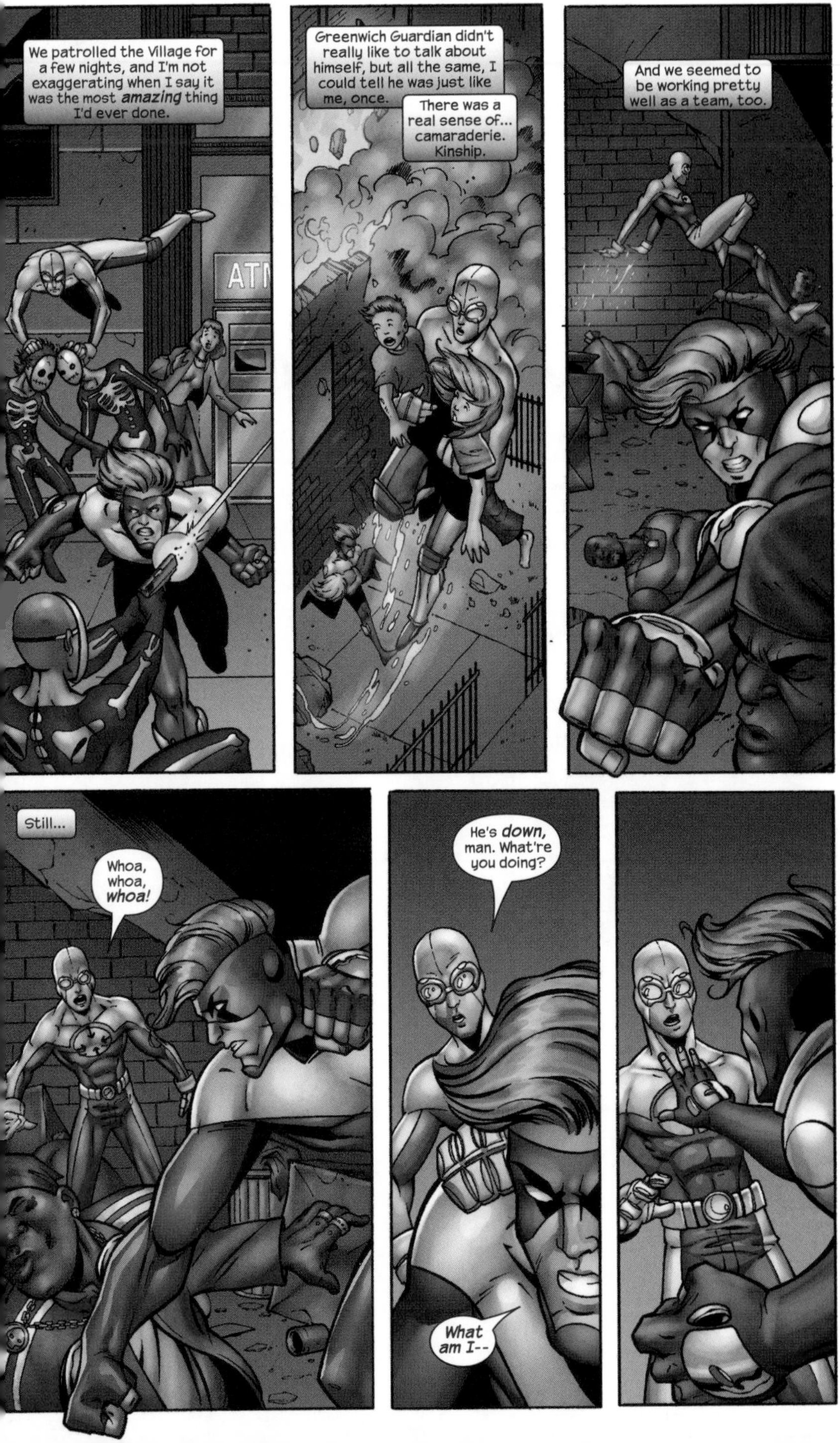
We patrolled the Village for a few nights, and I'm not exaggerating when I say it was the most *amazing* thing I'd ever done.
Greenwich Guardian didn't really like to talk about himself, but all the same, I could tell he was just like me, once.
There was a real sense of... camaraderie. Kinship.
ATM
And we seemed to be working pretty well as a team, too.
Still...
Whoa, whoa, *whoa!*
He's *down,* man. What're you doing?
What am I--

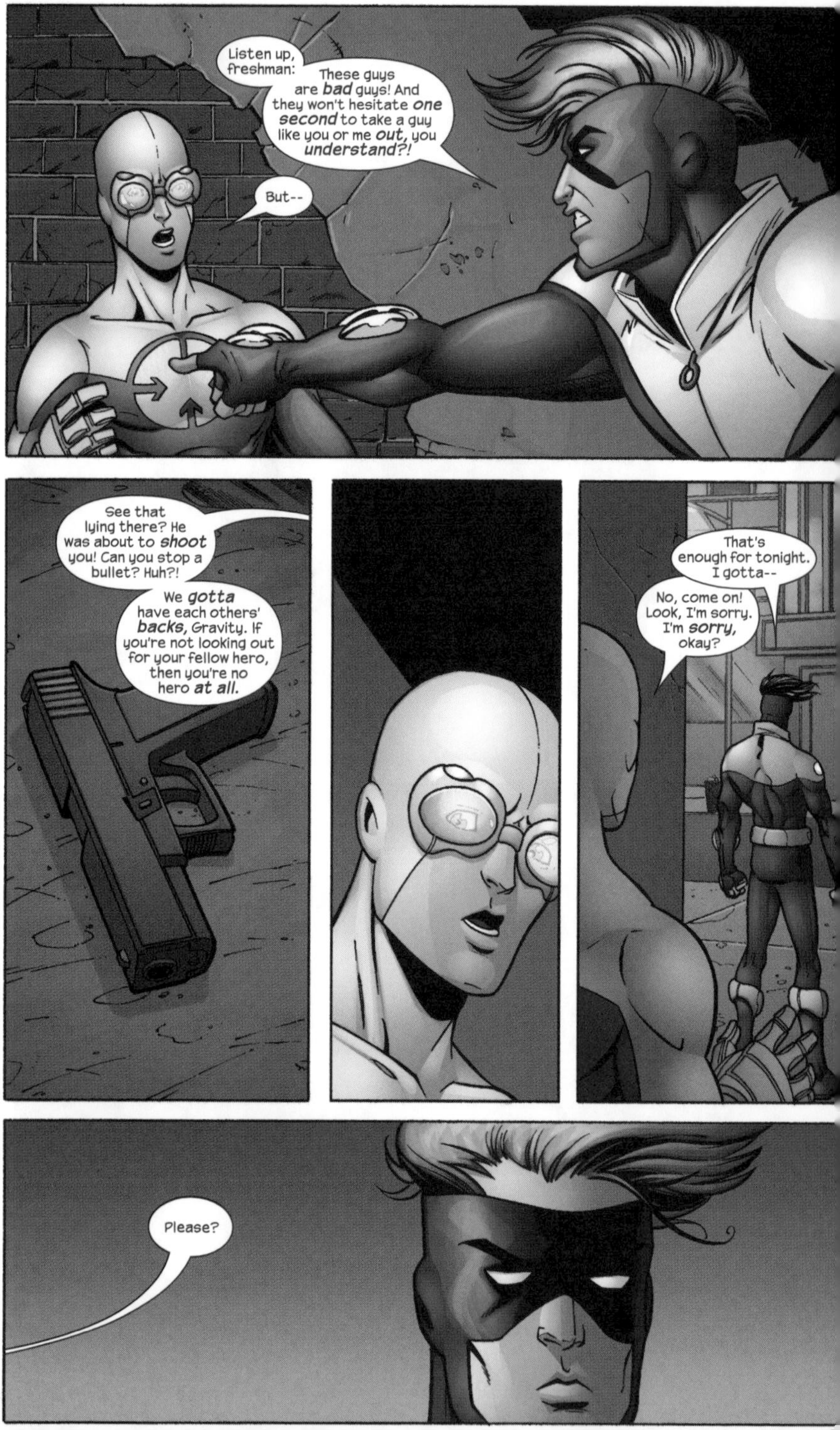

Listen up, freshman:
These guys are bad guys! And they won't hesitate one second to take a guy like you or me out, you understand?!
But--
See that lying there? He was about to shoot you! Can you stop a bullet? Huh?!
We gotta have each others' backs, Gravity. If you're not looking out for your fellow hero, then you're no hero at all.
That's enough for tonight. I gotta--
No, come on! Look, I'm sorry. I'm sorry, okay?
Please?

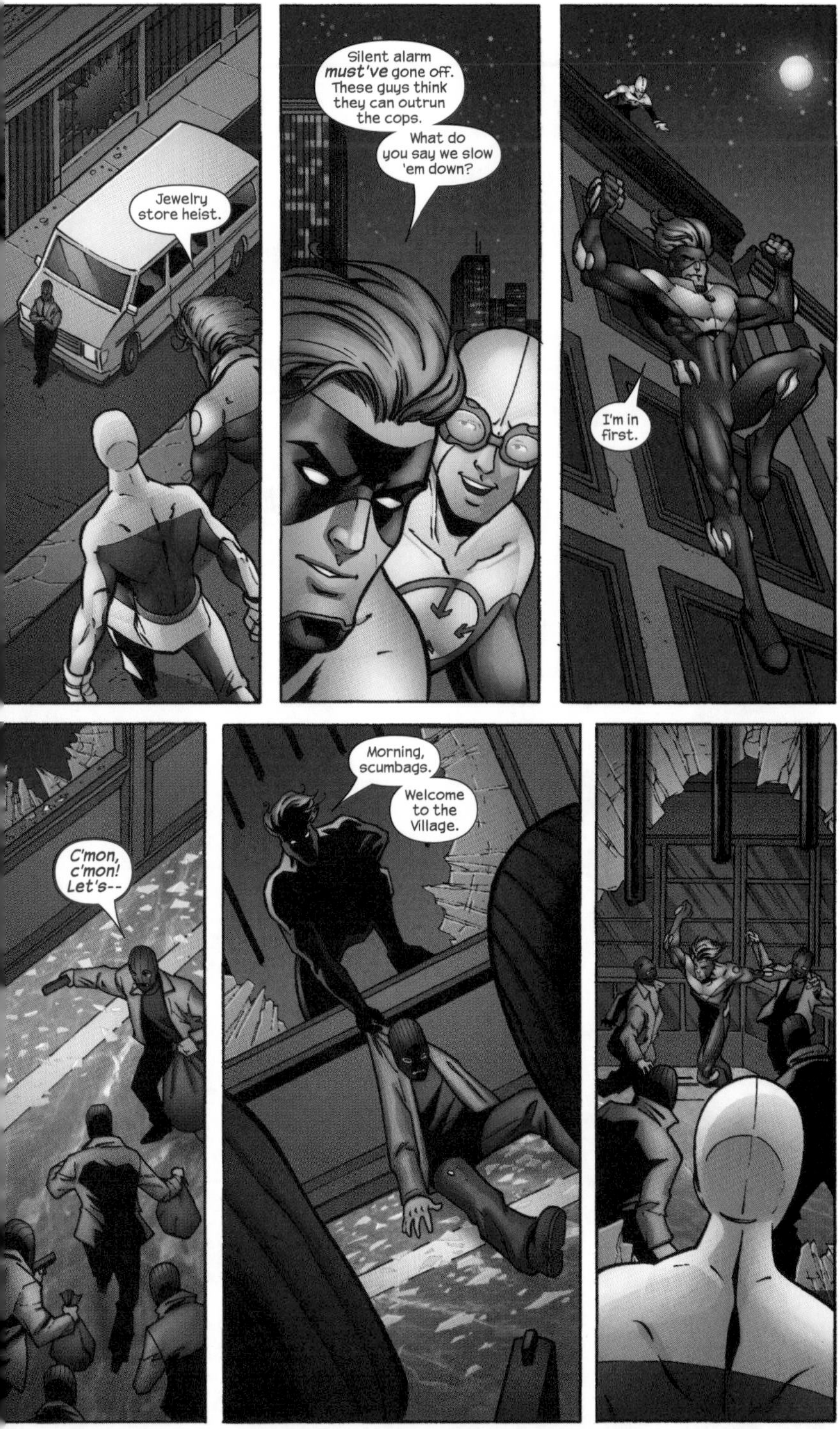

Jewelry store heist.
Silent alarm *must've* gone off. These guys think they can outrun the cops.
What do you say we slow 'em down?
I'm in first.
C'mon, c'mon! Let's--
Morning, scumbags.
Welcome to the Village.

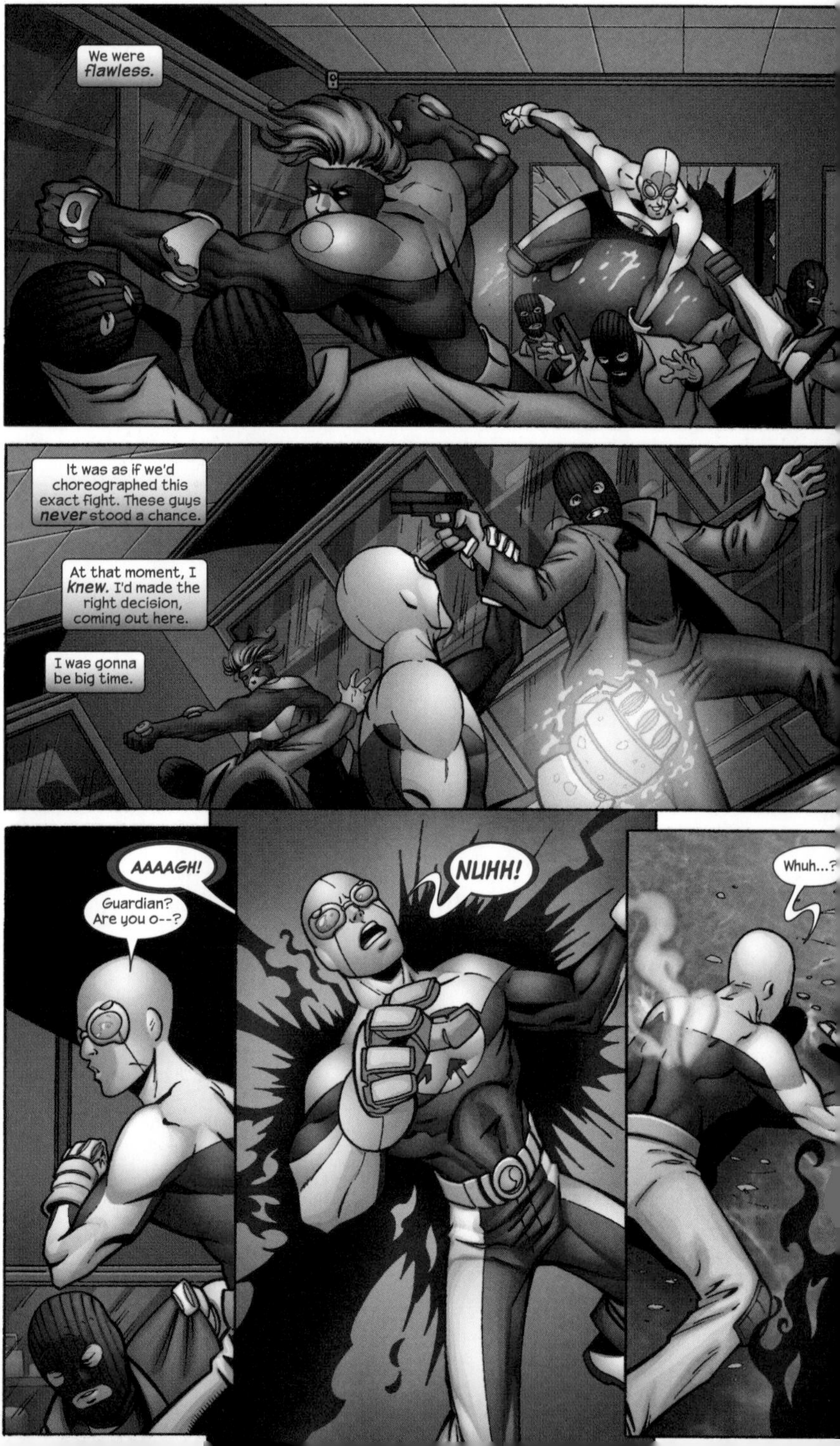
We were *flawless.*
It was as if we'd choreographed this exact fight. These guys *never* stood a chance.
At that moment, I *knew.* I'd made the right decision, coming out here.
I was gonna be big time.
AAAAGH!
Guardian? Are you o--?
NUHH!
Whuh...?

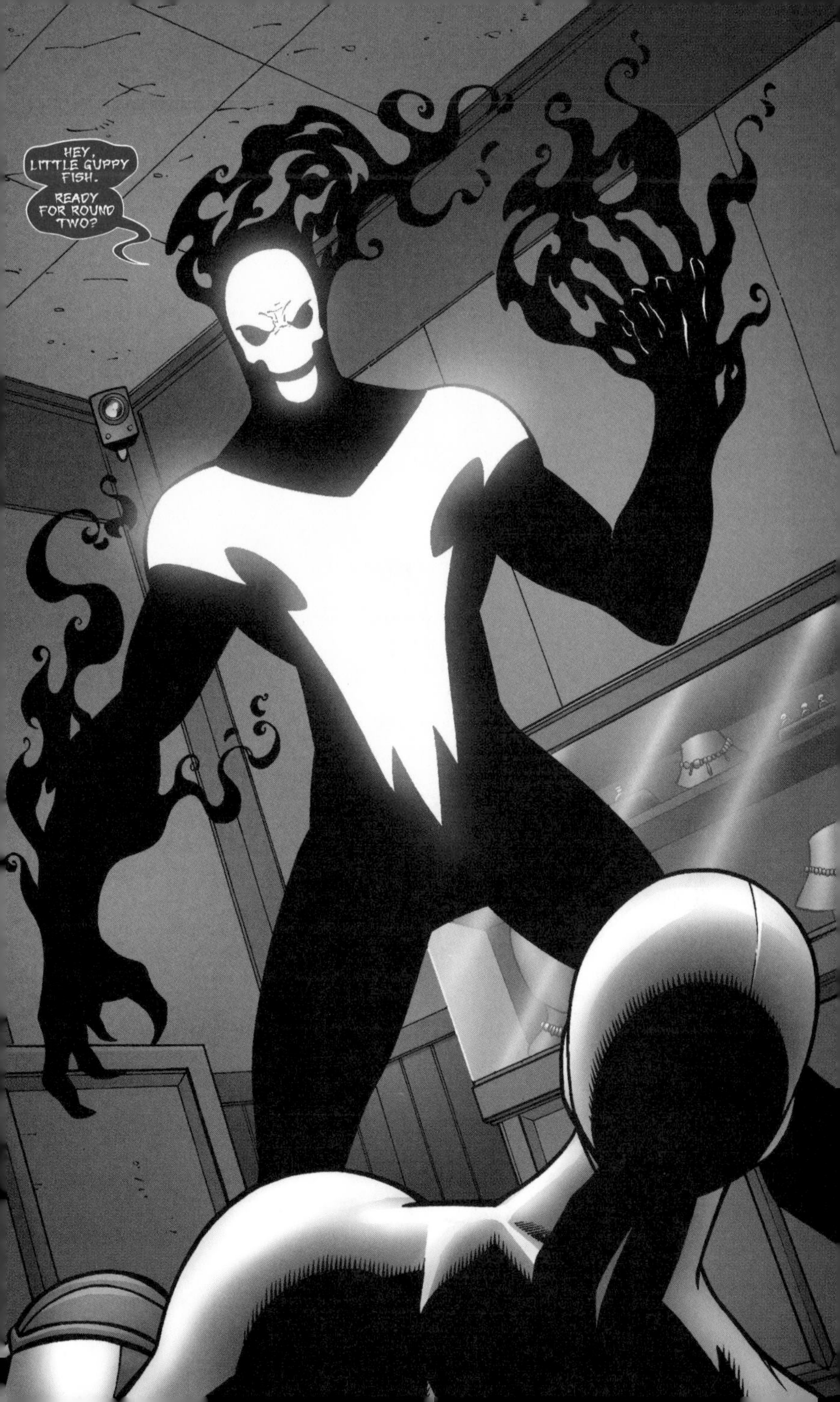
HEY, LITTLE GUPPY FISH.
READY FOR ROUND TWO?

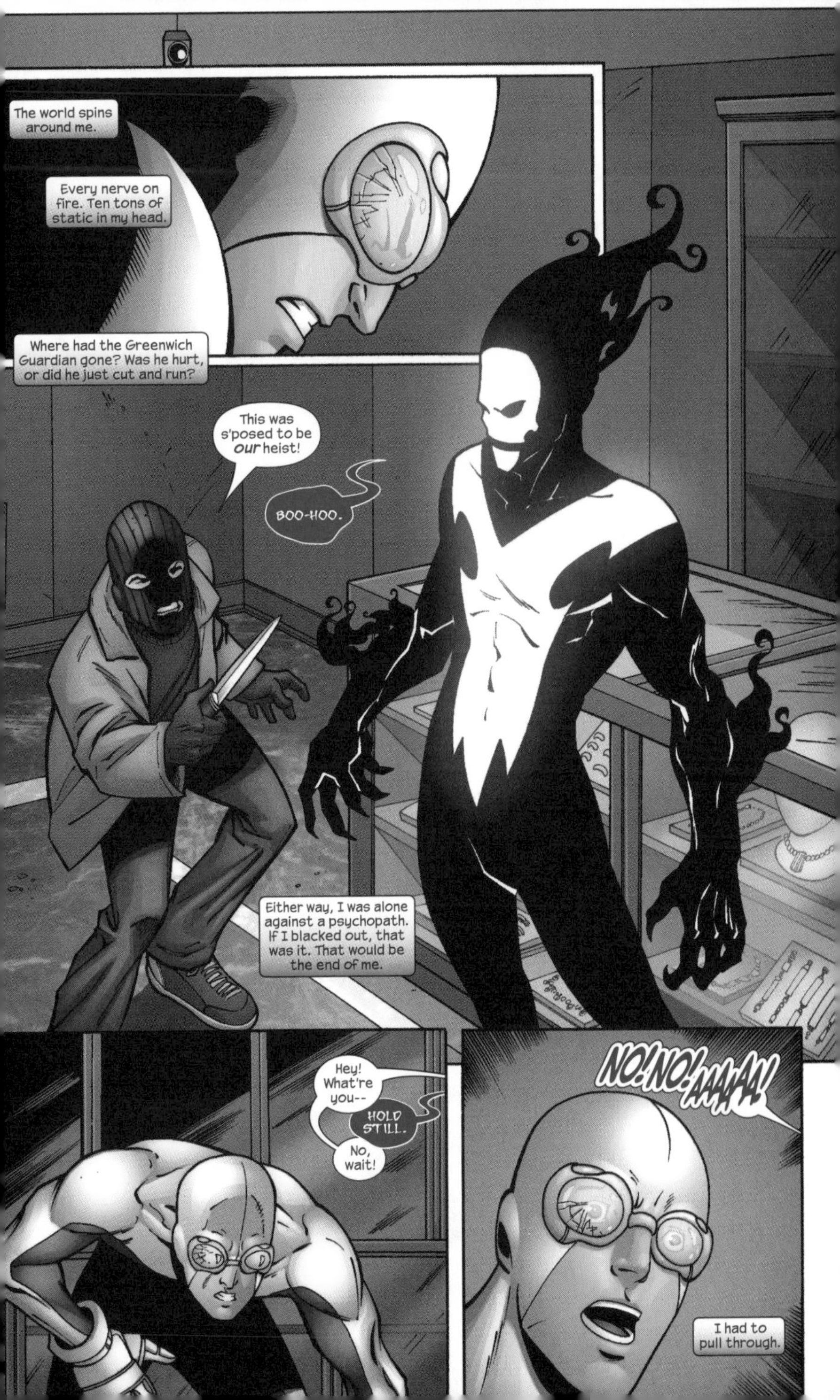
The world spins around me.
Every nerve on fire. Ten tons of static in my head.
Where had the Greenwich Guardian gone? Was he hurt, or did he just cut and run?
This was s'posed to be ***our*** heist!
BOO-HOO.
Either way, I was alone against a psychopath. If I blacked out, that was it. That would be the end of me.
Hey! What're you--
HOLD STILL.
No, wait!
NO! NO! AAAAA!
I had to pull through.

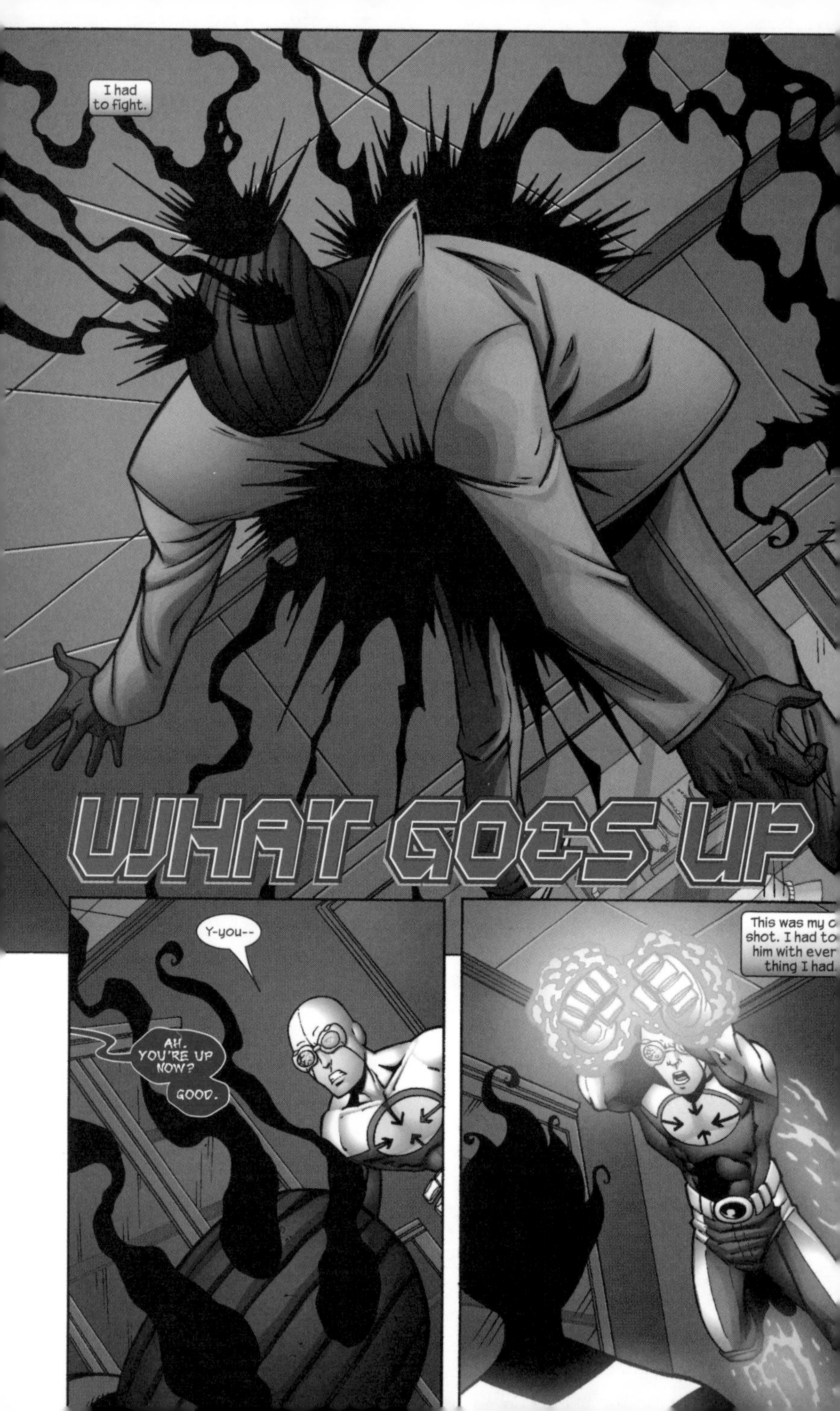
I had to fight.
WHAT GOES UP
Y-you--
AH. YOU'RE UP NOW?
GOOD.
This was my c
shot. I had to
him with ever
thing I had.

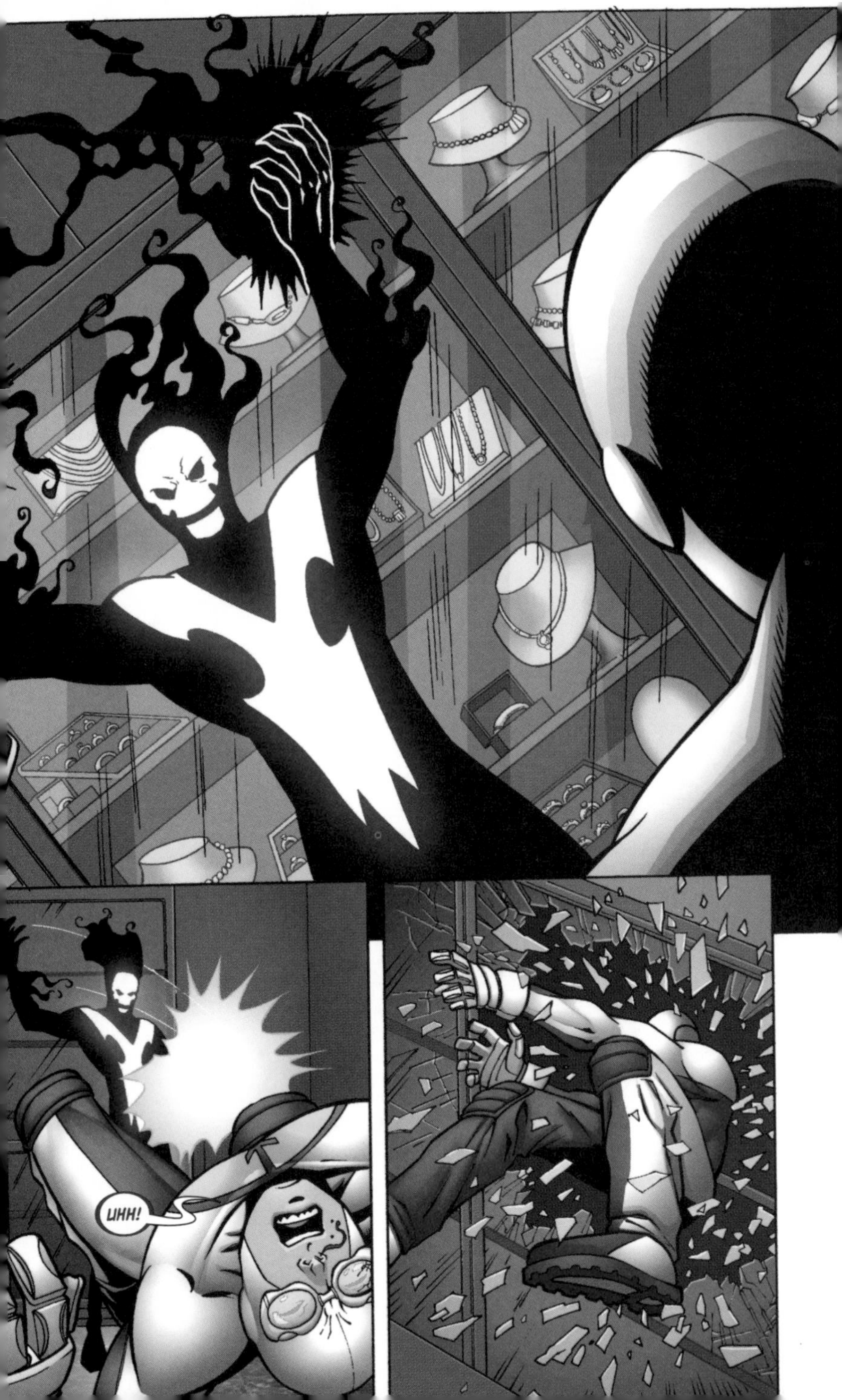
UHH!

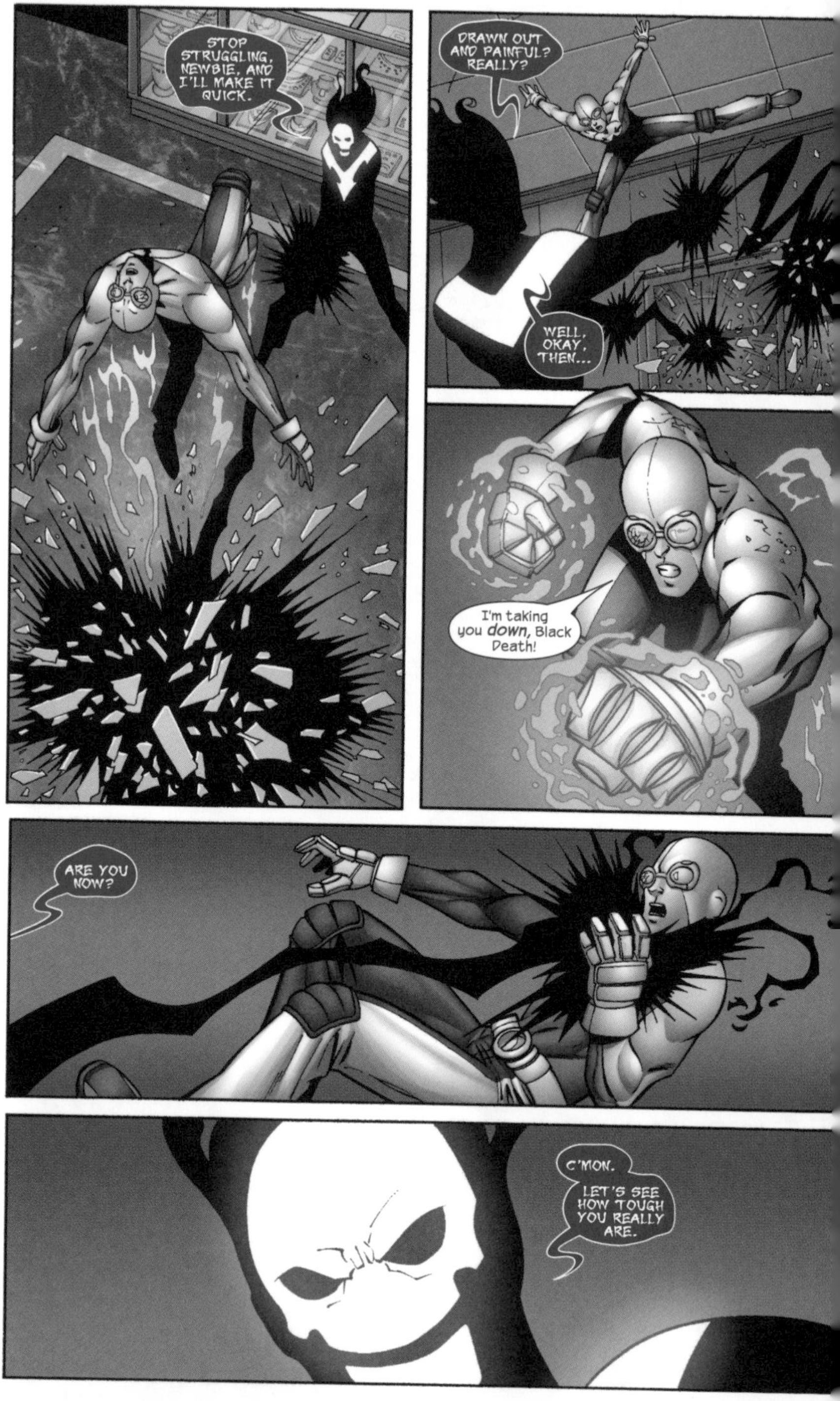
STOP STRUGGLING, NEWBIE, AND I'LL MAKE IT QUICK.
DRAWN OUT AND PAINFUL? REALLY?
WELL, OKAY, THEN...
I'm taking you *down,* Black Death!
ARE YOU NOW?
C'MON.
LET'S SEE HOW TOUGH YOU REALLY ARE.

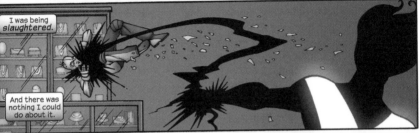

I was being *slaughtered.*

And there was nothing I could do about it.

He was so *fast...*

Why couldn't I break his hold? Was it something in his powers?

Or was it just fear?

If I didn't *free* myself, I'd be gone for sure. So...

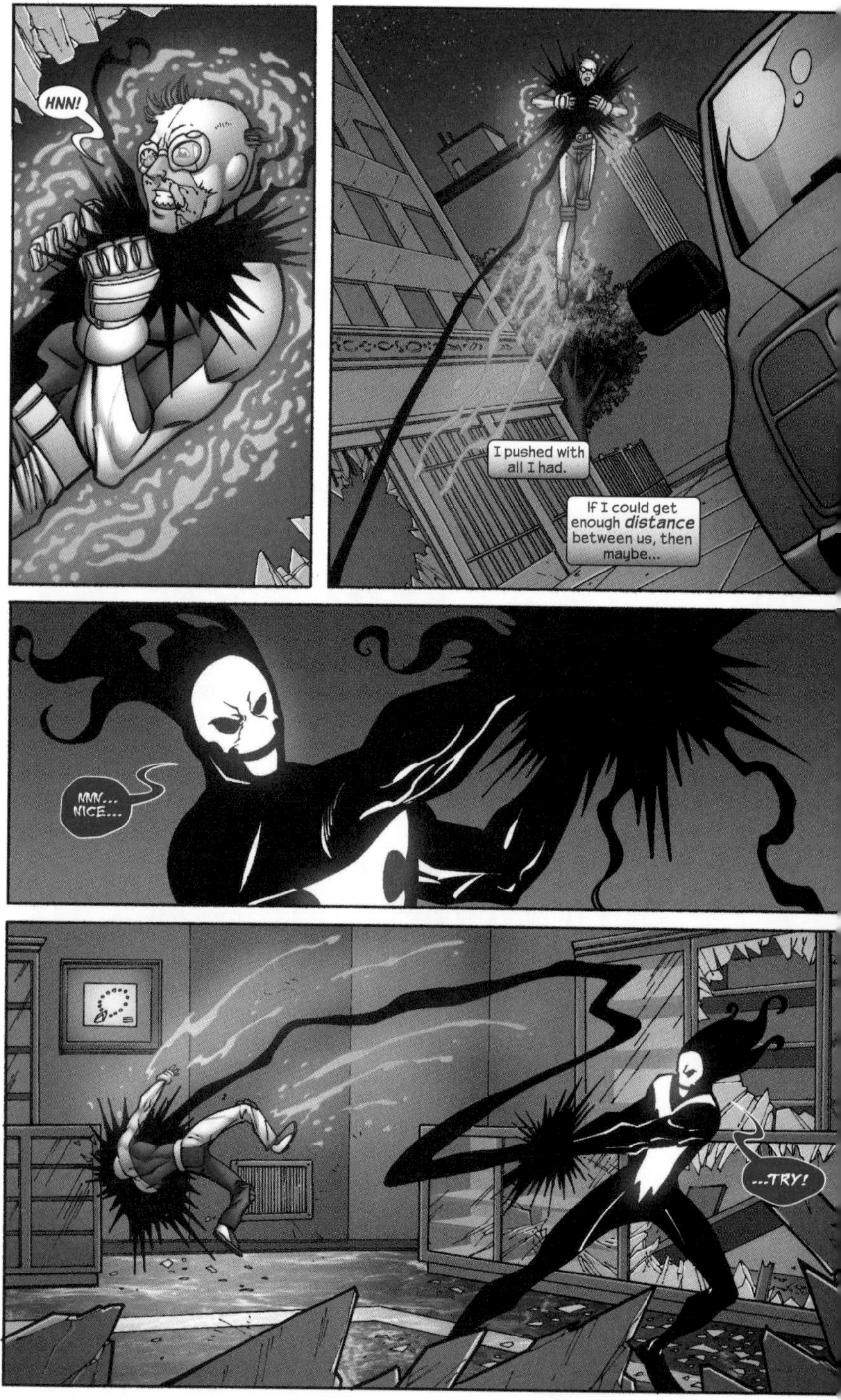
HNN!
I pushed with all I had.
If I could get enough *distance* between us, then maybe...
NNN... NICE...
...TRY!

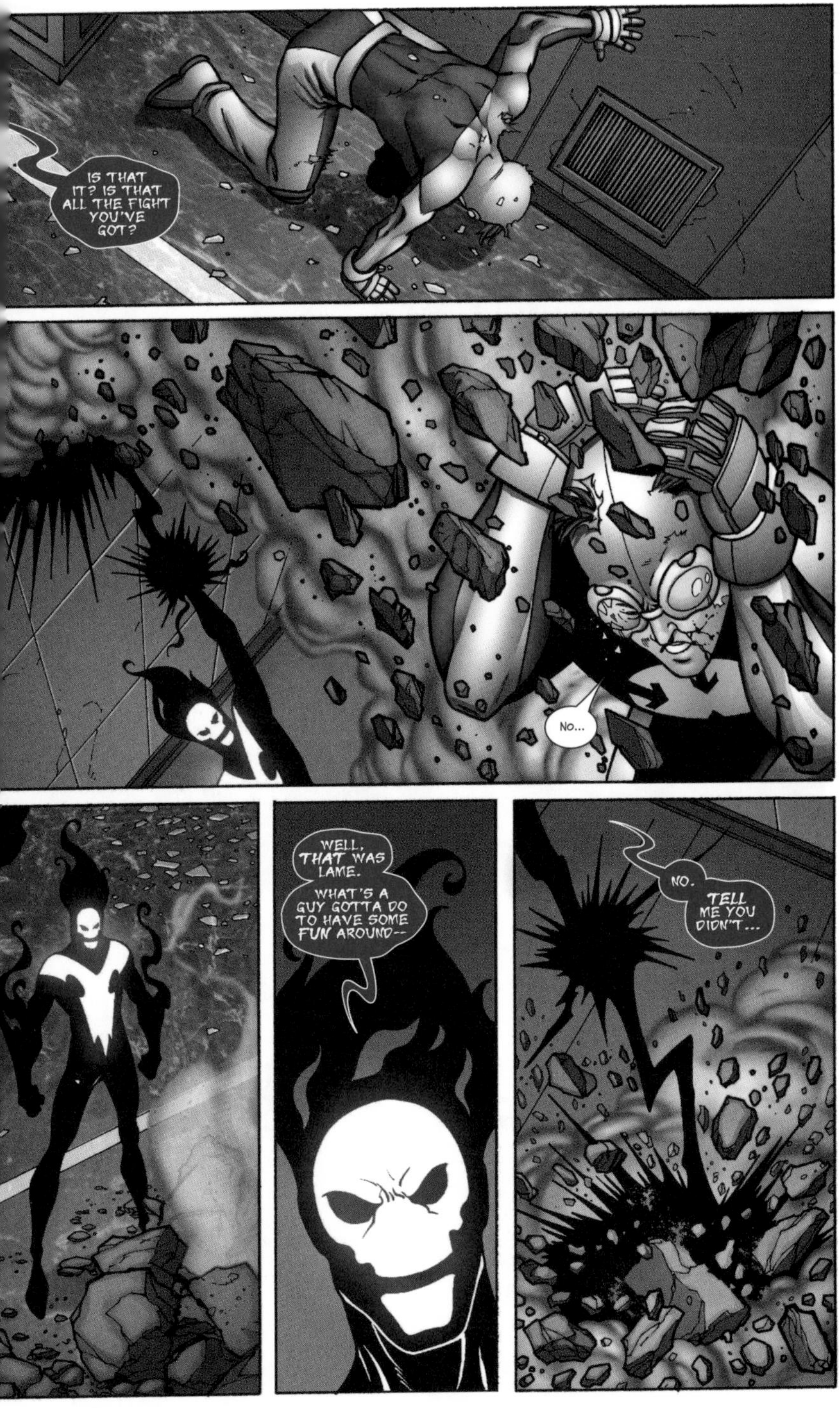
IS THAT IT? IS THAT ALL THE FIGHT YOU'VE GOT?
NO...
WELL, THAT WAS LAME.
WHAT'S A GUY GOTTA DO TO HAVE SOME FUN AROUND--
NO.
TELL ME YOU DIDN'T...

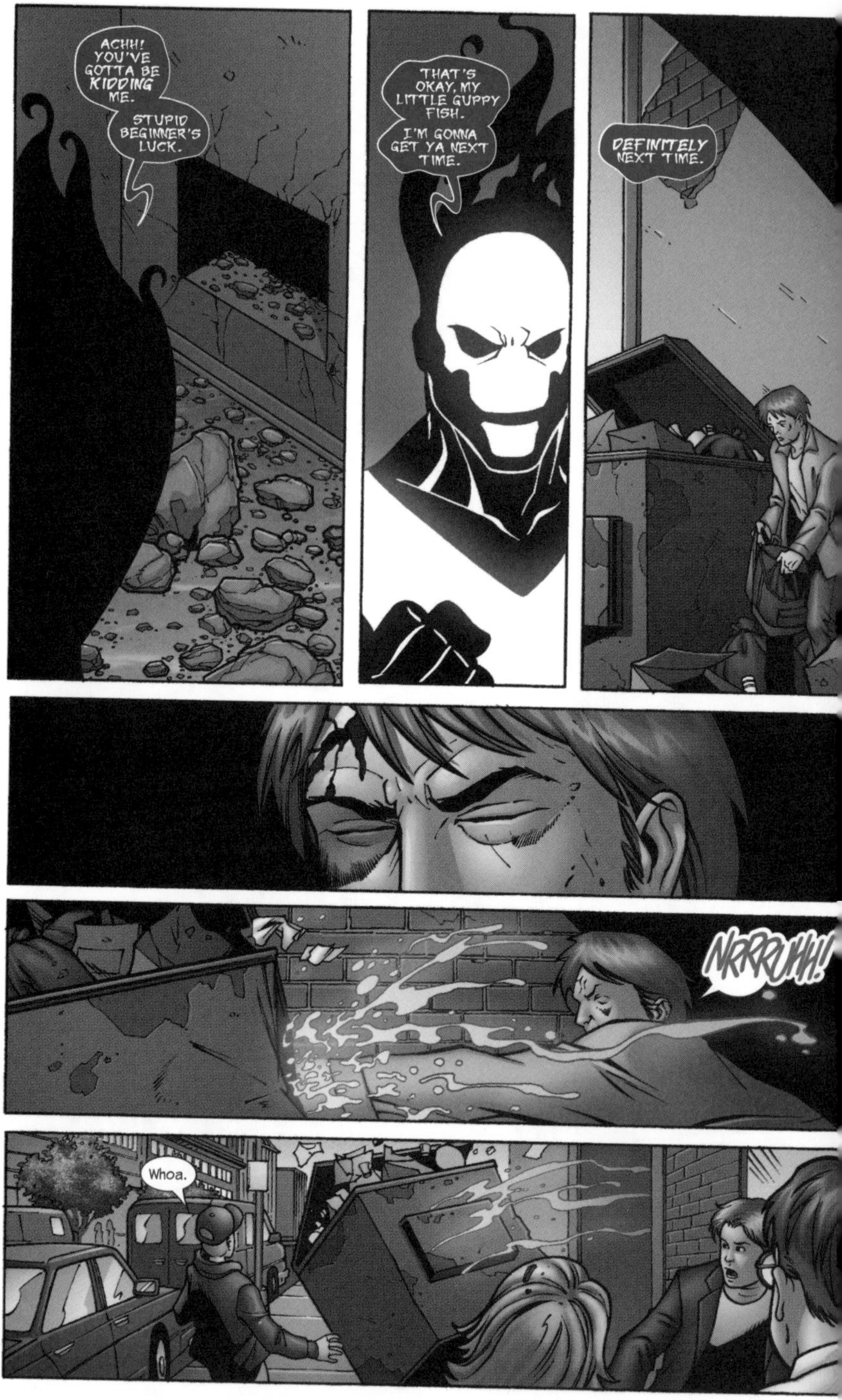
ACHH! YOU'VE GOTTA BE KIDDING ME.
STUPID BEGINNER'S LUCK.
THAT'S OKAY, MY LITTLE GUPPY FISH.
I'M GONNA GET YA NEXT TIME.
DEFINITELY NEXT TIME.
NRRRUHH!
Whoa.

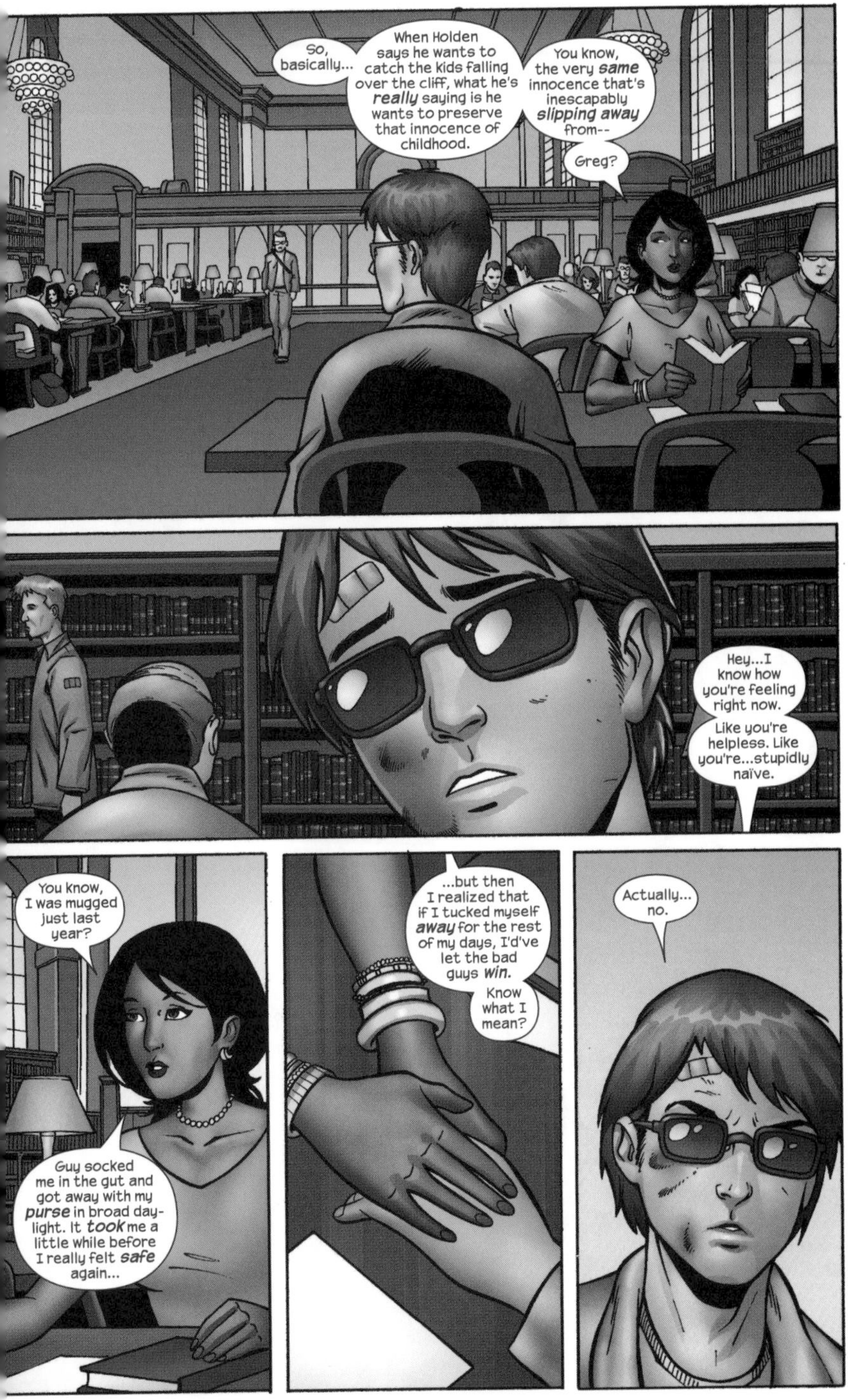
So, basically...
When Holden says he wants to catch the kids falling over the cliff, what he's *really* saying is he wants to preserve that innocence of childhood.
You know, the very *same* innocence that's inescapably *slipping away* from--
Greg?
Hey...I know how you're feeling right now.
Like you're helpless. Like you're...stupidly naïve.
You know, I was mugged just last year?
Guy socked me in the gut and got away with my *purse* in broad daylight. It *took* me a little while before I really felt *safe* again...
...but then I realized that if I tucked myself *away* for the rest of my days, I'd've let the bad guys *win.*
Know what I mean?
Actually... no.

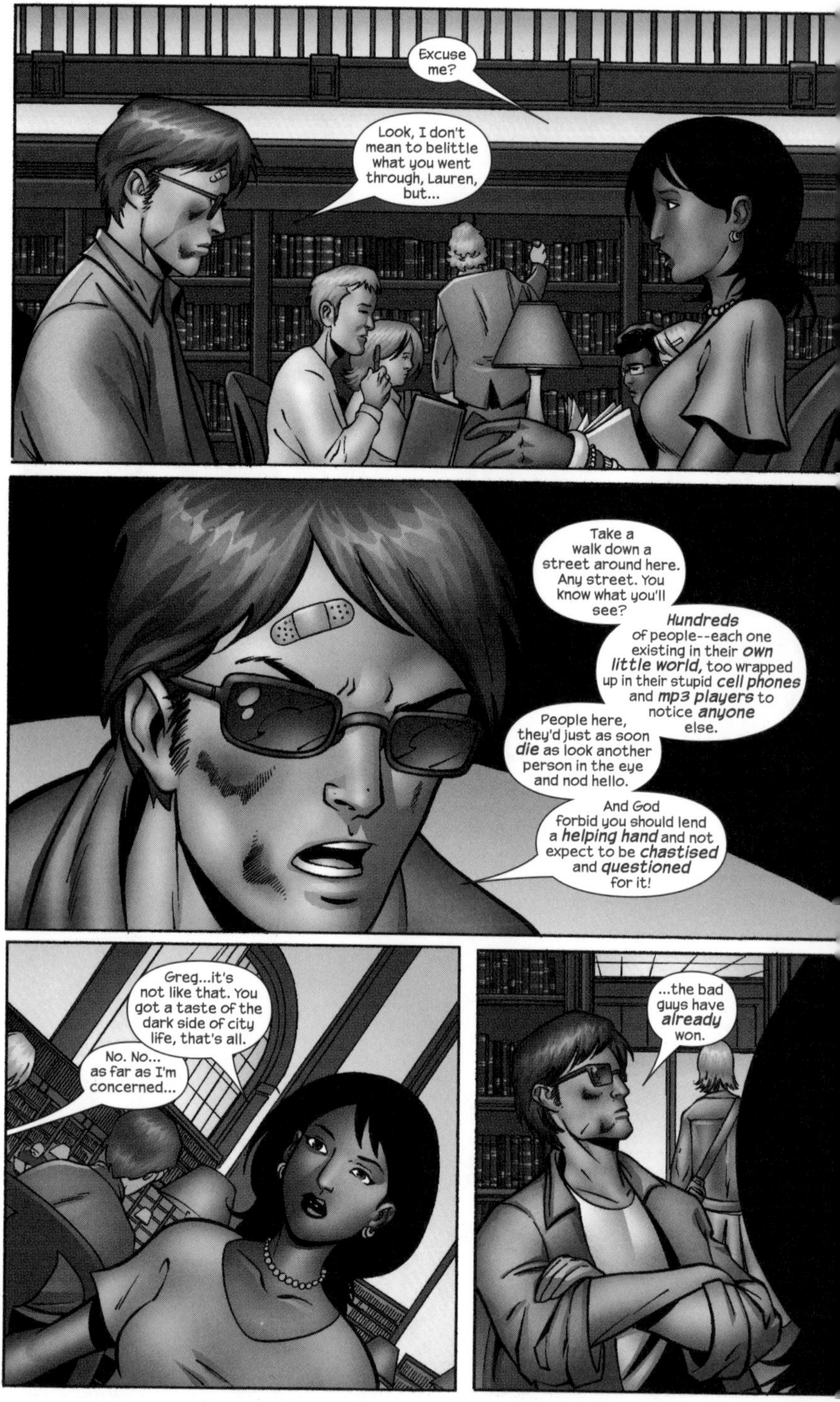
Excuse me?
Look, I don't mean to belittle what you went through, Lauren, but...
Take a walk down a street around here. Any street. You know what you'll see?
Hundreds of people--each one existing in their own little world, too wrapped up in their stupid cell phones and mp3 players to notice anyone else.
People here, they'd just as soon die as look another person in the eye and nod hello.
And God forbid you should lend a helping hand and not expect to be chastised and questioned for it!
Greg...it's not like that. You got a taste of the dark side of city life, that's all.
No. No... as far as I'm concerned...
...the bad guys have already won.

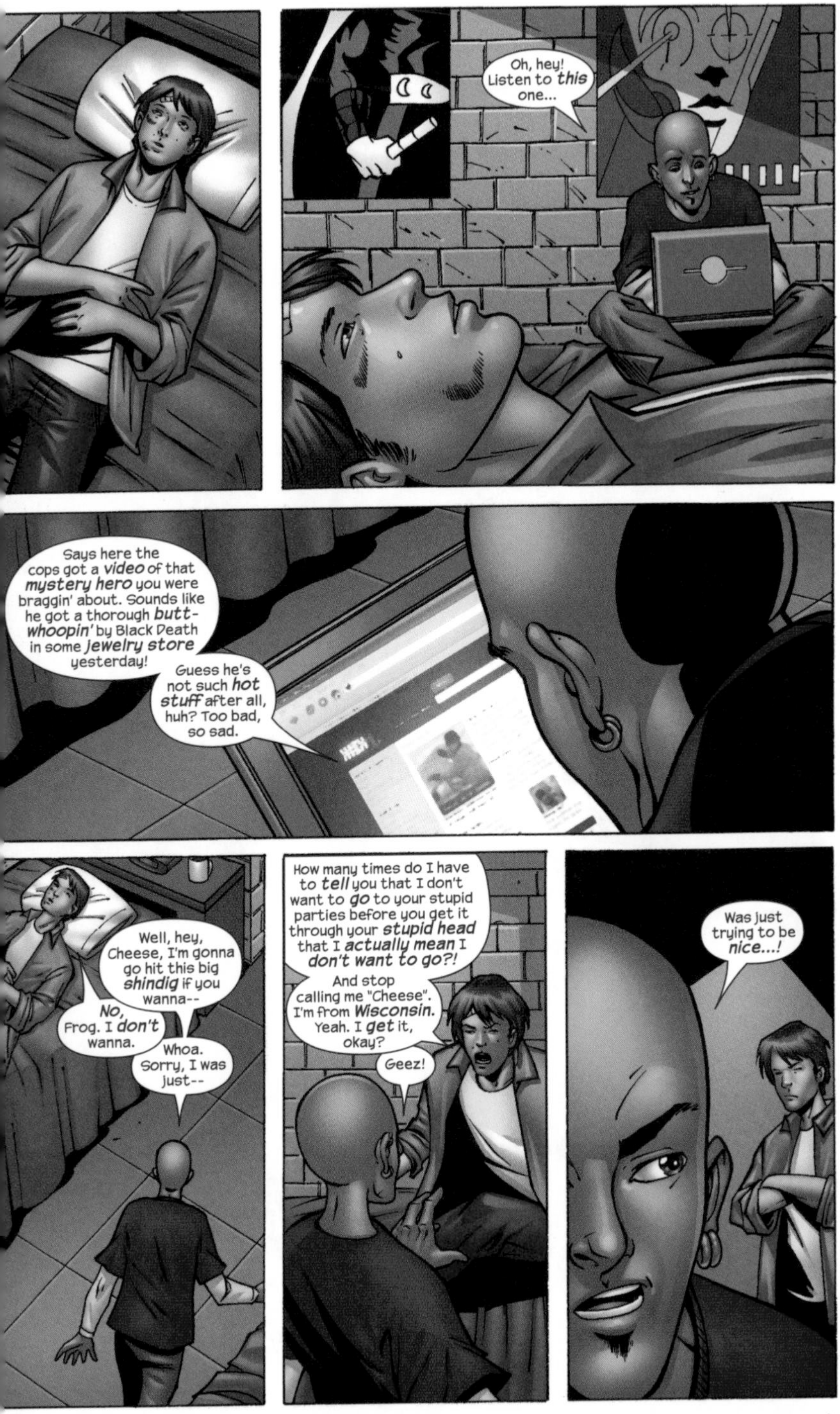

Oh, hey! Listen to *this* one...
Says here the cops got a *video* of that *mystery hero* you were braggin' about. Sounds like he got a thorough *butt-whoopin'* by Black Death in some *jewelry store* yesterday!
Guess he's not such *hot stuff* after all, huh? Too bad, so sad.
Well, hey, Cheese, I'm gonna go hit this big *shindig* if you wanna--
No, Frog. I *don't* wanna.
Whoa. Sorry, I was just--
How many times do I have to *tell* you that I don't want to *go* to your stupid parties before you get it through your *stupid head* that I *actually mean* I *don't want to go?!*
And stop calling me "Cheese". I'm from *Wisconsin*. Yeah. I *get* it, okay?
Geez!
Was just trying to be *nice...!*

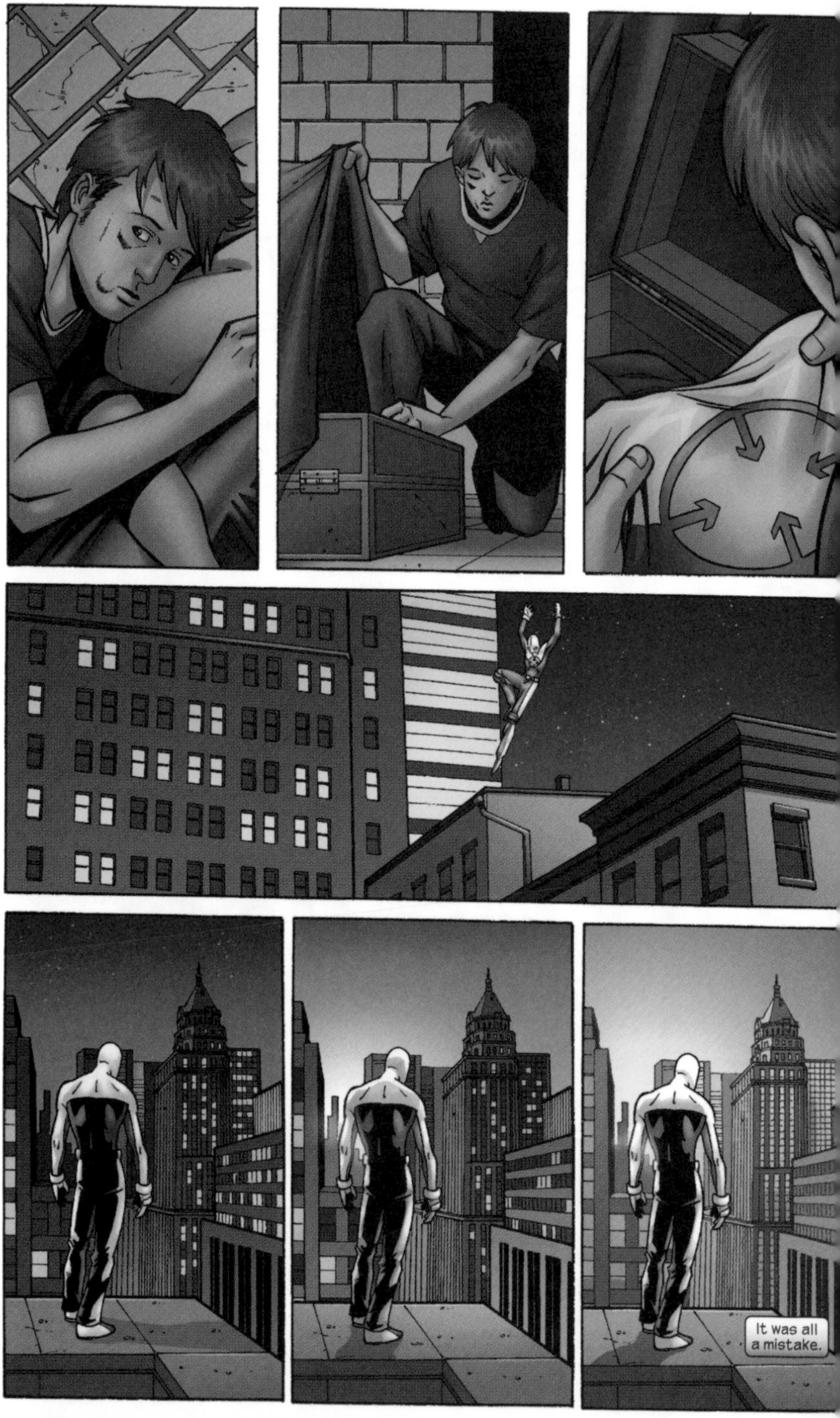
It was all
a mistake.

I mean...what kind of super hero was I?

I never stood a *chance* against Black Death. If it wasn't for that air duct, I'd be *dead* right now.

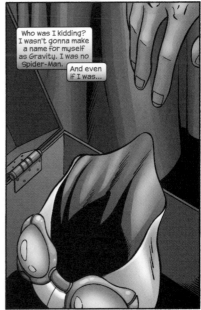

Who was I kidding? I wasn't gonna make a name for myself as Gravity. I was no Spider-Man.

And even if I was...

...how was I supposed to help people *and* make it through college, too?

How could anyone?

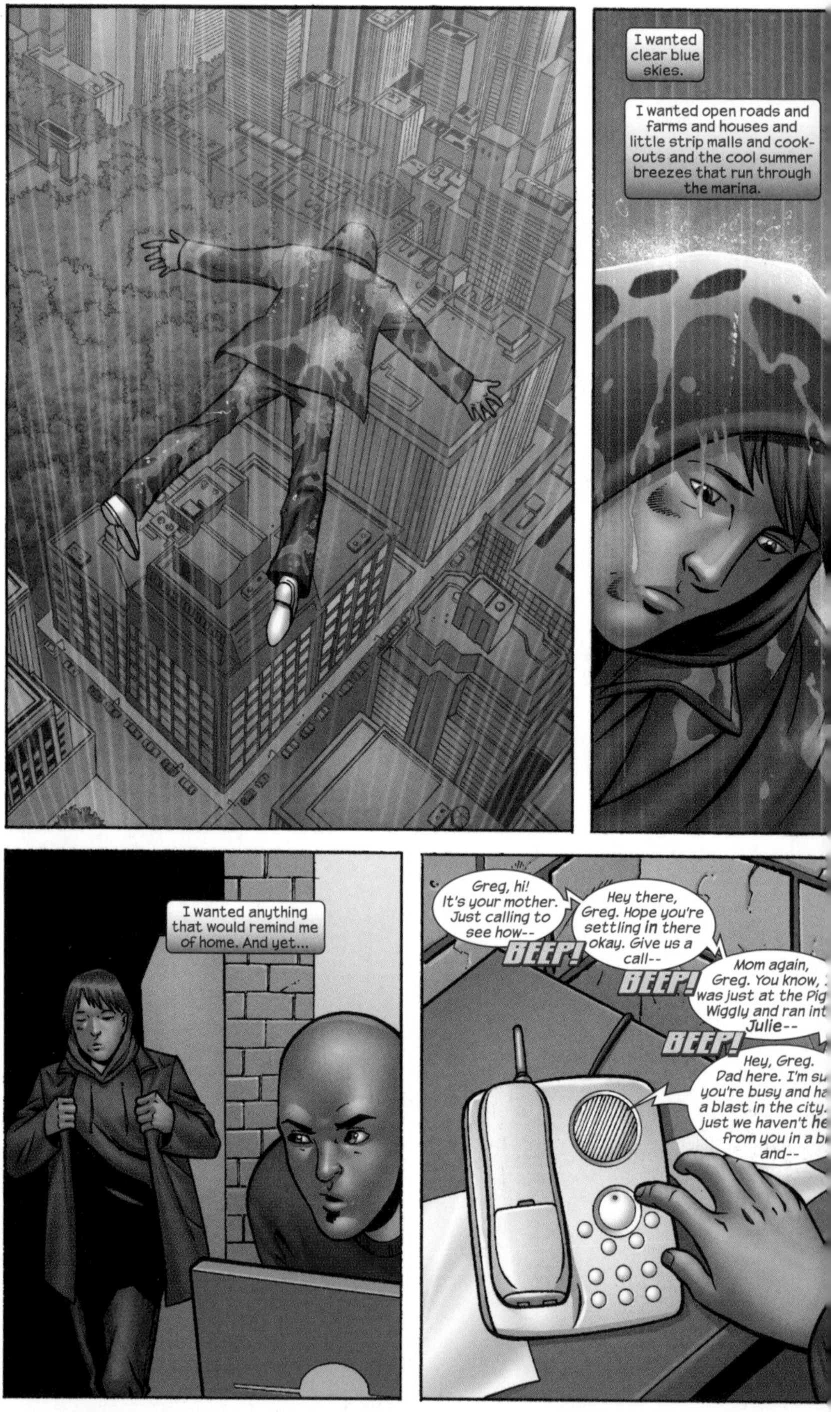
I wanted clear blue skies.
I wanted open roads and farms and houses and little strip malls and cook-outs and the cool summer breezes that run through the marina.
I wanted anything that would remind me of home. And yet...
Greg, hi! It's your mother. Just calling to see how--
BEEP!
Hey there, Greg. Hope you're settling in there okay. Give us a call--
BEEP!
Mom again, Greg. You know,
was just at the Pig
Wiggly and ran int
Julie--
BEEP!
Hey, Greg. Dad here. I'm su
you're busy and ha
a blast in the city.
just we haven't he
from you in a b
and--

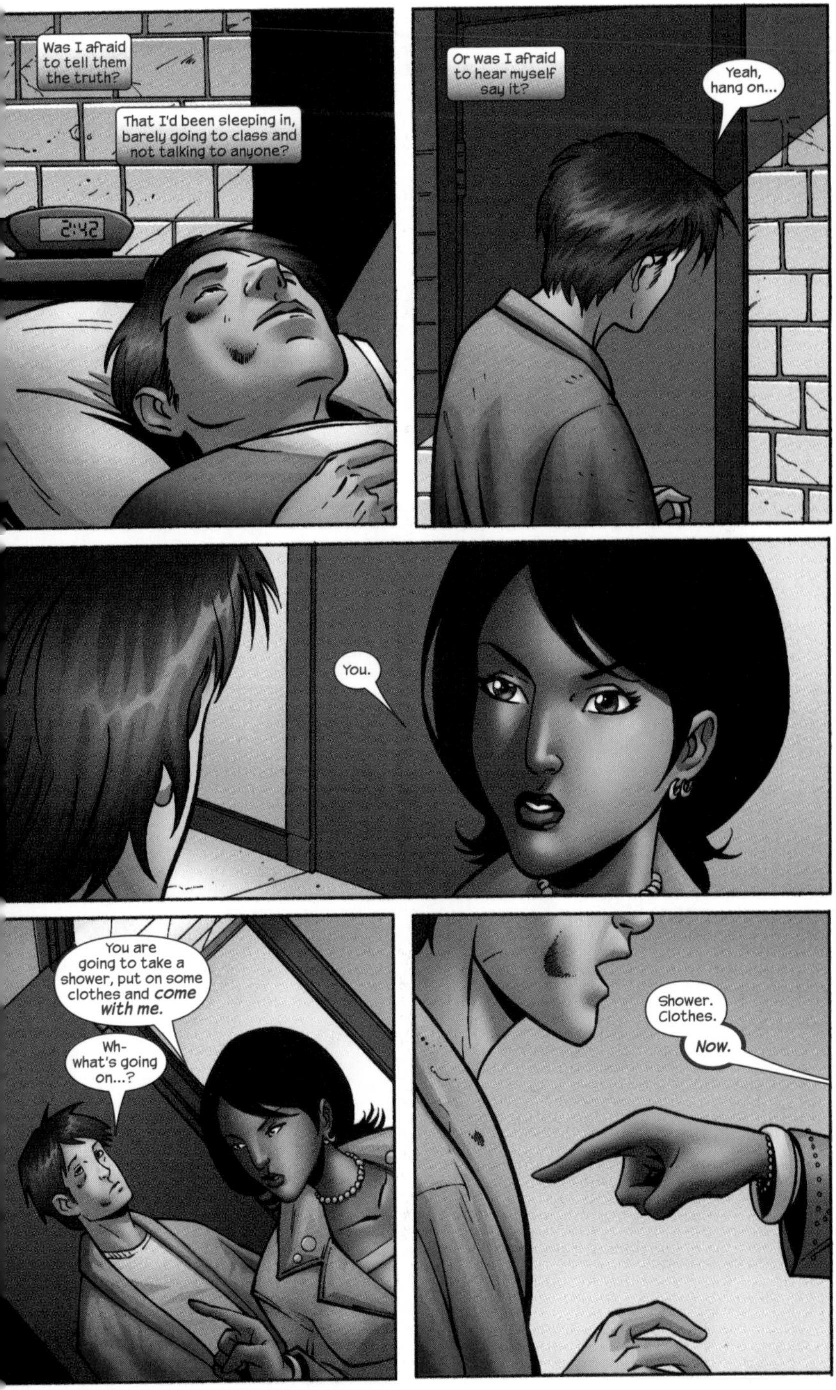
Was I afraid to tell them the truth?
That I'd been sleeping in, barely going to class and not talking to anyone?
2:42
Or was I afraid to hear myself say it?
Yeah, hang on...
You.
You are going to take a shower, put on some clothes and *come with me.*
Wh- what's going on...?
Shower. Clothes.
Now.

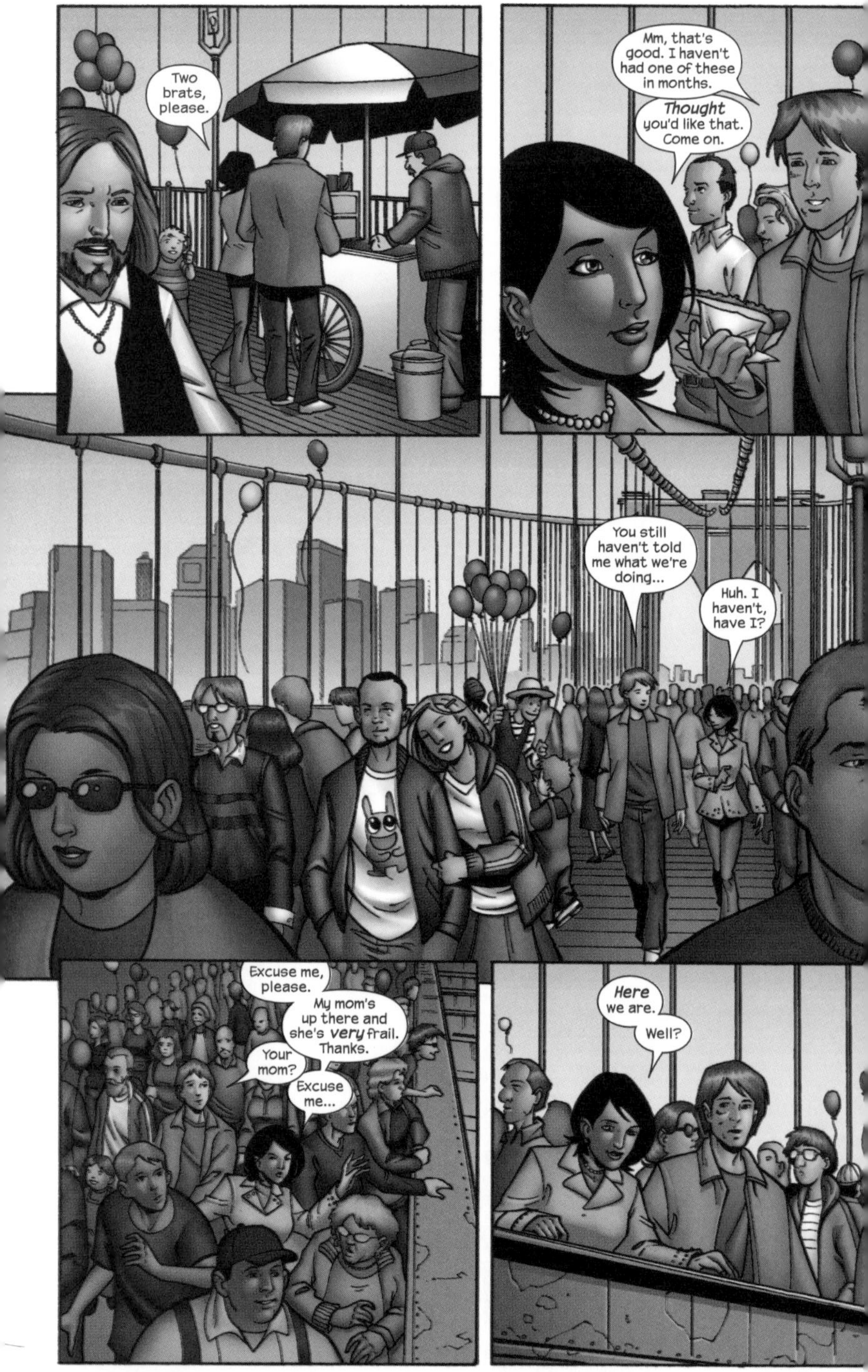
Two brats, please.
Mm, that's good. I haven't had one of these in months.
Thought you'd like that. Come on.
You still haven't told me what we're doing...
Huh. I haven't, have I?
Excuse me, please.
My mom's up there and she's *very* frail. Thanks.
Your mom?
Excuse me...
Here we are.
Well?

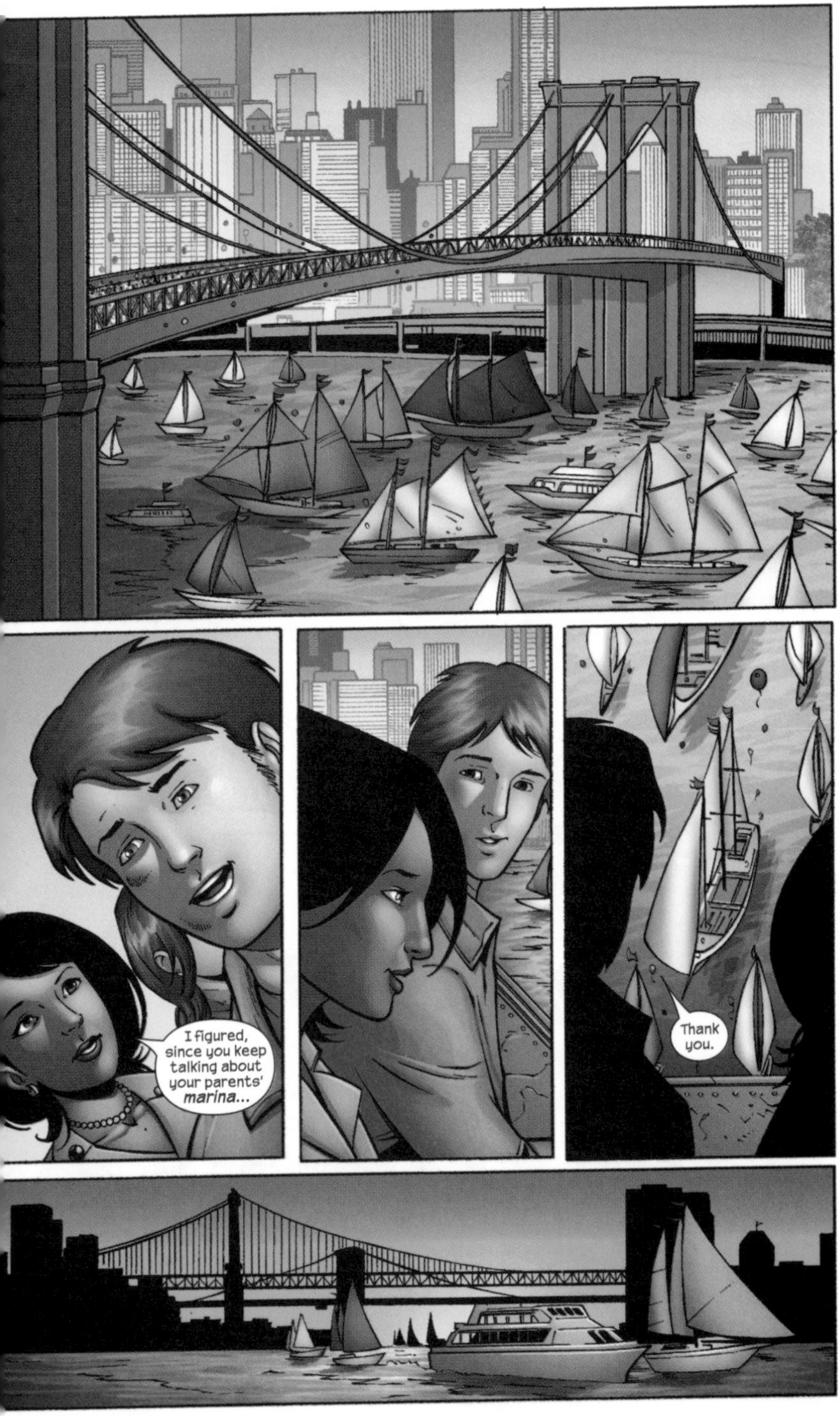
I figured, since you keep talking about your parents' *marina*...
Thank you.

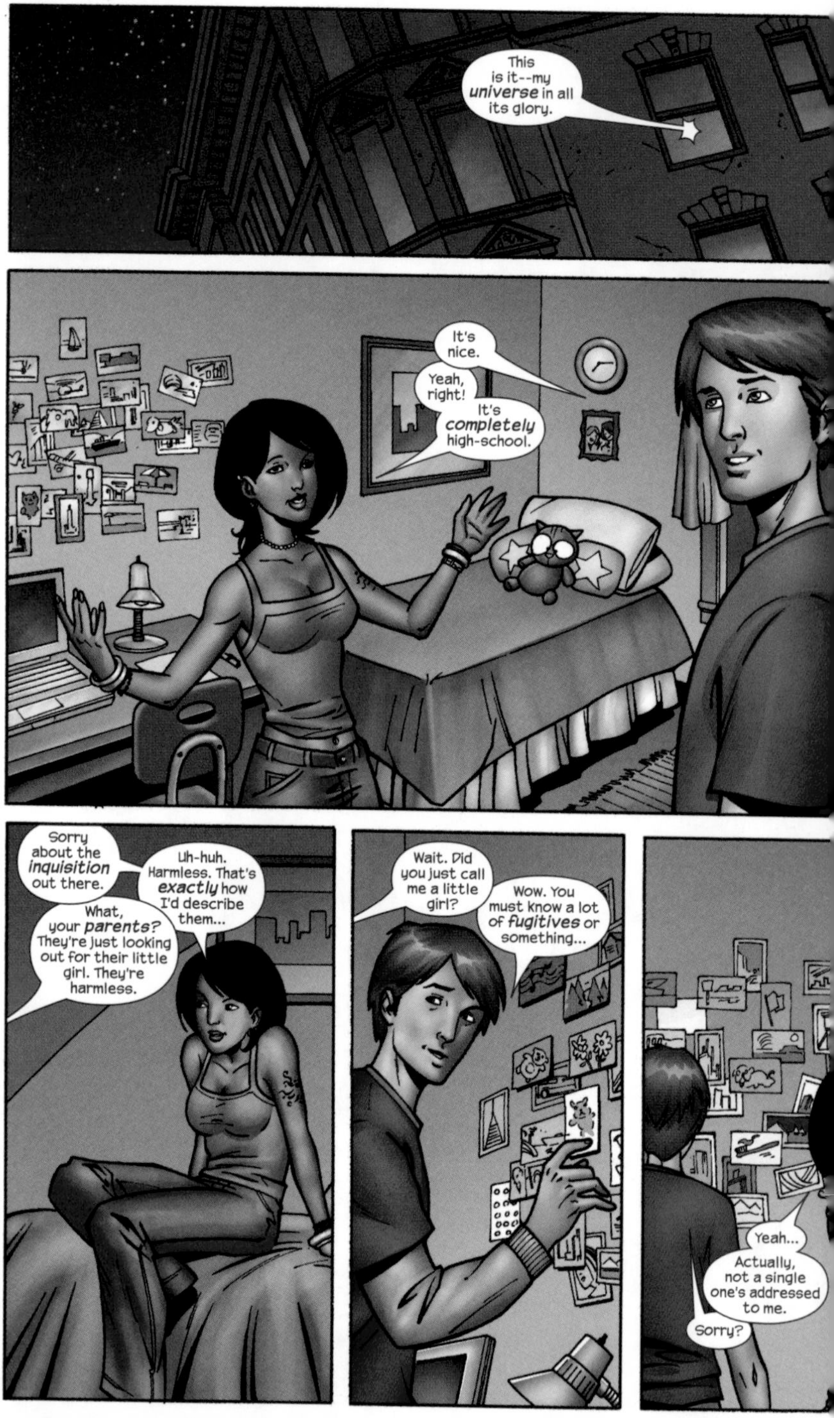
This is it--my universe in all its glory.
It's nice.
Yeah, right! It's completely high-school.
Sorry about the inquisition out there.
What, your parents? They're just looking out for their little girl. They're harmless.
Uh-huh. Harmless. That's exactly how I'd describe them...
Wait. Did you just call me a little girl?
Wow. You must know a lot of fugitives or something...
Yeah... Actually, not a single one's addressed to me.
Sorry?

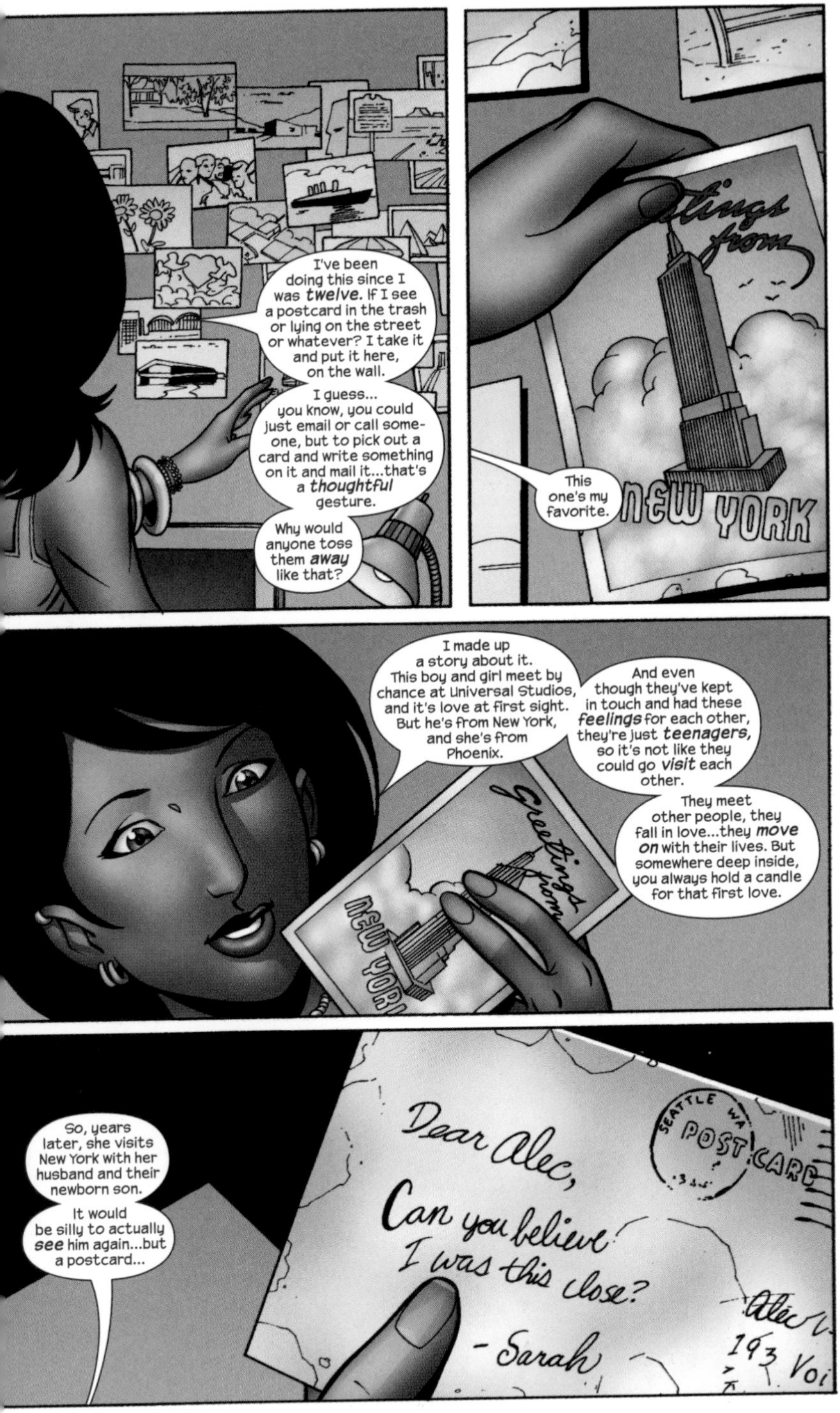
I've been doing this since I was *twelve.* If I see a postcard in the trash or lying on the street or whatever? I take it and put it here, on the wall.
I guess... you know, you could just email or call someone, but to pick out a card and write something on it and mail it...that's a *thoughtful* gesture.
Why would anyone toss them *away* like that?
NEW YORK
This one's my favorite.
I made up a story about it. This boy and girl meet by chance at Universal Studios, and it's love at first sight. But he's from New York, and she's from Phoenix.
And even though they've kept in touch and had these *feelings* for each other, they're just *teenagers,* so it's not like they could go *visit* each other.
They meet other people, they fall in love...they *move on* with their lives. But somewhere deep inside, you always hold a candle for that first love.
Greetings from
NEW YORK
So, years later, she visits New York with her husband and their newborn son.
It would be silly to actually *see* him again...but a postcard...
Dear Alec,
Can you believe I was this close?
- Sarah
SEATTLE WA
POST CARD

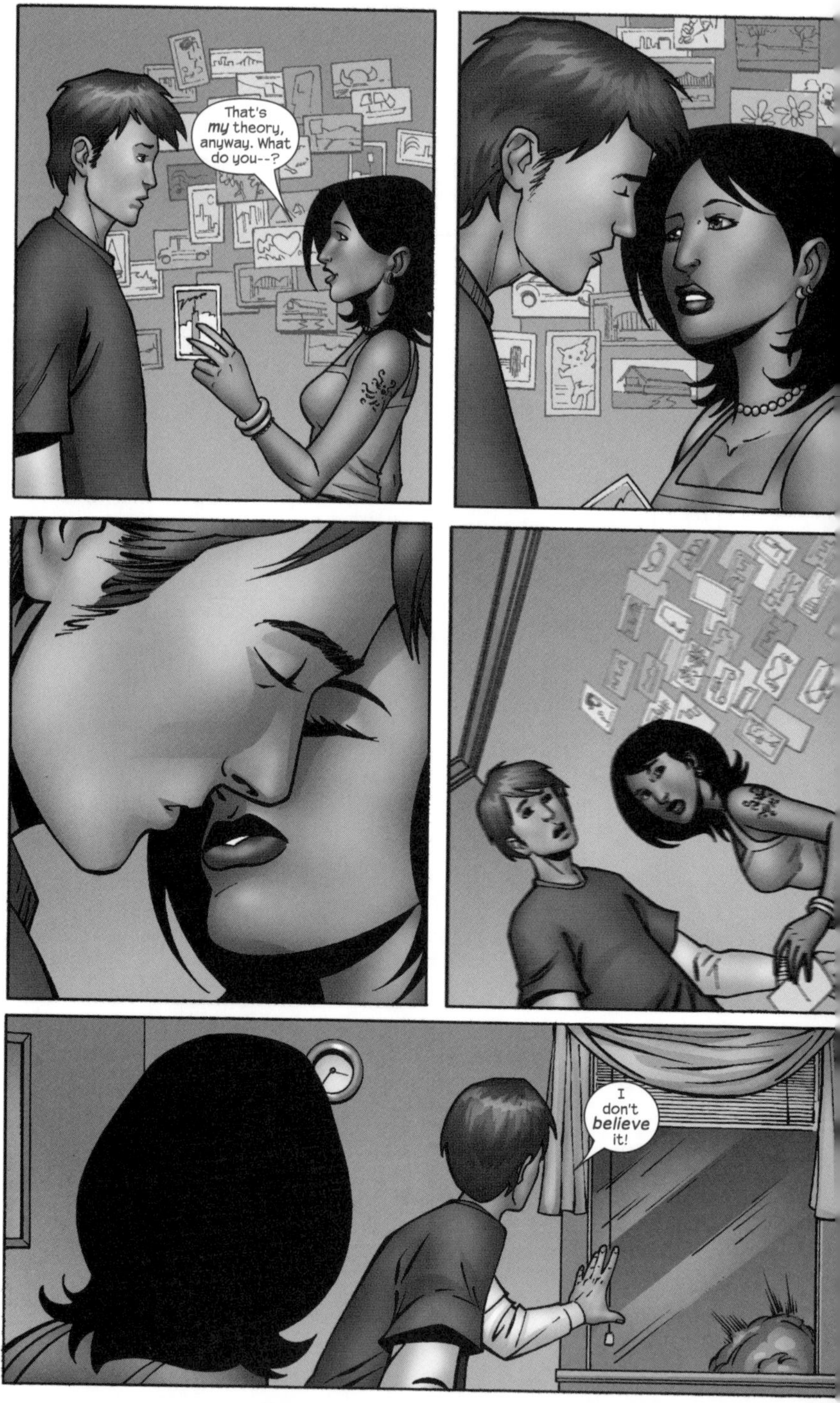
That's *my* theory, anyway. What do you--?
I don't *believe* it!

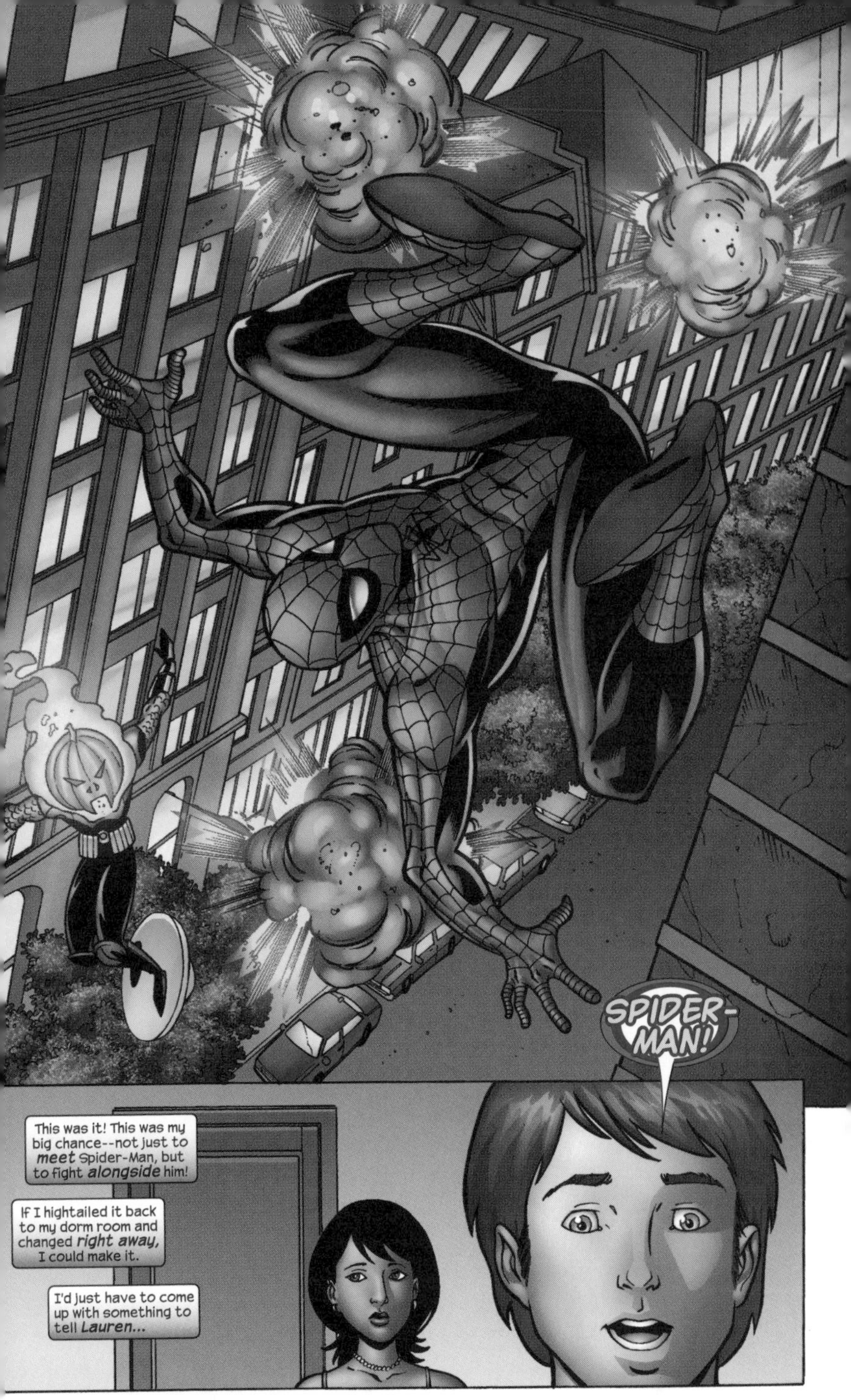
SPIDER-MAN!
This was it! This was my big chance--not just to *meet* Spider-Man, but to fight *alongside* him!
If I hightailed it back to my dorm room and changed *right away,* I could make it.
I'd just have to come up with something to tell *Lauren*...

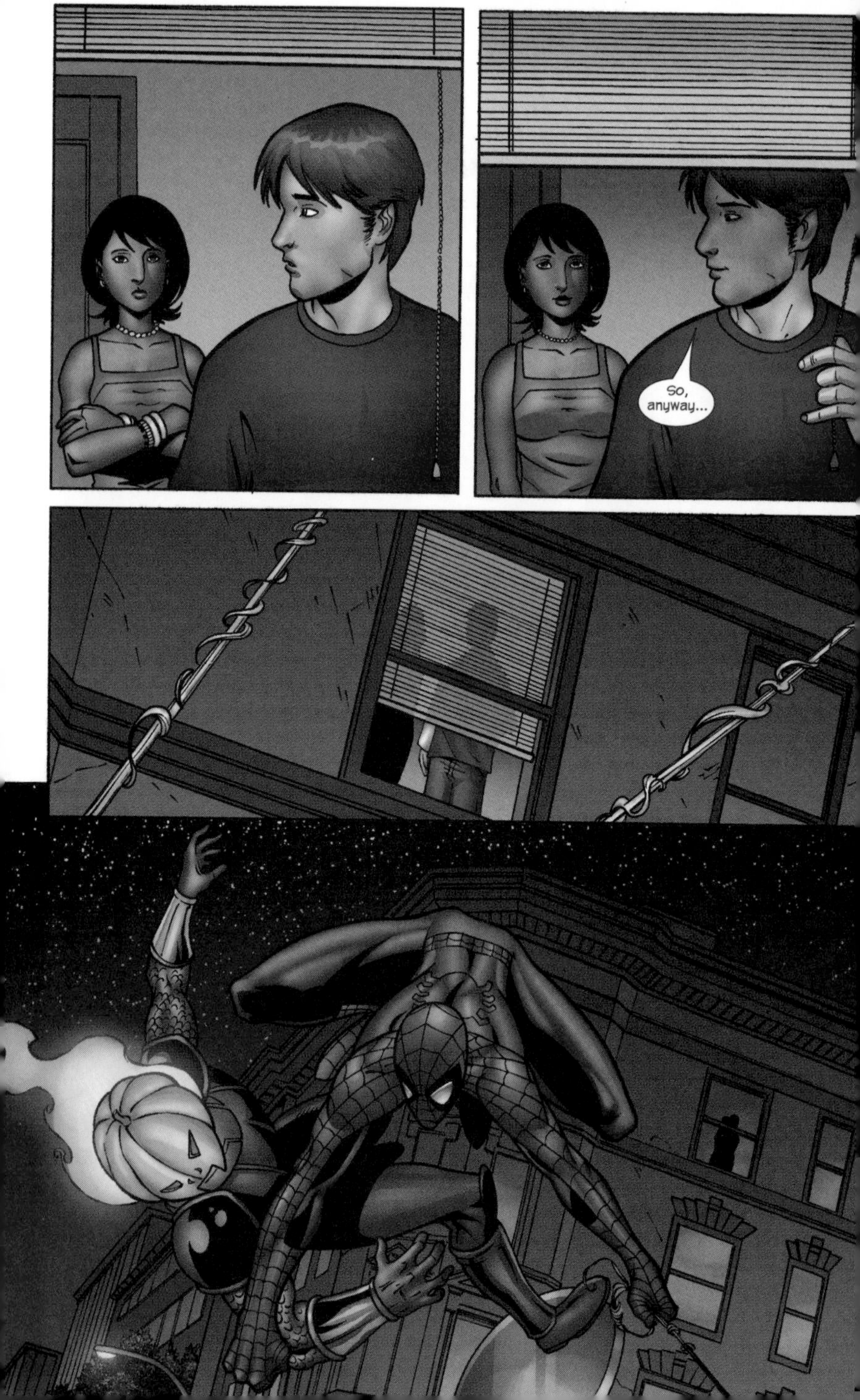
So, anyway...

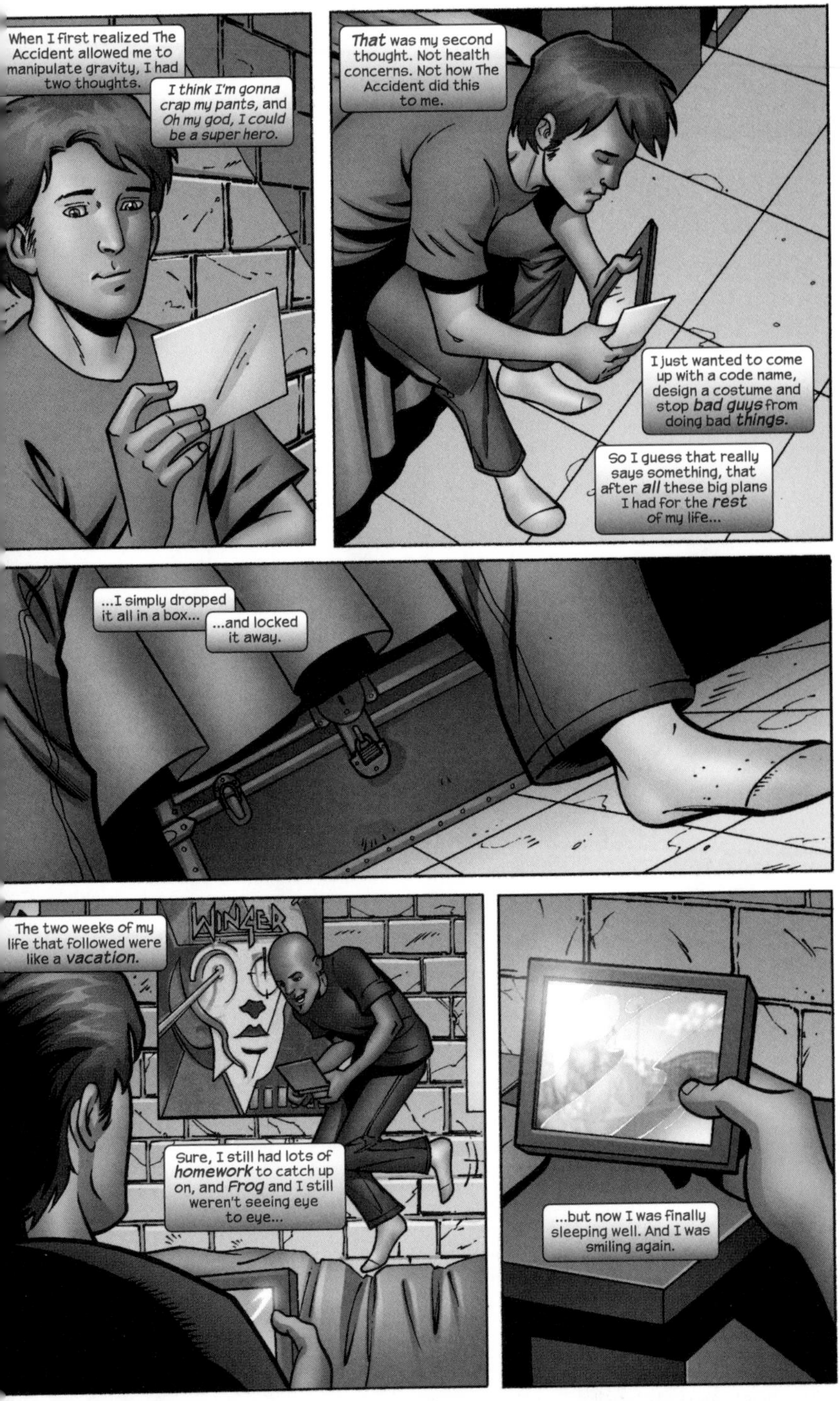
When I first realized The Accident allowed me to manipulate gravity, I had two thoughts.
I think I'm gonna crap my pants, and *Oh my god, I could be a super hero.*
That was my second thought. Not health concerns. Not how The Accident did this to me.
I just wanted to come up with a code name, design a costume and stop *bad guys* from doing bad *things.*
So I guess that really says something, that after *all* these big plans I had for the *rest* of my life...
...I simply dropped it all in a box...
...and locked it away.
The two weeks of my life that followed were like a *vacation.*
WINGER
Sure, I still had lots of *homework* to catch up on, and *Frog* and I still weren't seeing eye to eye...
...but now I was finally sleeping well. And I was smiling again.

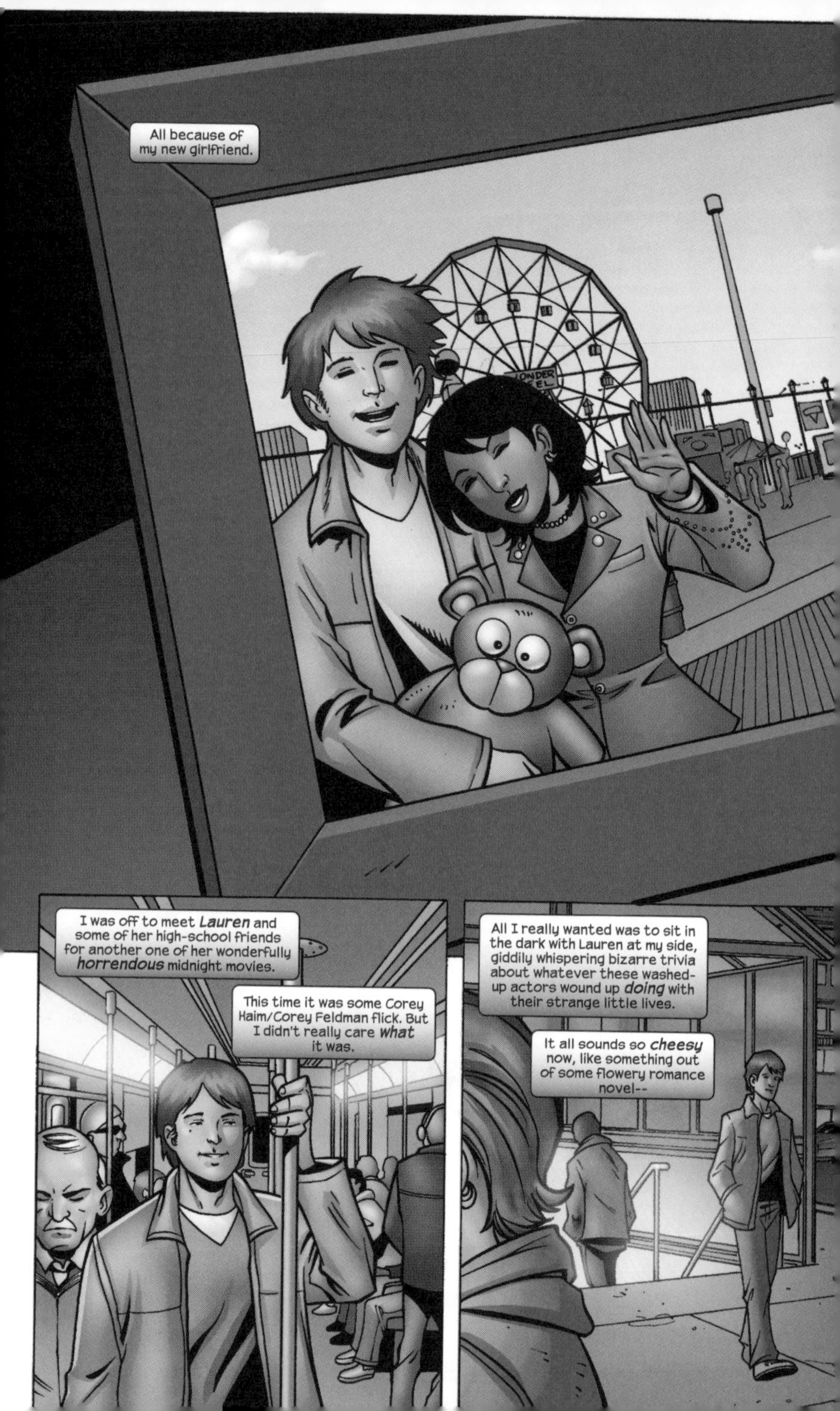
All because of my new girlfriend.
WONDER
I was off to meet *Lauren* and some of her high-school friends for another one of her wonderfully *horrendous* midnight movies.
This time it was some Corey Haim/Corey Feldman flick. But I didn't really care *what* it was.
All I really wanted was to sit in the dark with Lauren at my side, giddily whispering bizarre trivia about whatever these washed-up actors wound up *doing* with their strange little lives.
It all sounds so *cheesy* now, like something out of some flowery romance novel--

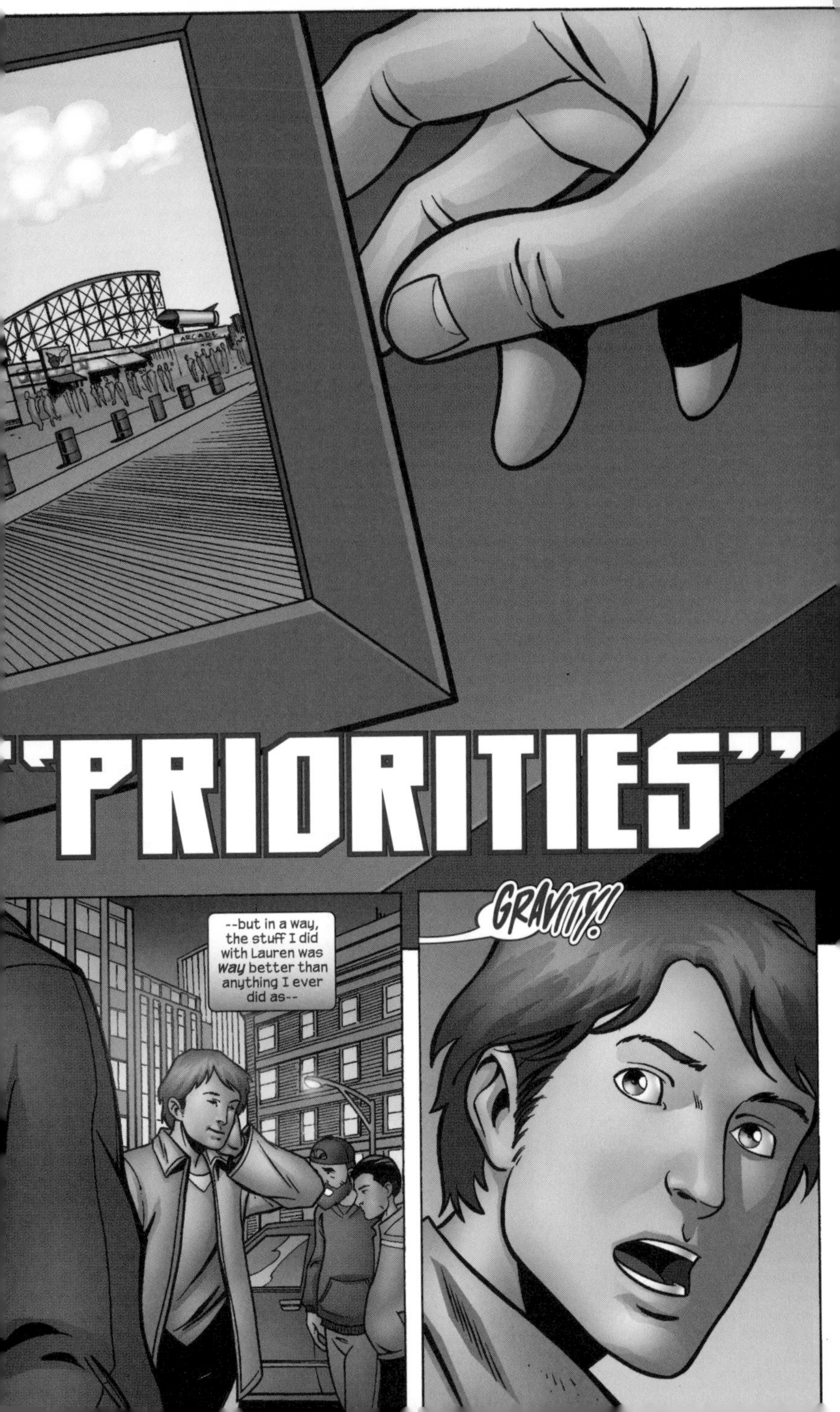
"PRIORITIES"
--but in a way, the stuff I did with Lauren was *way* better than anything I ever did as--
GRAVITY!

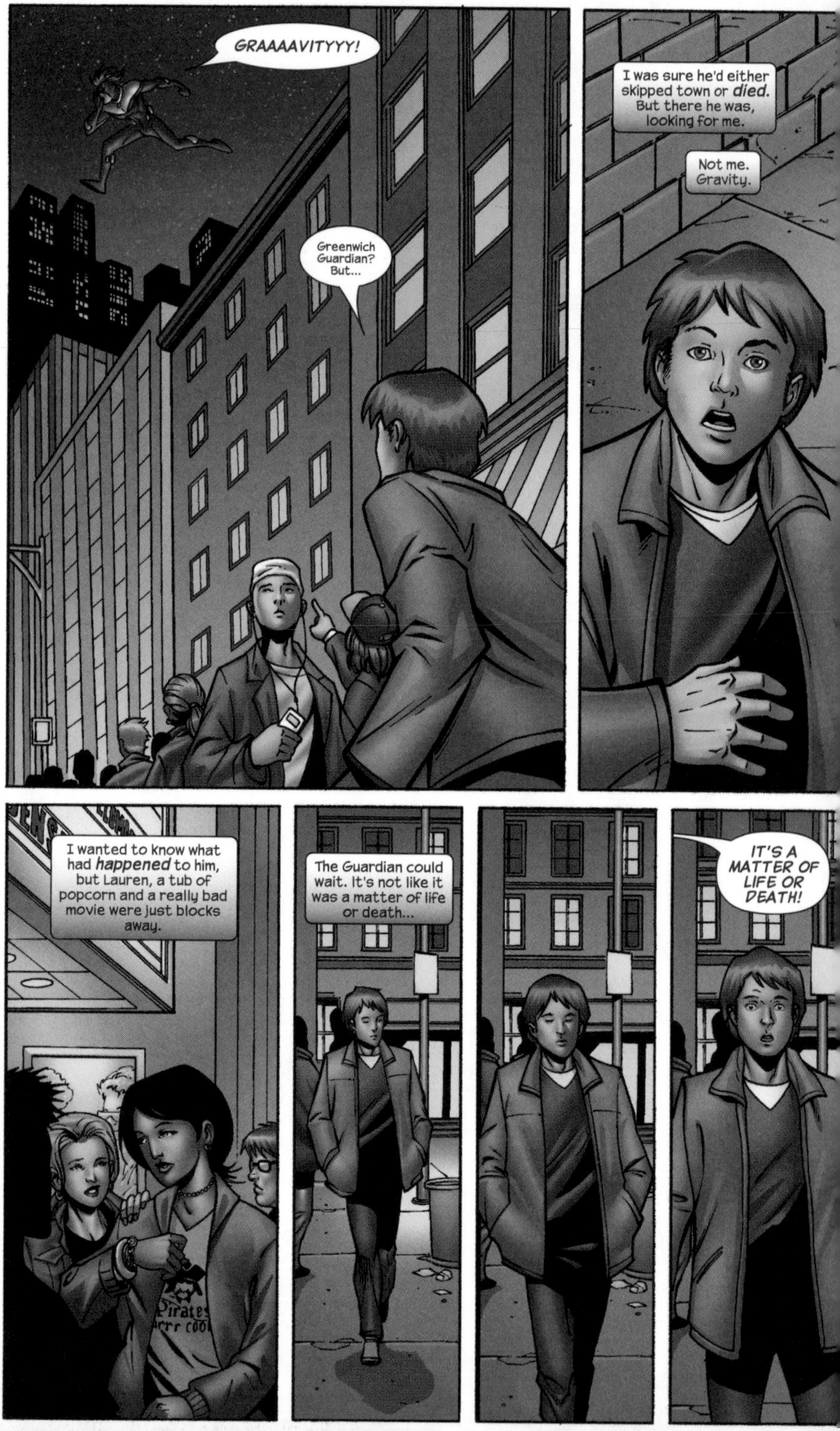
GRAAAAVITYYY!
Greenwich Guardian? But...
I was sure he'd either skipped town or *died*. But there he was, looking for me.
Not me. Gravity.
I wanted to know what had *happened* to him, but Lauren, a tub of popcorn and a really bad movie were just blocks away.
The Guardian could wait. It's not like it was a matter of life or death...
IT'S A MATTER OF LIFE OR DEATH!
Pirates

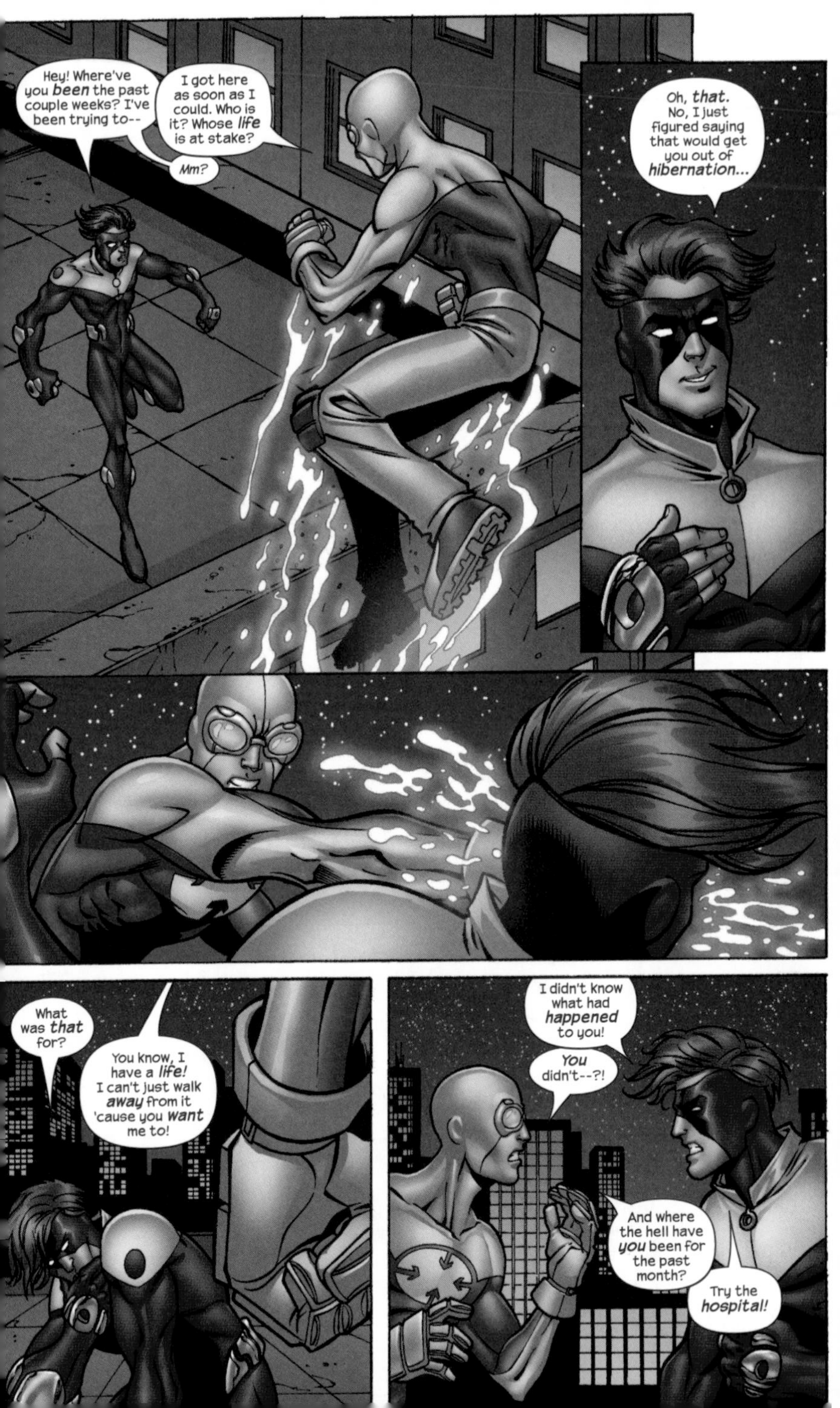
Hey! Where've you been the past couple weeks? I've been trying to--
I got here as soon as I could. Who is it? Whose life is at stake?
Mm?
Oh, that. No, I just figured saying that would get you out of hibernation...
What was that for?
You know, I have a life! I can't just walk away from it 'cause you want me to!
I didn't know what had happened to you!
You didn't--?!
And where the hell have you been for the past month?
Try the hospital!

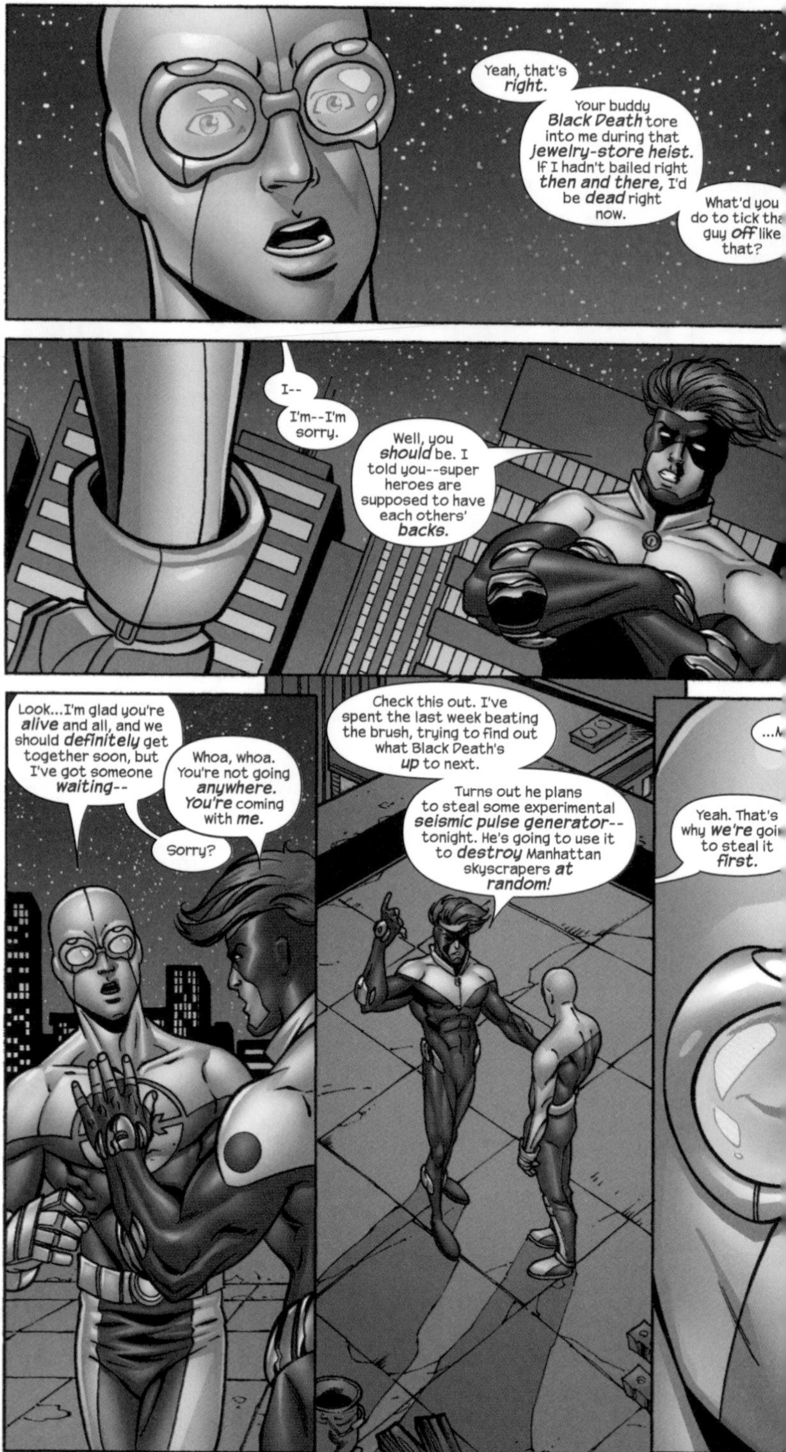
Yeah, that's *right.*
Your buddy *Black Death* tore into me during that *jewelry-store heist.* If I hadn't bailed right *then and there,* I'd be *dead* right now.
What'd you do to tick tha guy *off* like that?
I--
I'm--I'm sorry.
Well, you *should* be. I told you--super heroes are supposed to have each others' *backs.*
Look...I'm glad you're *alive* and all, and we should *definitely* get together soon, but I've got someone *waiting*--
Whoa, whoa. You're not going *anywhere. You're* coming with *me.*
Sorry?
Check this out. I've spent the last week beating the brush, trying to find out what Black Death's *up* to next.
Turns out he plans to steal some experimental *seismic pulse generator*--tonight. He's going to use it to *destroy* Manhattan skyscrapers *at random!*
Yeah. That's why *we're* goi to steal it *first.*

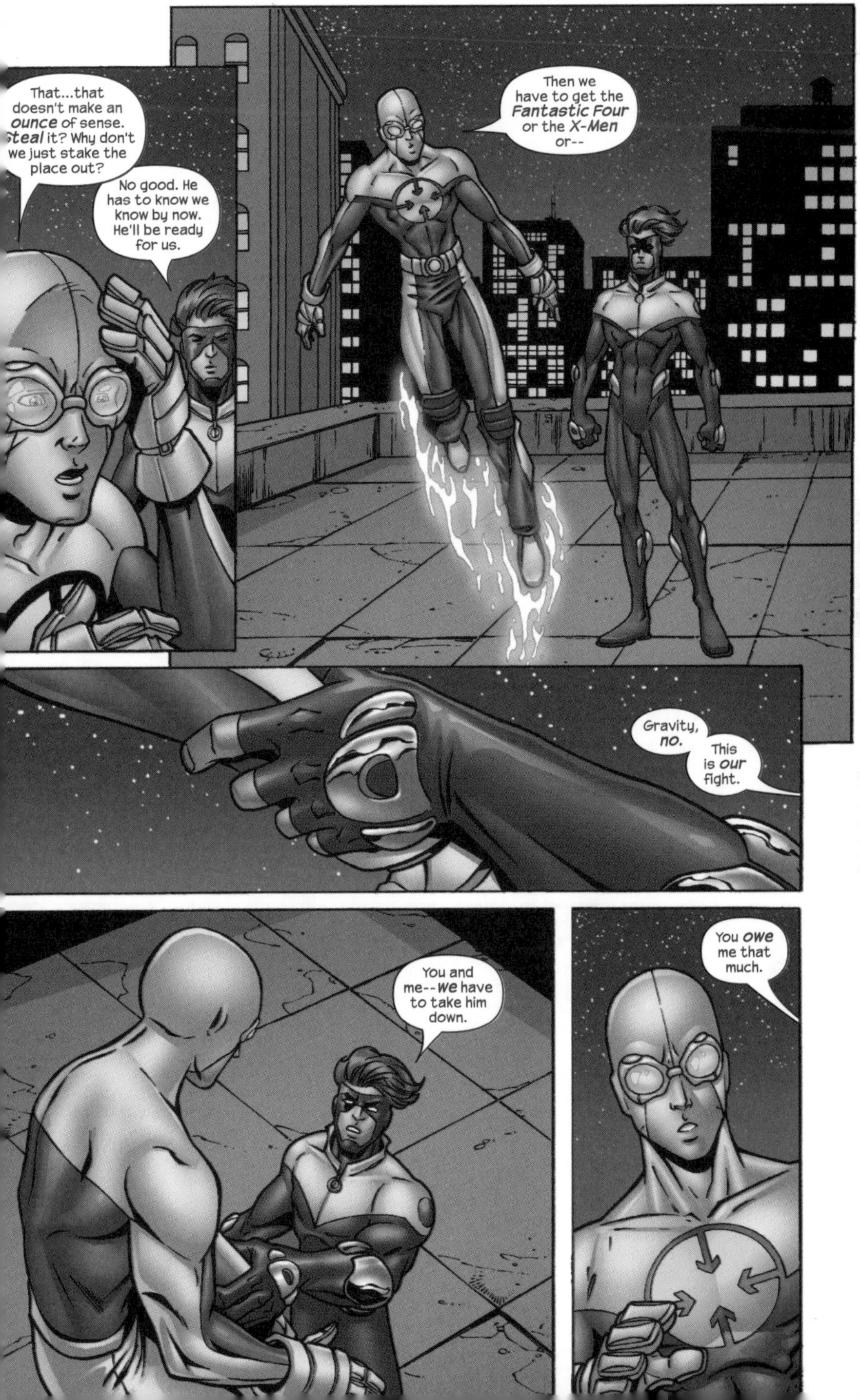
That...that doesn't make an ounce of sense. Steal it? Why don't we just stake the place out?
No good. He has to know we know by now. He'll be ready for us.
Then we have to get the Fantastic Four or the X-Men or--
Gravity, no.
This is our fight.
You and me--we have to take him down.
You owe me that much.

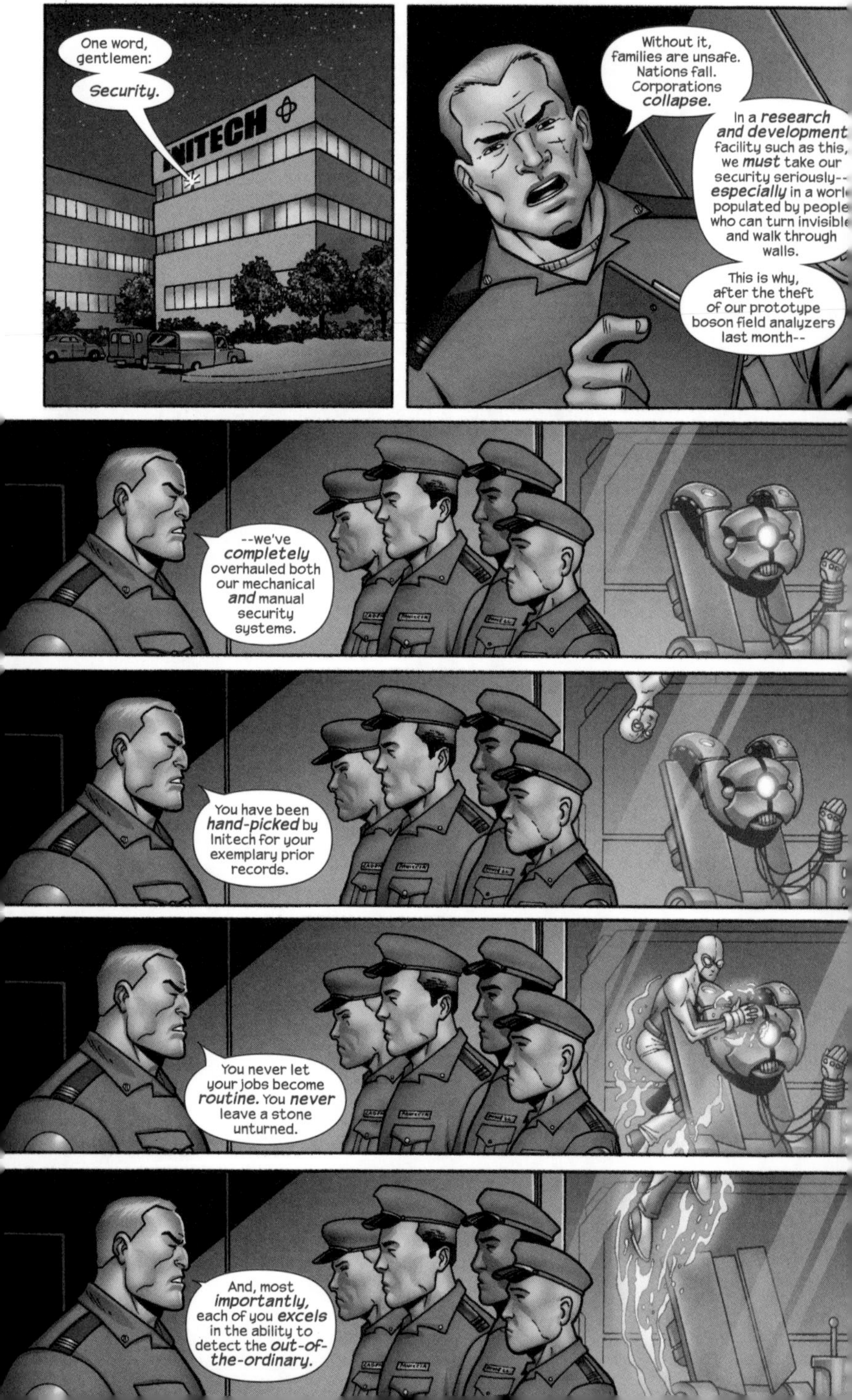
One word, gentlemen:
Security.
INITECH
Without it, families are unsafe. Nations fall. Corporations collapse.
In a research and development facility such as this, we must take our security seriously--especially in a world populated by people who can turn invisible and walk through walls.
This is why, after the theft of our prototype boson field analyzers last month--
--we've completely overhauled both our mechanical and manual security systems.
You have been hand-picked by Initech for your exemplary prior records.
You never let your jobs become routine. You never leave a stone unturned.
And, most importantly, each of you excels in the ability to detect the out-of-the-ordinary.

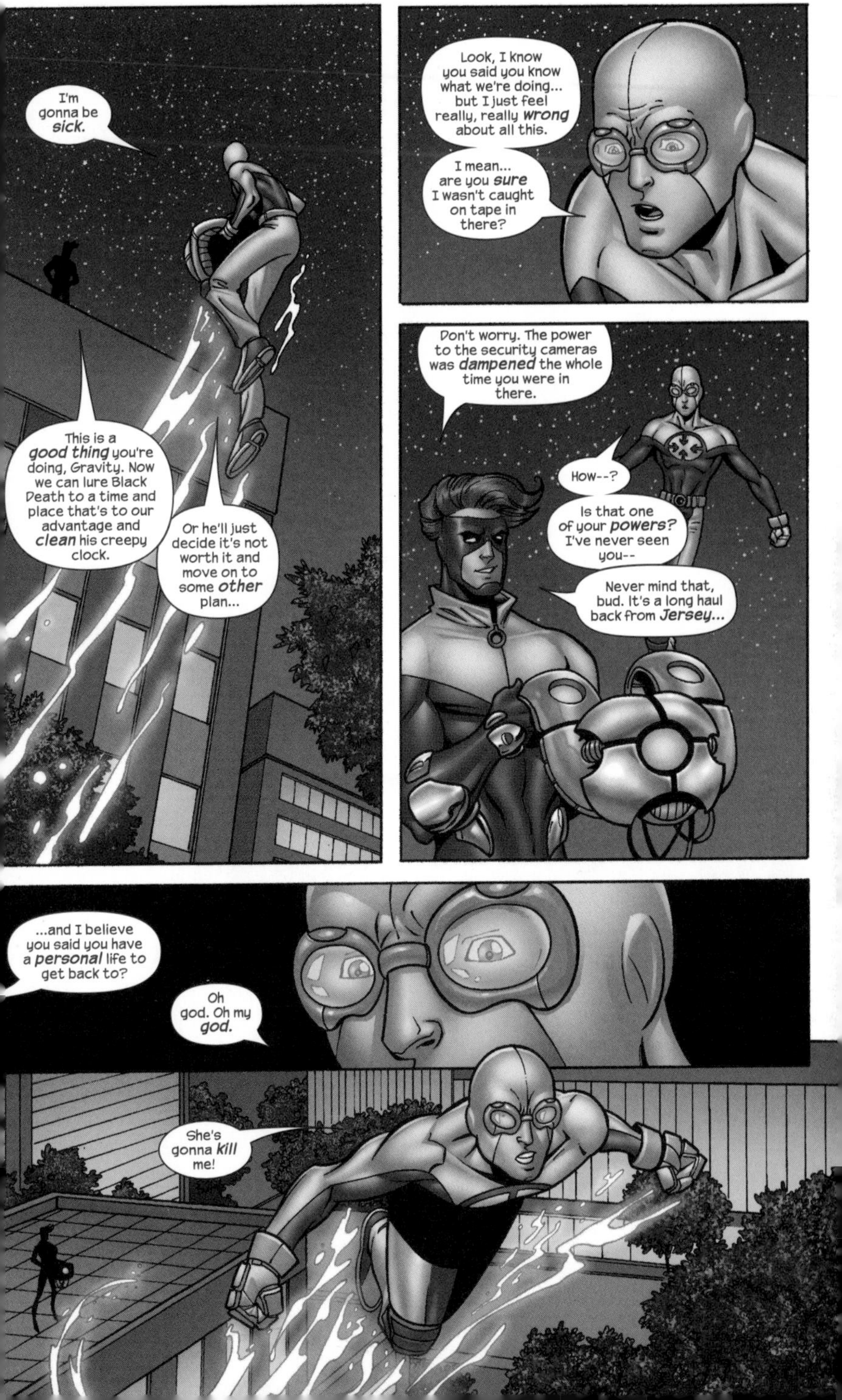

I'm gonna be *sick.*
This is a *good thing* you're doing, Gravity. Now we can lure Black Death to a time and place that's to our advantage and *clean* his creepy clock.
Or he'll just decide it's not worth it and move on to some *other* plan...
Look, I know you said you know what we're doing... but I just feel really, really *wrong* about all this.
I mean... are you *sure* I wasn't caught on tape in there?
Don't worry. The power to the security cameras was *dampened* the whole time you were in there.
How--?
Is that one of your *powers?* I've never seen you--
Never mind that, bud. It's a long haul back from *Jersey...*
...and I believe you said you have a *personal* life to get back to?
Oh god. Oh my *god.*
She's gonna *kill* me!

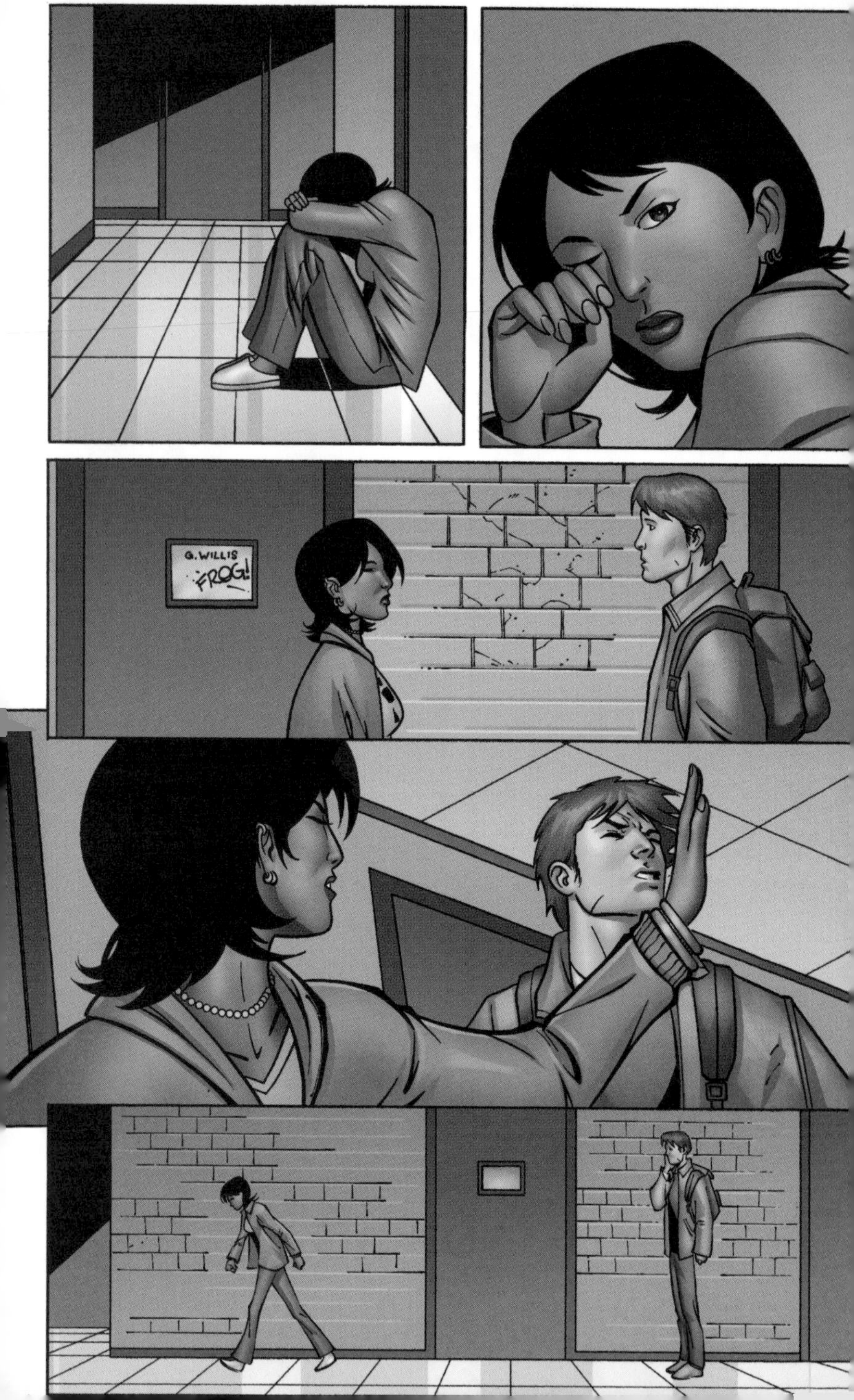
G. WILLIS
FROG!

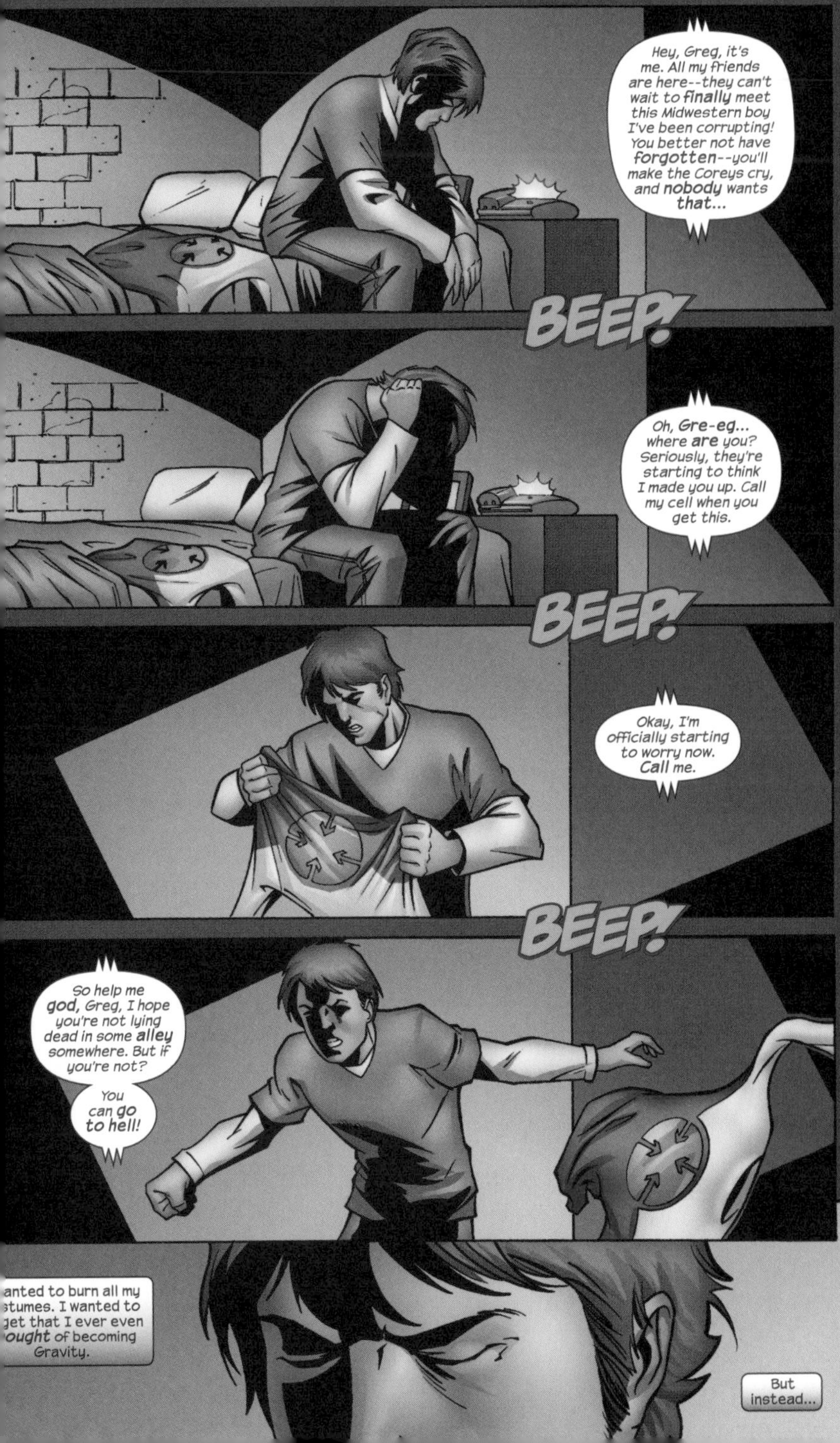
Hey, Greg, it's me. All my friends are here--they can't wait to finally meet this Midwestern boy I've been corrupting! You better not have forgotten--you'll make the Coreys cry, and nobody wants that...
BEEP!
Oh, Gre-eg... where are you? Seriously, they're starting to think I made you up. Call my cell when you get this.
BEEP!
Okay, I'm officially starting to worry now. Call me.
BEEP!
So help me god, Greg, I hope you're not lying dead in some alley somewhere. But if you're not?
You can go to hell!
anted to burn all my stumes. I wanted to get that I ever even ought of becoming Gravity.
But instead...

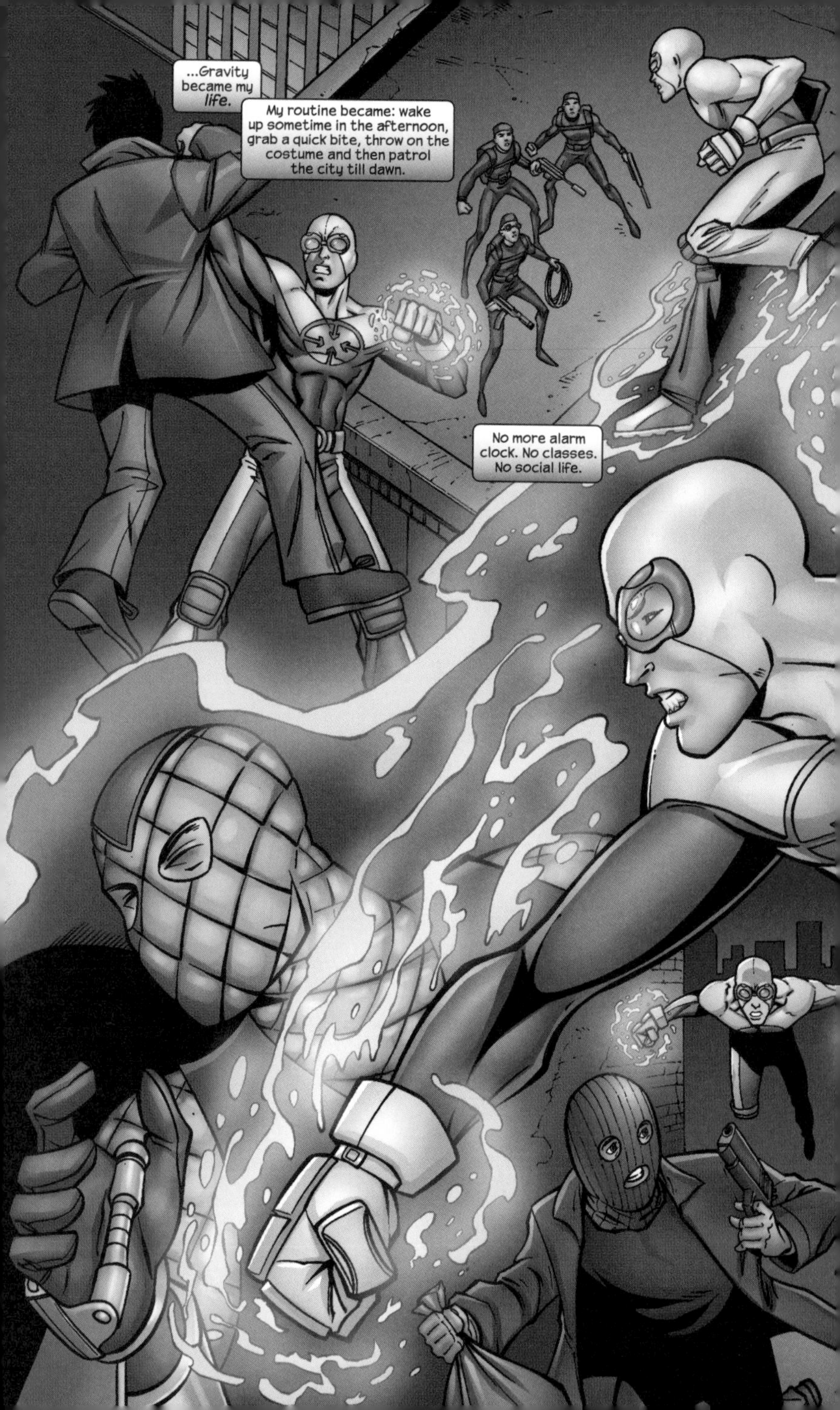
...Gravity became my *life*.
My routine became: wake up sometime in the afternoon, grab a quick bite, throw on the costume and then patrol the city till dawn.
No more alarm clock. No classes. No social life.

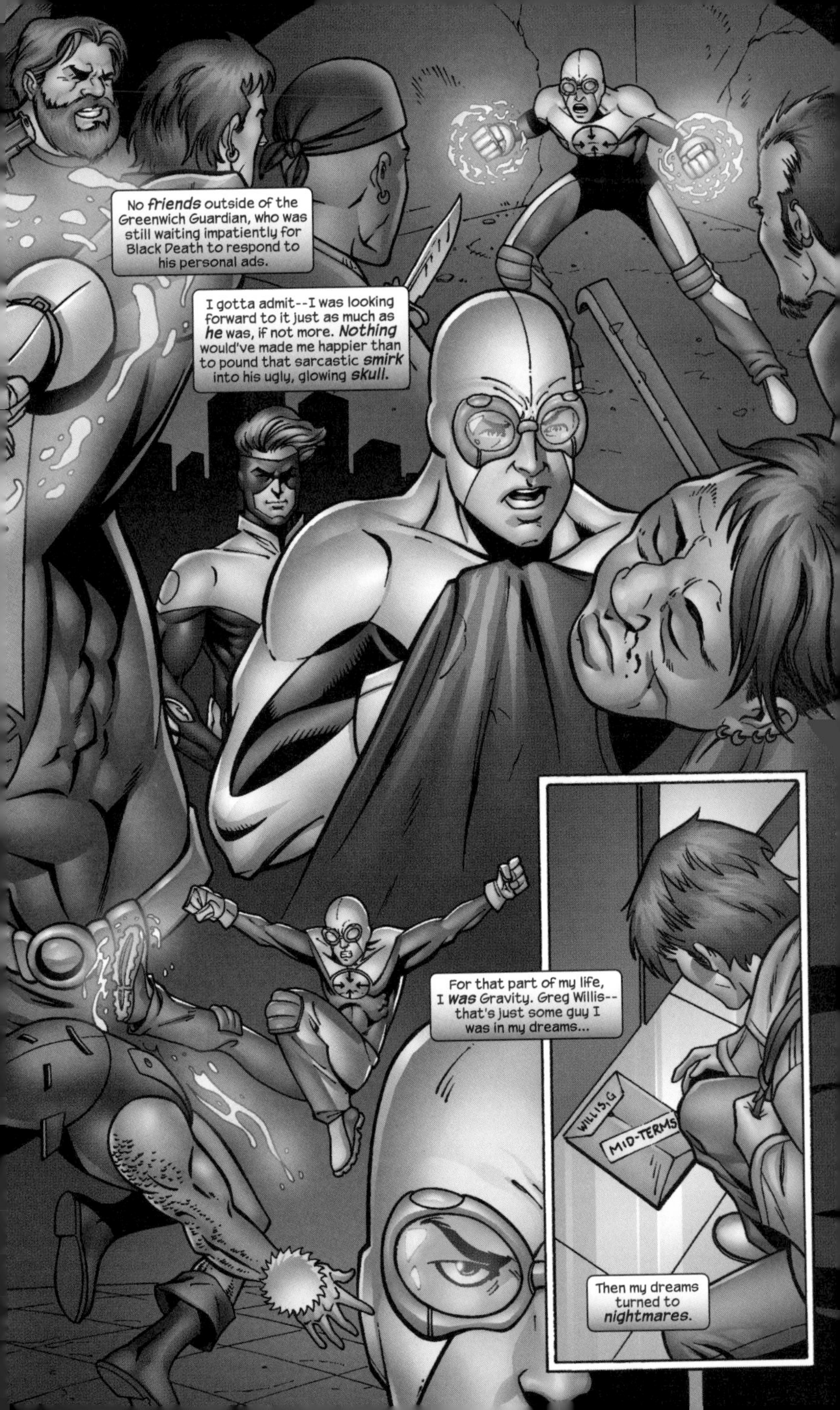
No *friends* outside of the Greenwich Guardian, who was still waiting impatiently for Black Death to respond to his personal ads.
I gotta admit--I was looking forward to it just as much as *he* was, if not more. *Nothing* would've made me happier than to pound that sarcastic *smirk* into his ugly, glowing *skull*.
For that part of my life, I *was* Gravity. Greg Willis--that's just some guy I was in my dreams...
WILLIS, G
MID-TERMS
Then my dreams turned to *nightmares*.

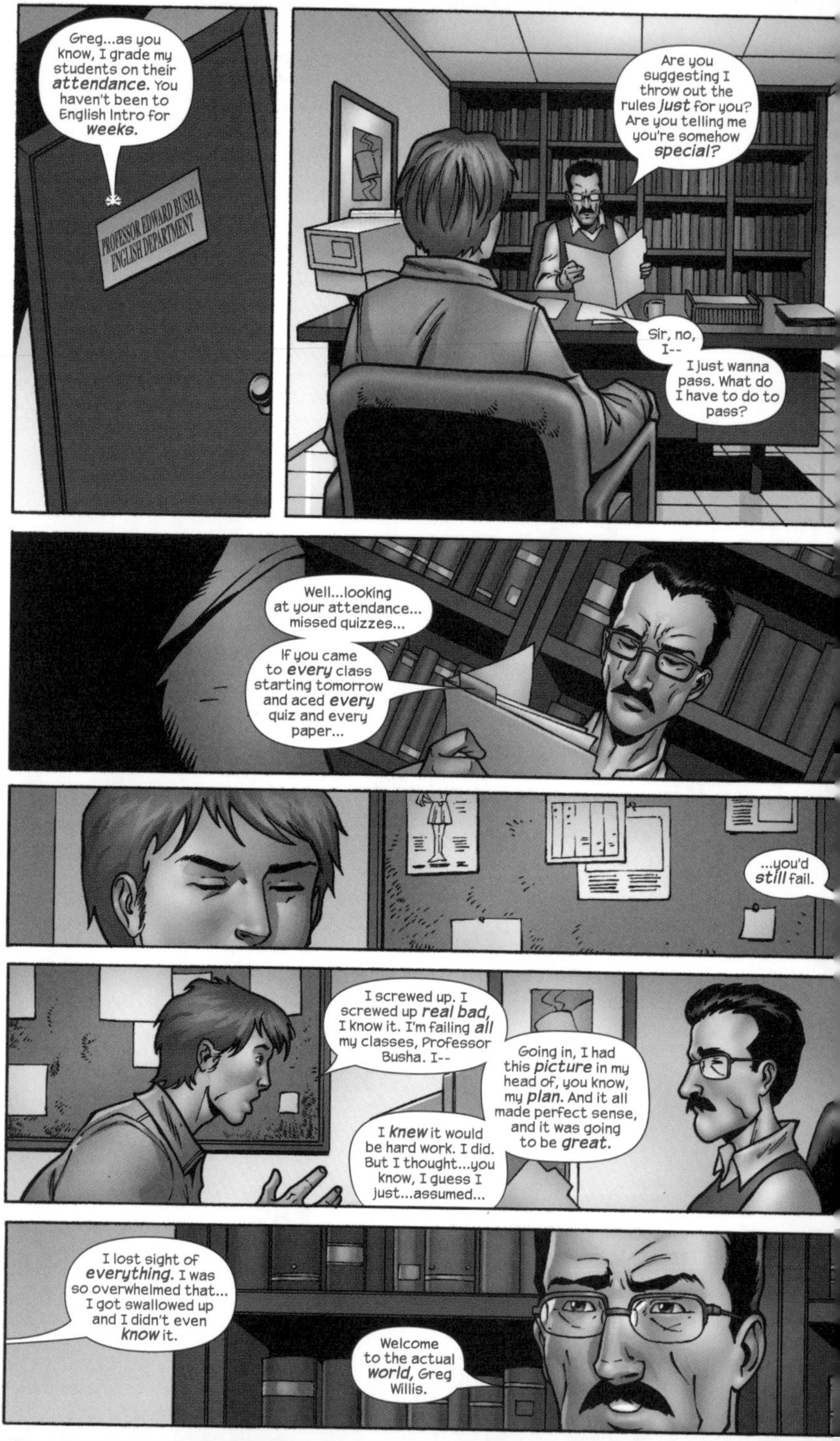
Greg...as you know, I grade my students on their *attendance*. You haven't been to English Intro for *weeks*.
PROFESSOR EDWARD BUSHA ENGLISH DEPARTMENT
Are you suggesting I throw out the rules *just* for you? Are you telling me you're somehow *special*?
Sir, no, I--
I just wanna pass. What do I have to do to pass?
Well...looking at your attendance... missed quizzes...
If you came to *every* class starting tomorrow and aced *every* quiz and every paper...
...you'd *still* fail.
I screwed up. I screwed up *real bad*, I know it. I'm failing *all* my classes, Professor Busha. I--
Going in, I had this *picture* in my head of, you know, my *plan*. And it all made perfect sense, and it was going to be *great*.
I *knew* it would be hard work. I did. But I thought...you know, I guess I just...assumed...
I lost sight of *everything*. I was so overwhelmed that... I got swallowed up and I didn't even *know* it.
Welcome to the actual *world*, Greg Willis.

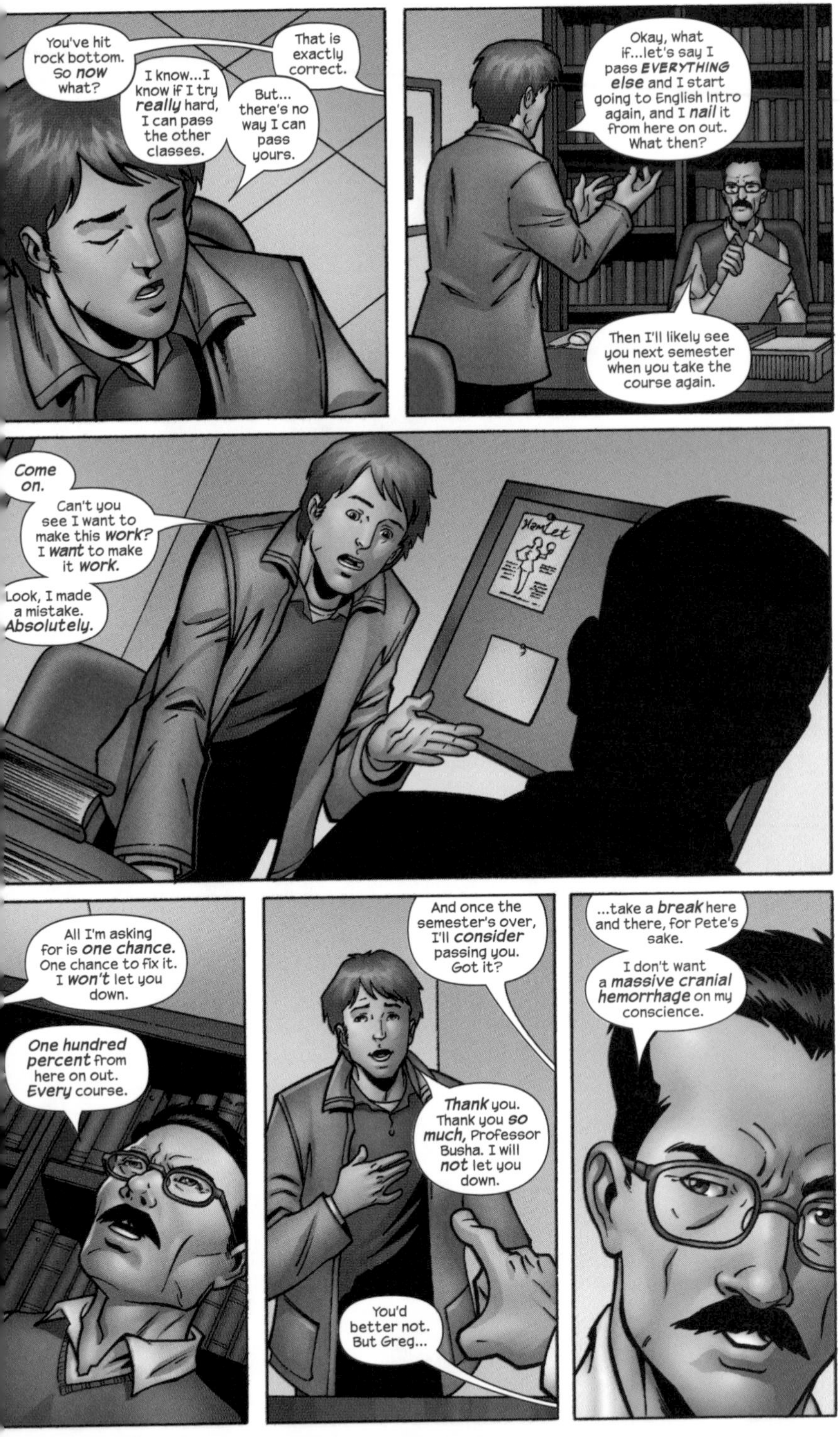
You've hit rock bottom. So now what?
That is exactly correct.
I know...I know if I try really hard, I can pass the other classes.
But... there's no way I can pass yours.
Okay, what if...let's say I pass EVERYTHING else and I start going to English Intro again, and I nail it from here on out. What then?
Then I'll likely see you next semester when you take the course again.
Come on.
Can't you see I want to make this work? I want to make it work.
Look, I made a mistake. Absolutely.
Hamlet
All I'm asking for is one chance. One chance to fix it. I won't let you down.
One hundred percent from here on out. Every course.
And once the semester's over, I'll consider passing you. Got it?
Thank you. Thank you so much, Professor Busha. I will not let you down.
You'd better not. But Greg...
...take a break here and there, for Pete's sake.
I don't want a massive cranial hemorrhage on my conscience.

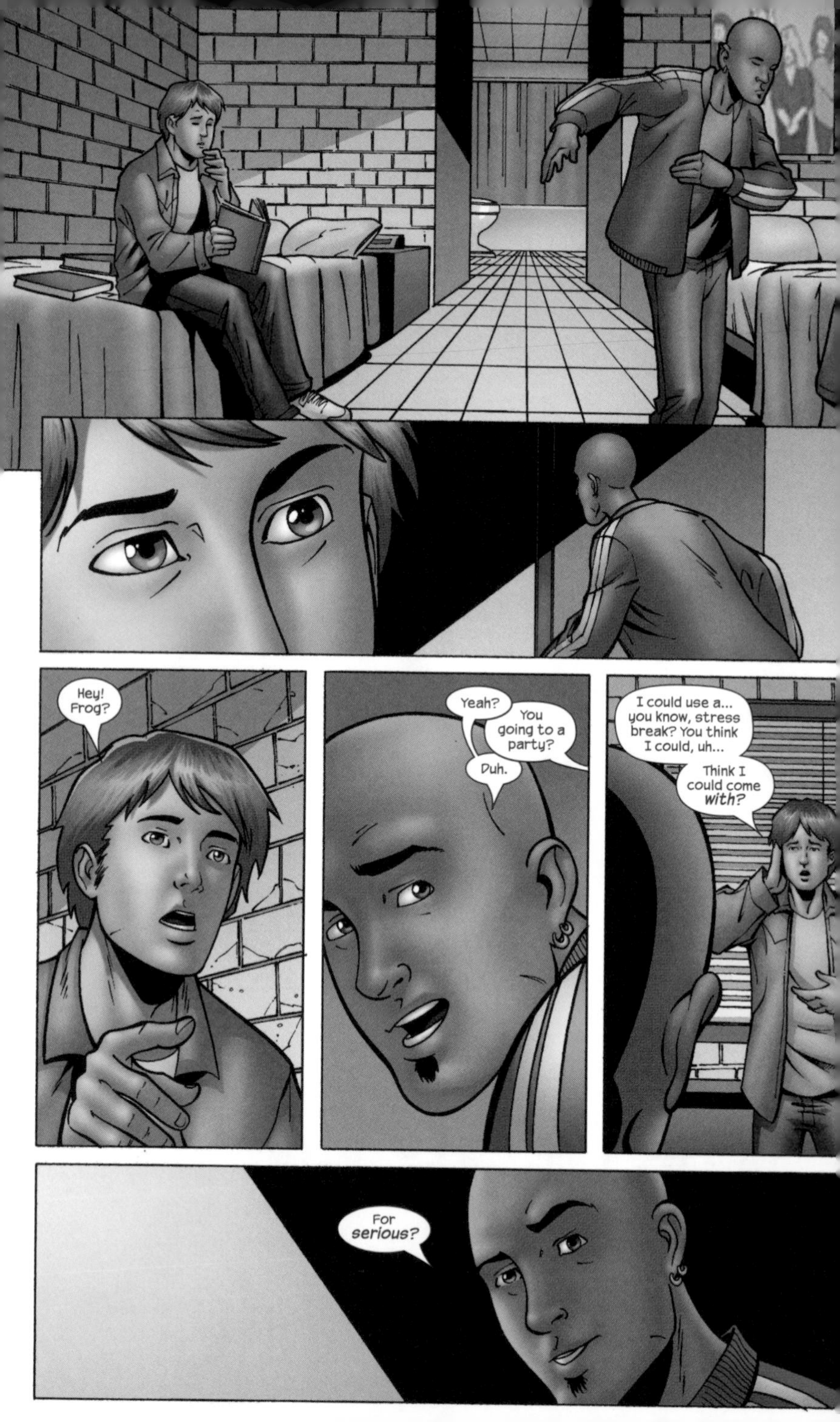
Hey! Frog?
Yeah?
You going to a party?
Duh.
I could use a... you know, stress break? You think I could, uh...
Think I could come *with?*
For *serious?*

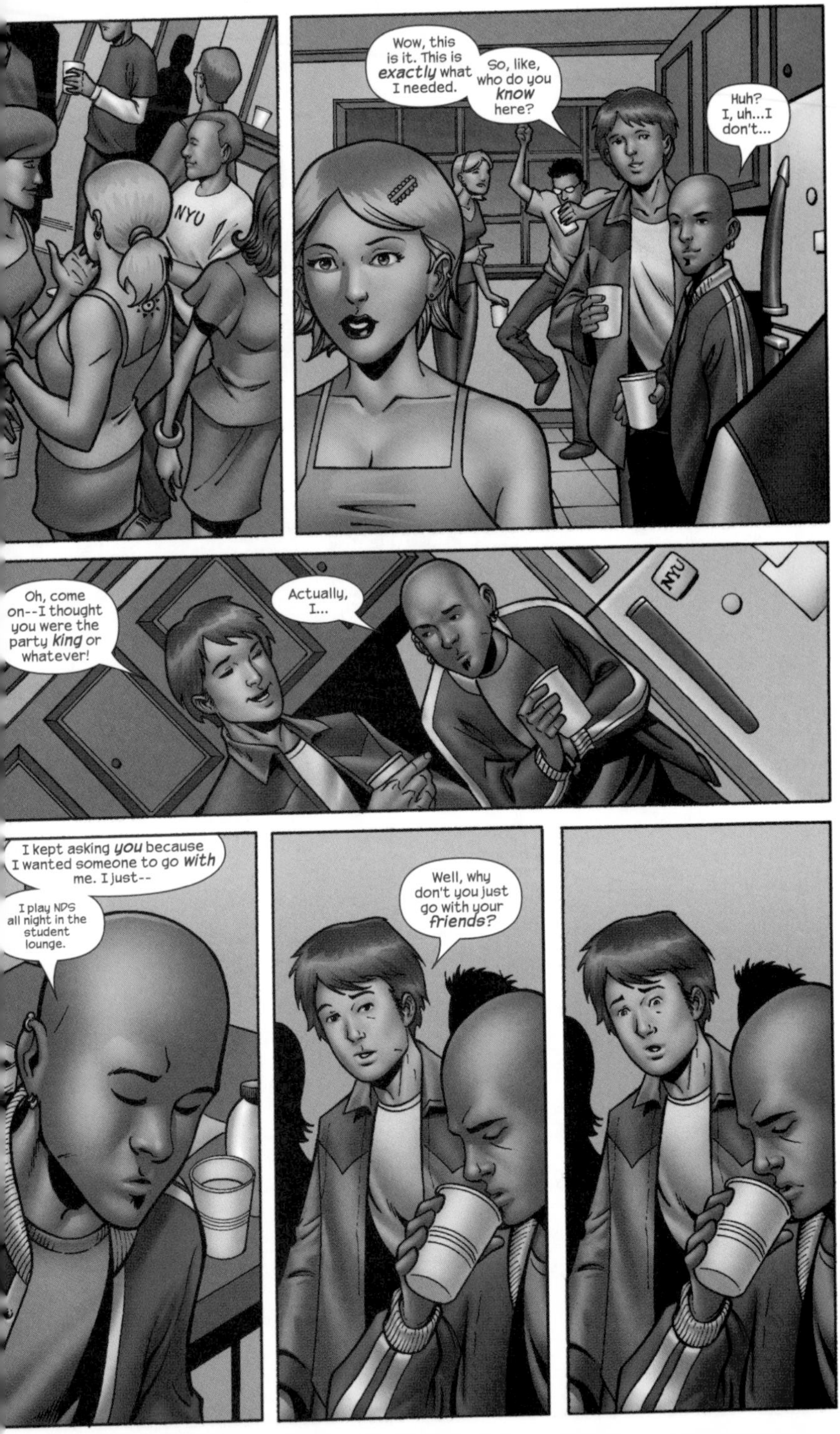
Wow, this is it. This is *exactly* what I needed.
So, like, who do you *know* here?
Huh? I, uh...I don't...
Oh, come on--I thought you were the party *king* or whatever!
Actually, I...
I kept asking *you* because I wanted someone to go *with* me. I just--
I play NDS all night in the student lounge.
Well, why don't you just go with your *friends*?
NYU
NYU

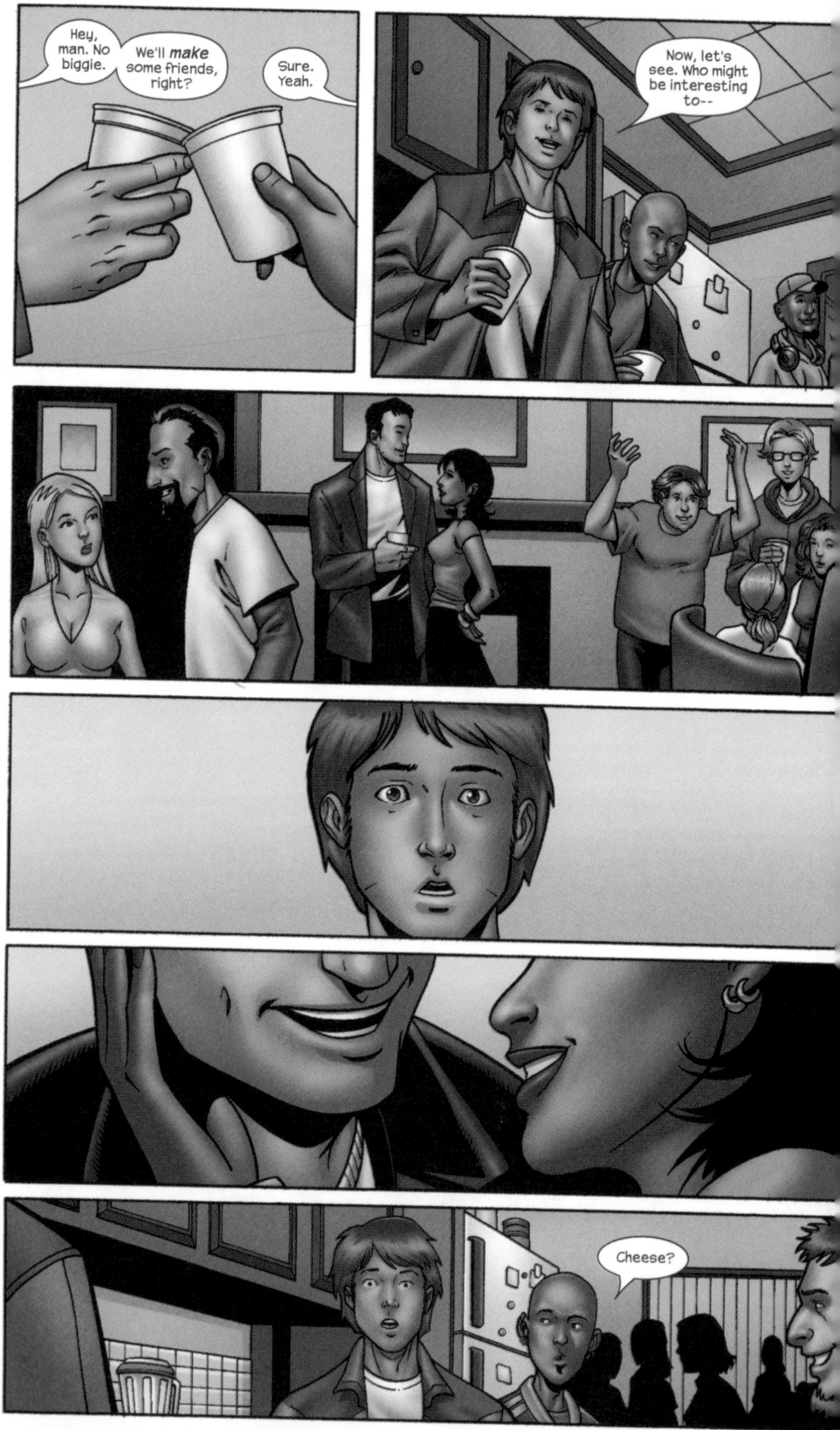
Hey, man. No biggie.
We'll *make* some friends, right?
Sure. Yeah.
Now, let's see. Who might be interesting to--
Cheese?

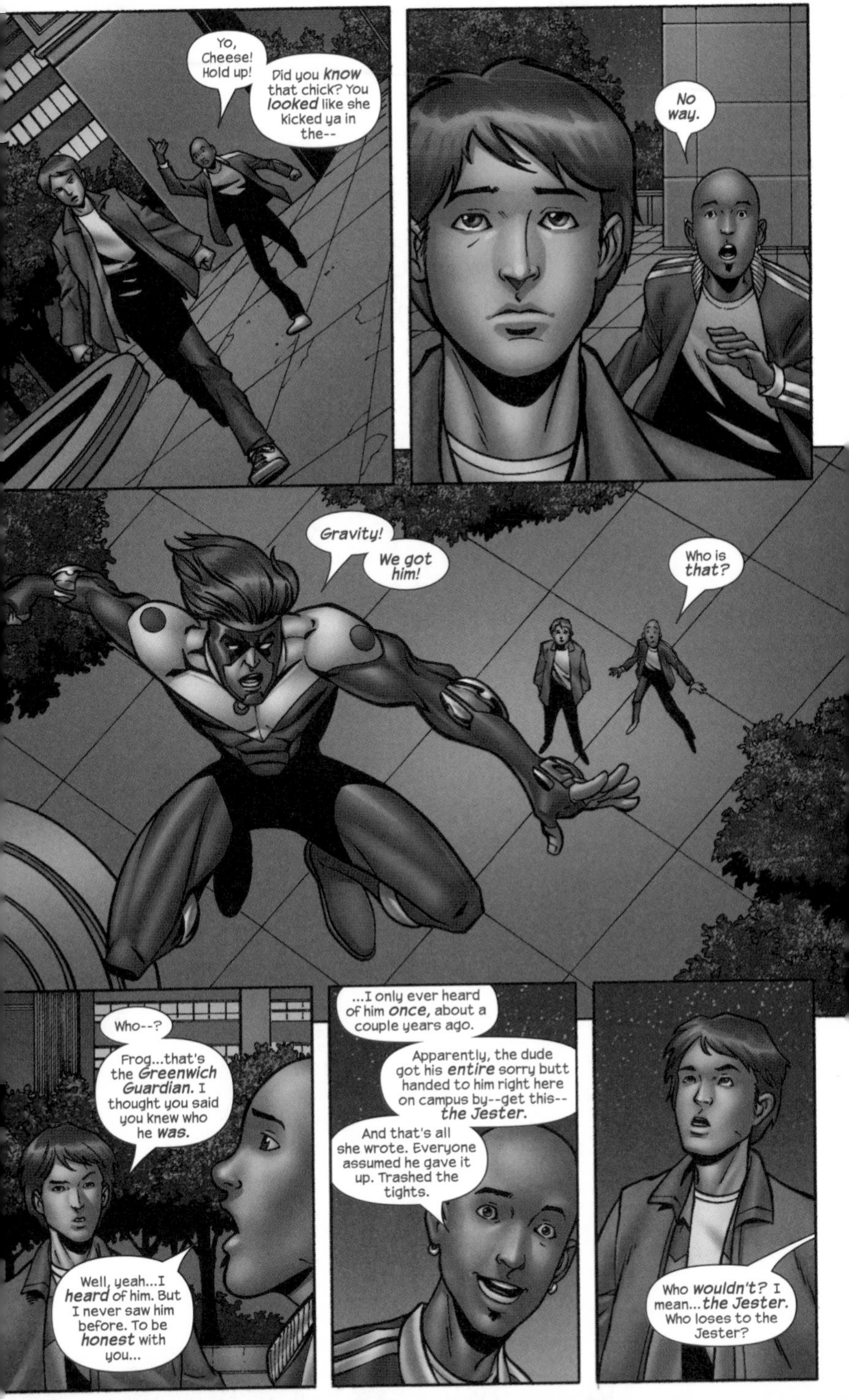
Yo, Cheese! Hold up!
Did you know that chick? You looked like she kicked ya in the--
No way.
Gravity!
We got him!
Who is that?
Who--?
Frog...that's the Greenwich Guardian. I thought you said you knew who he was.
Well, yeah...I heard of him. But I never saw him before. To be honest with you...
...I only ever heard of him once, about a couple years ago.
Apparently, the dude got his entire sorry butt handed to him right here on campus by--get this-- the Jester.
And that's all she wrote. Everyone assumed he gave it up. Trashed the tights.
Who wouldn't? I mean...the Jester. Who loses to the Jester?

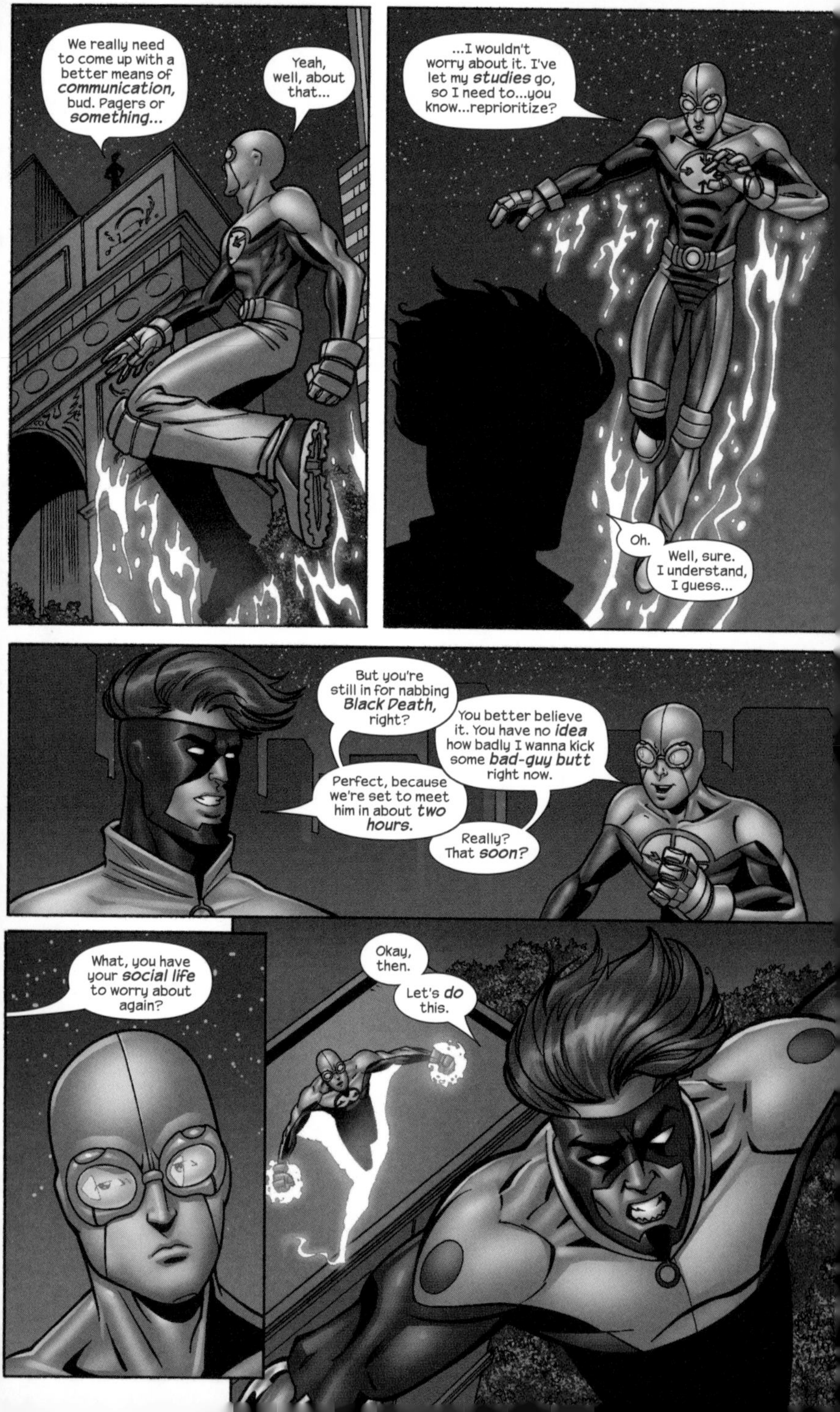
We really need to come up with a better means of communication, bud. Pagers or something...
Yeah, well, about that...
...I wouldn't worry about it. I've let my studies go, so I need to...you know...reprioritize?
Oh.
Well, sure. I understand, I guess...
But you're still in for nabbing Black Death, right?
You better believe it. You have no idea how badly I wanna kick some bad-guy butt right now.
Perfect, because we're set to meet him in about two hours.
Really? That soon?
What, you have your social life to worry about again?
Okay, then.
Let's do this.

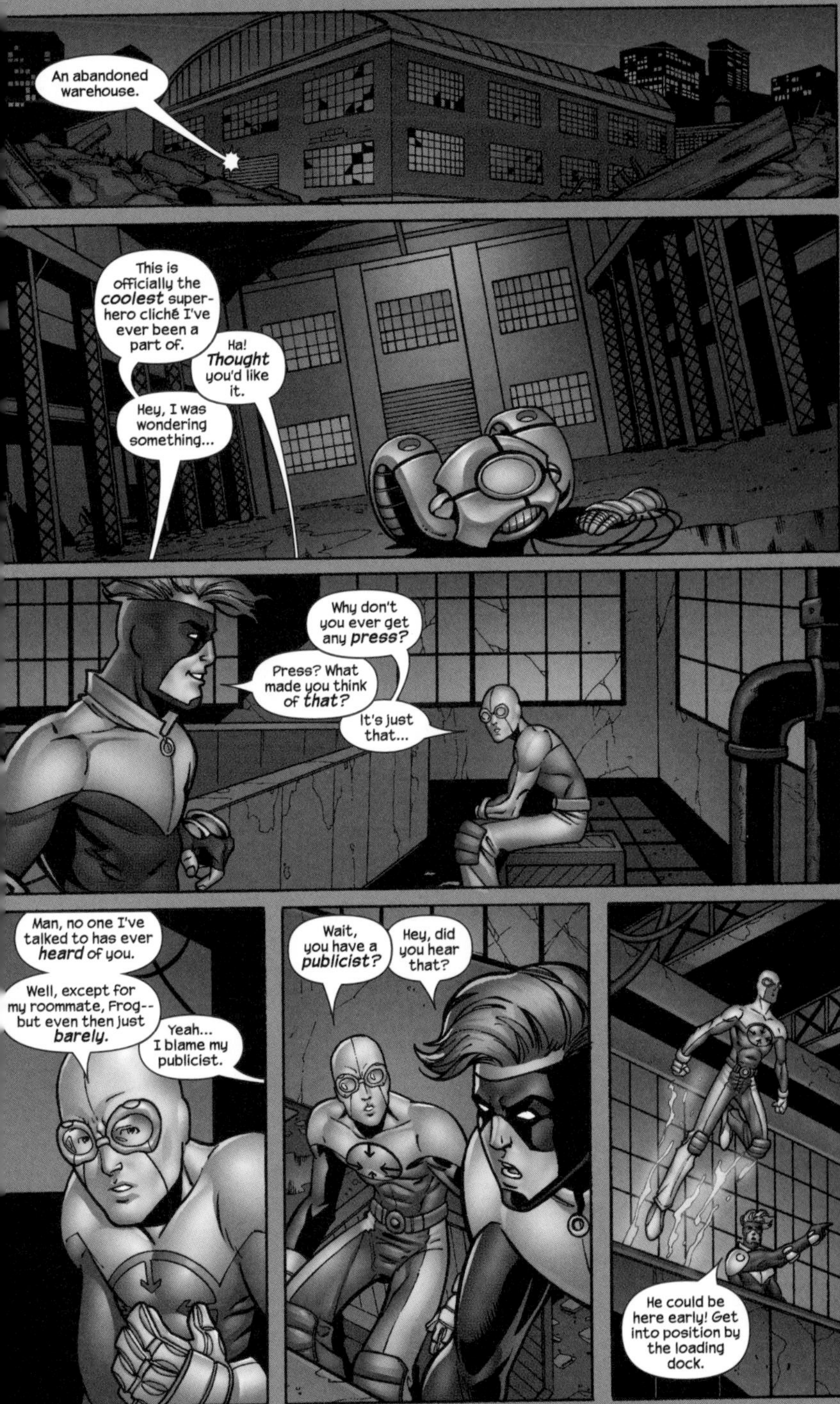

An abandoned warehouse.
This is officially the coolest super-hero cliché I've ever been a part of.
Ha! Thought you'd like it.
Hey, I was wondering something...
Why don't you ever get any press?
Press? What made you think of that?
It's just that...
Man, no one I've talked to has ever heard of you.
Well, except for my roommate, Frog-- but even then just barely.
Yeah... I blame my publicist.
Wait, you have a publicist?
Hey, did you hear that?
He could be here early! Get into position by the loading dock.

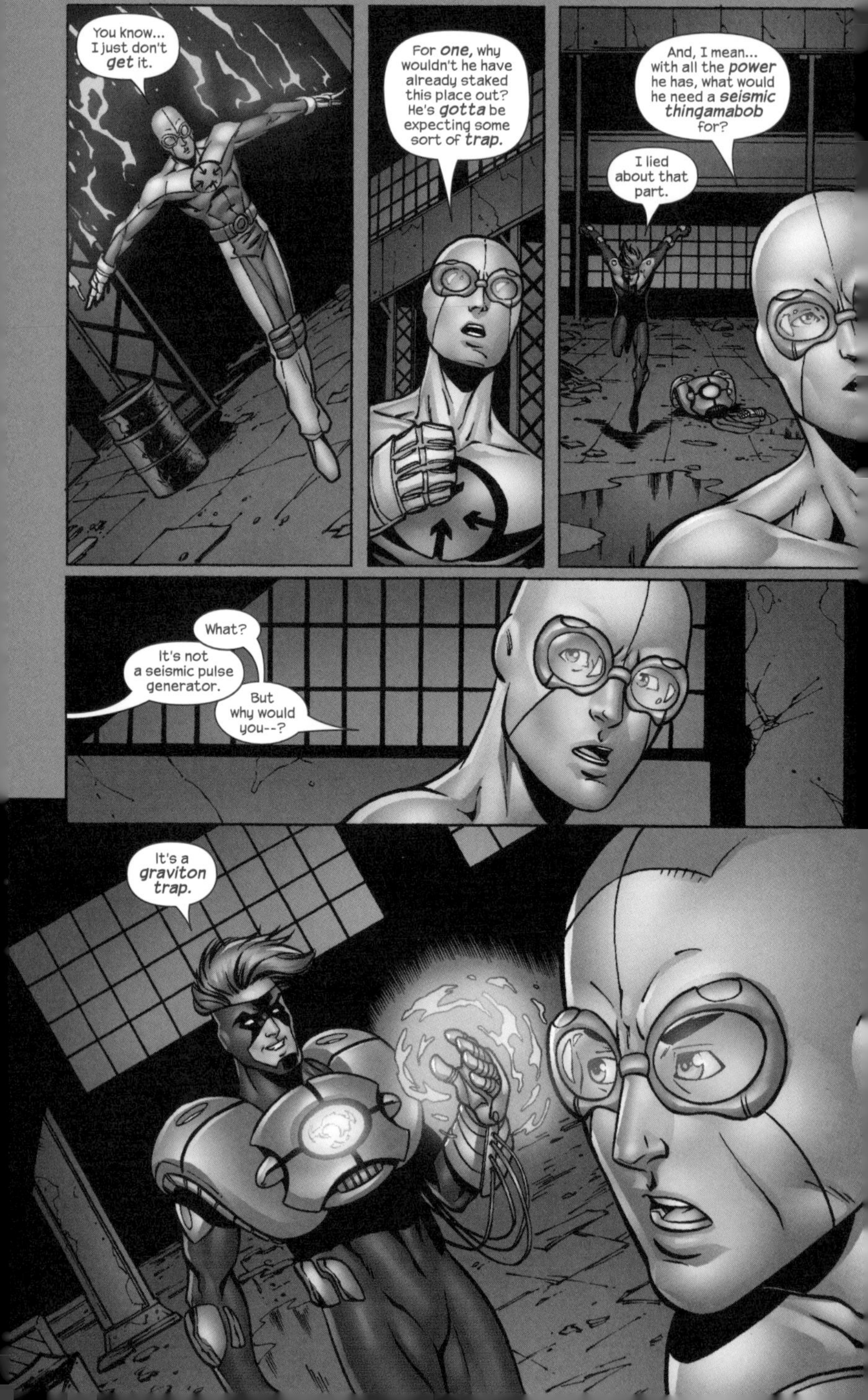

You know... I just don't *get* it.
For *one,* why wouldn't he have already staked this place out? He's *gotta* be expecting some sort of *trap.*
And, I mean... with all the *power* he has, what would he need a *seismic thingamabob* for?
I lied about that part.
What?
It's not a seismic pulse generator.
But why would you--?
It's a *graviton trap.*

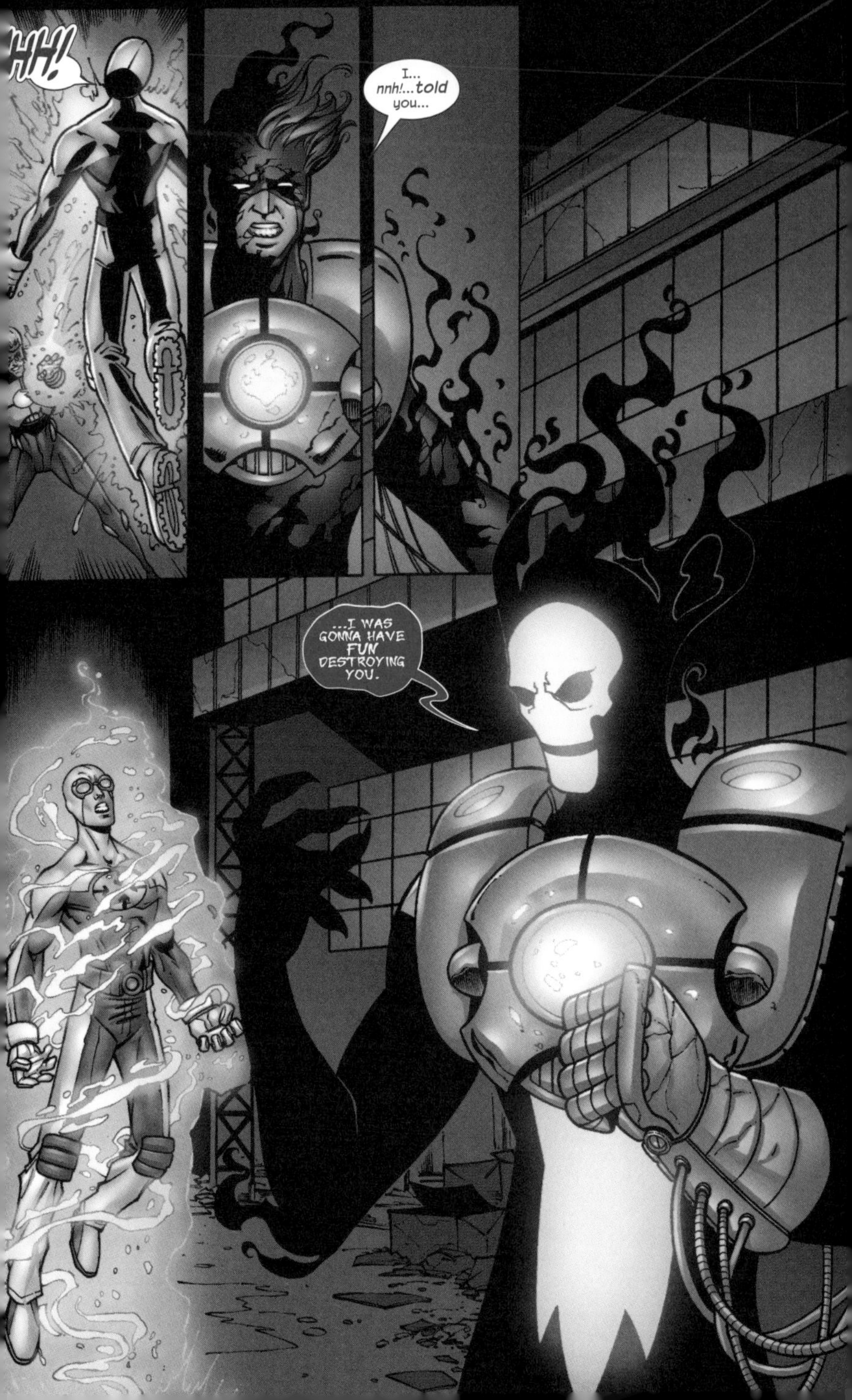
HH!
I... nnh!...told you...
...I WAS GONNA HAVE FUN DESTROYING YOU.

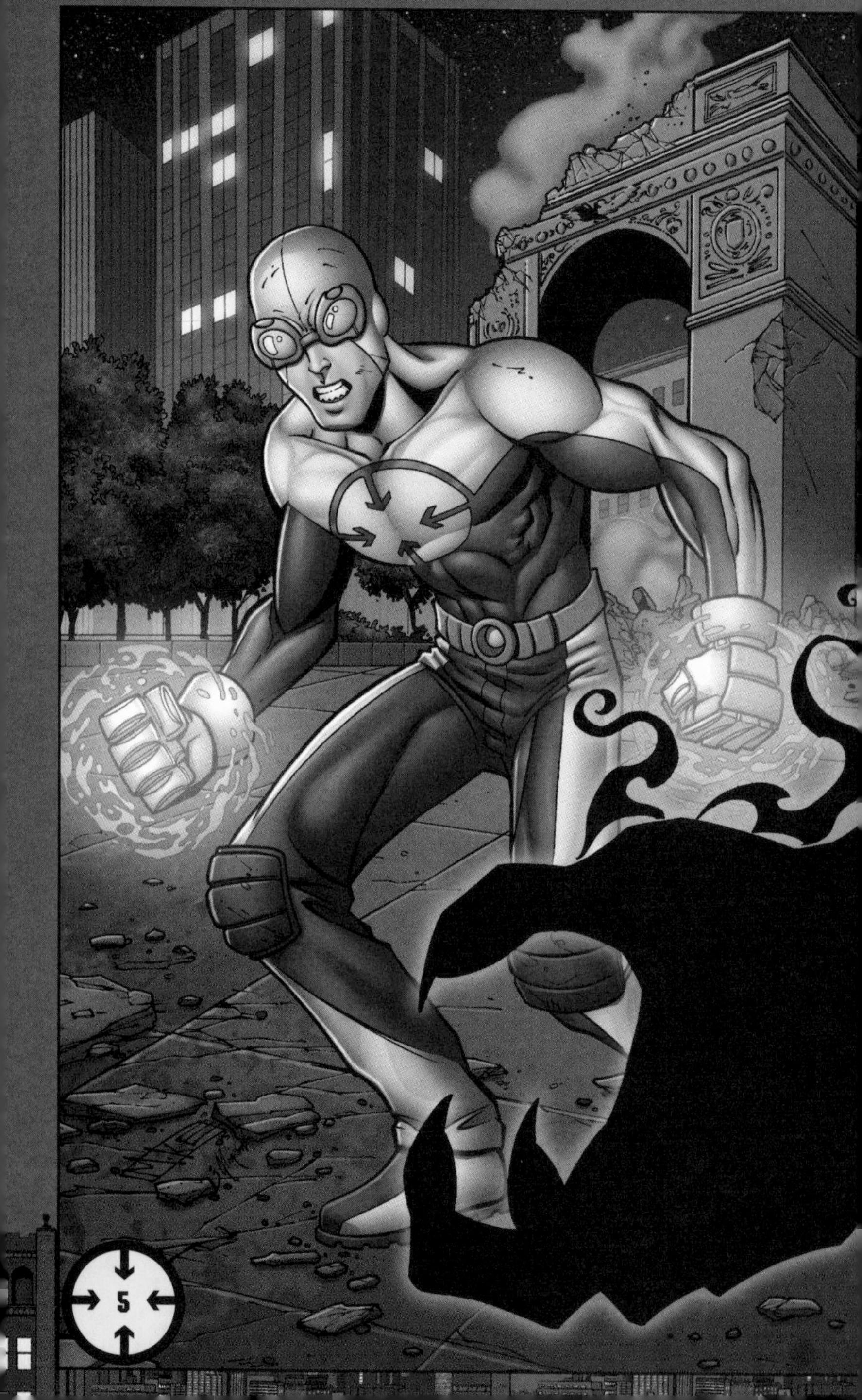
5

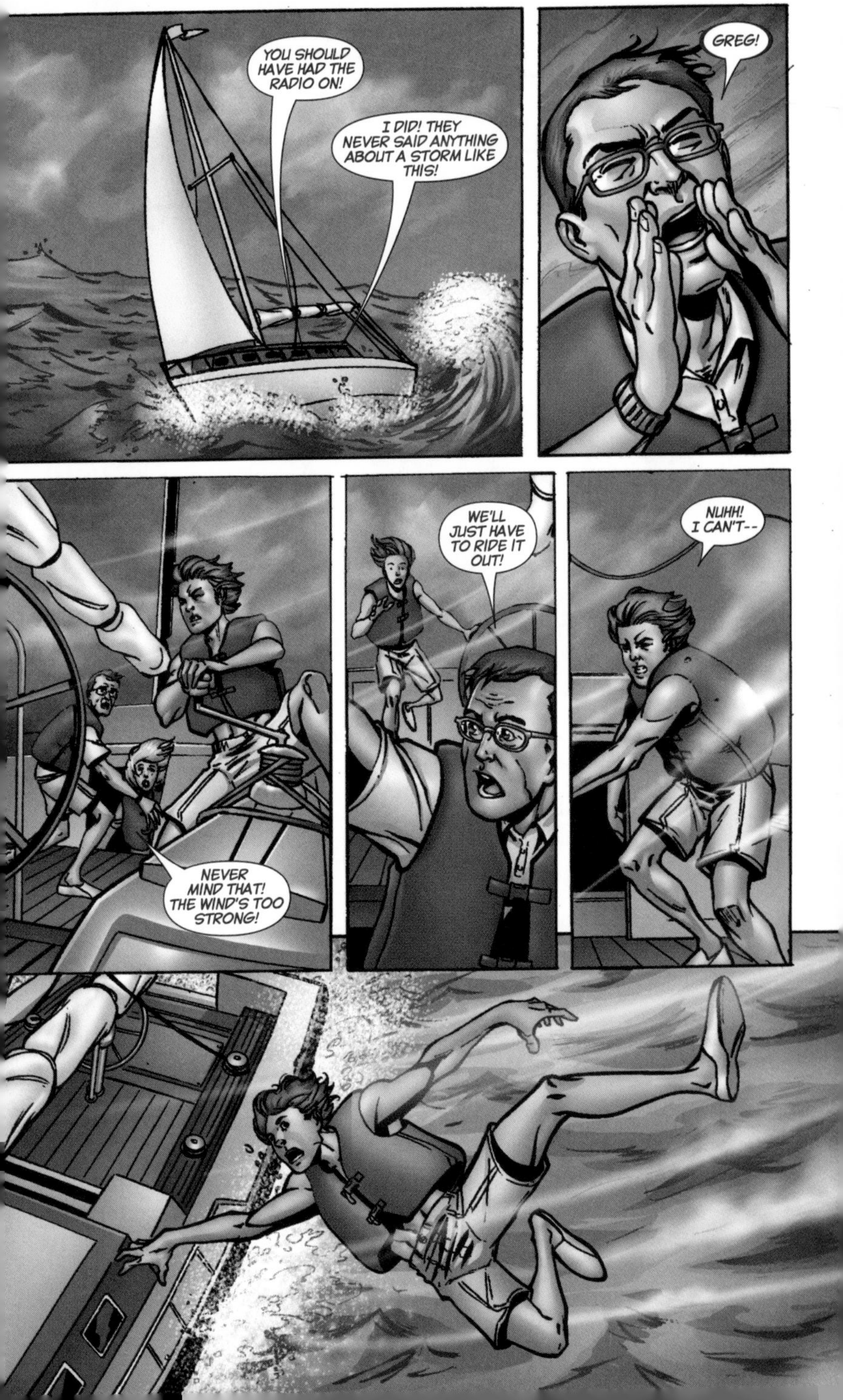
YOU SHOULD HAVE HAD THE RADIO ON!
I DID! THEY NEVER SAID ANYTHING ABOUT A STORM LIKE THIS!
GREG!
NEVER MIND THAT! THE WIND'S TOO STRONG!
WE'LL JUST HAVE TO RIDE IT OUT!
NUHH! I CAN'T--

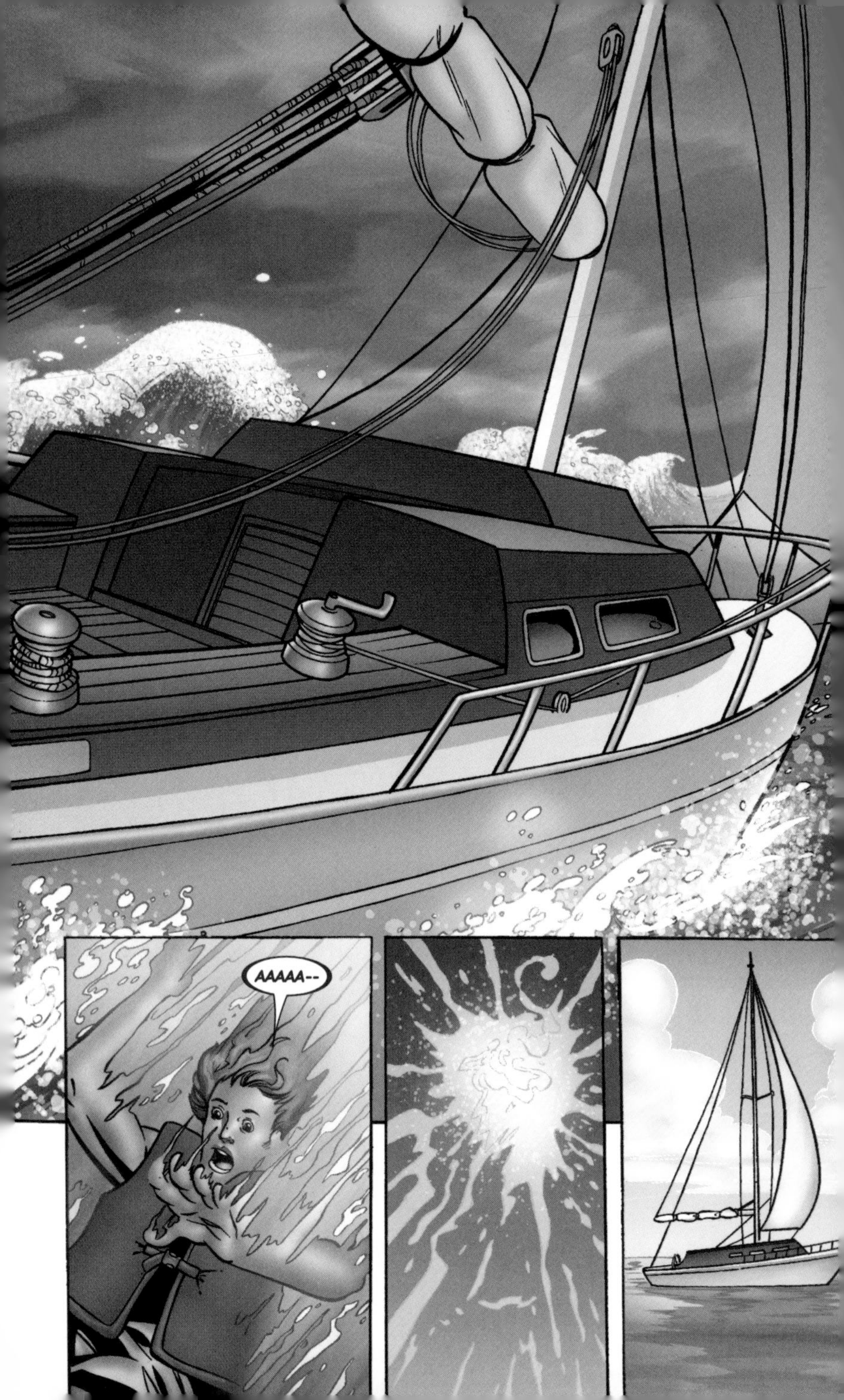
AAAAA--

CHEWED UP AND SPIT OUT

GREG!

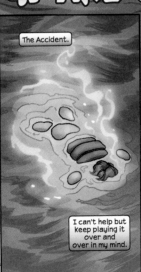

The Accident.

I can't help but keep playing it over and over in my mind.

But that's the past.

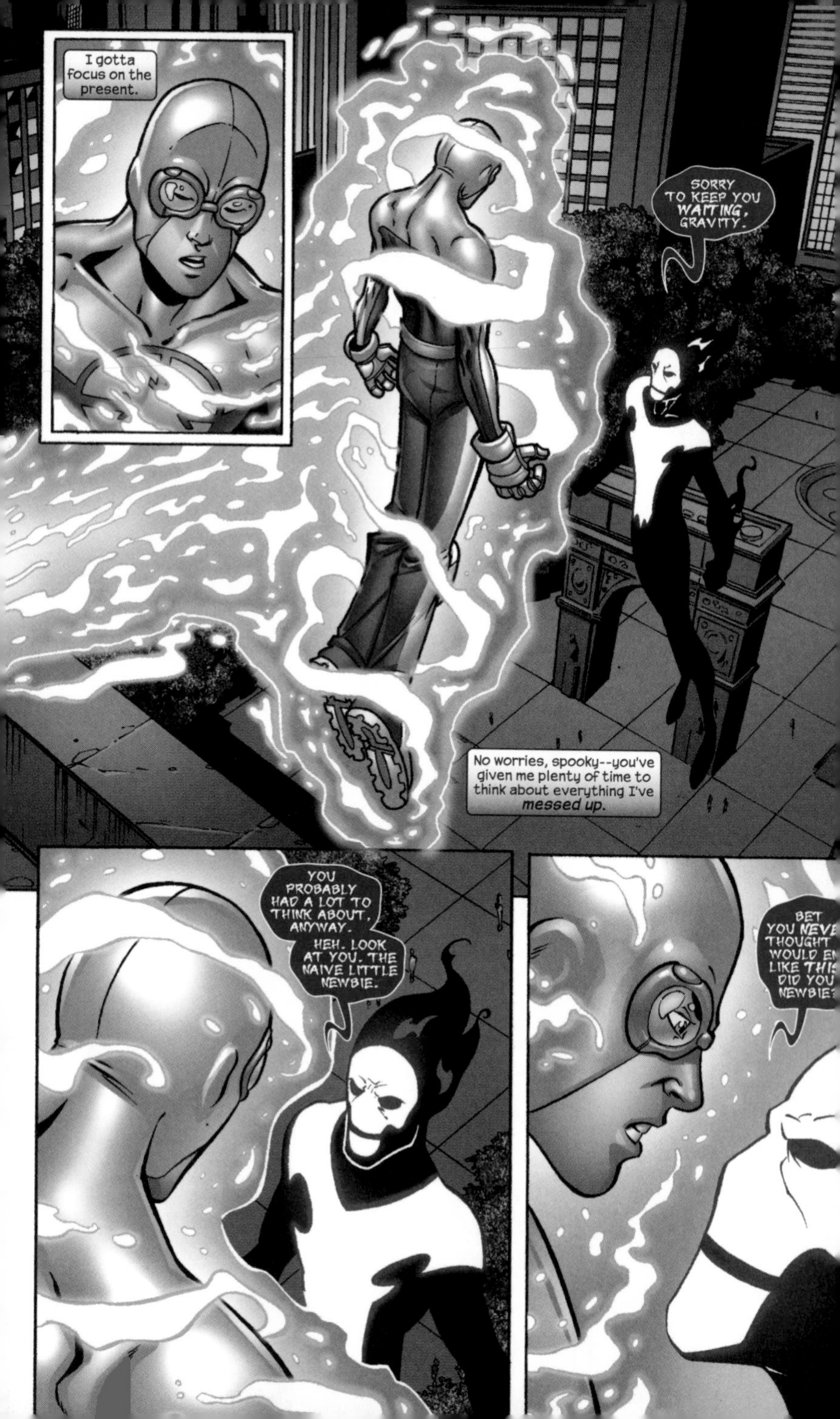
I gotta focus on the present.
SORRY TO KEEP YOU WAITING, GRAVITY.
No worries, spooky--you've given me plenty of time to think about everything I've messed up.
YOU PROBABLY HAD A LOT TO THINK ABOUT, ANYWAY.
HEH. LOOK AT YOU. THE NAIVE LITTLE NEWBIE.
BET YOU NEVE THOUGHT WOULD E LIKE THI DID YOU NEWBIE

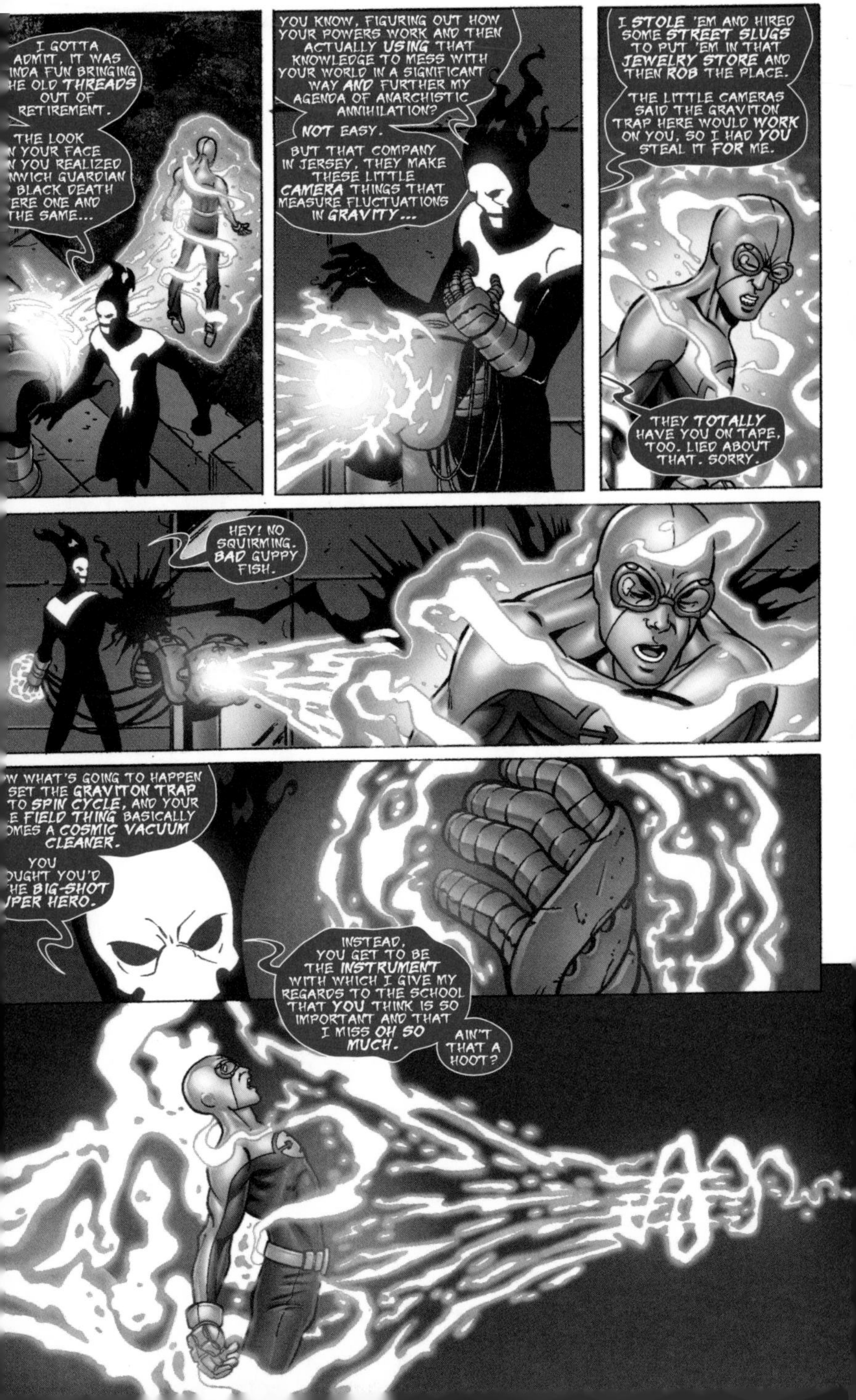

I GOTTA ADMIT, IT WAS INDA FUN BRINGING HE OLD THREADS OUT OF RETIREMENT.
THE LOOK N YOUR FACE N YOU REALIZED NWICH GUARDIAN BLACK DEATH ERE ONE AND THE SAME...
YOU KNOW, FIGURING OUT HOW YOUR POWERS WORK AND THEN ACTUALLY USING THAT KNOWLEDGE TO MESS WITH YOUR WORLD IN A SIGNIFICANT WAY AND FURTHER MY AGENDA OF ANARCHISTIC ANNIHILATION?
NOT EASY.
BUT THAT COMPANY IN JERSEY, THEY MAKE THESE LITTLE CAMERA THINGS THAT MEASURE FLUCTUATIONS IN GRAVITY...
I STOLE 'EM AND HIRED SOME STREET SLUGS TO PUT 'EM IN THAT JEWELRY STORE AND THEN ROB THE PLACE.
THE LITTLE CAMERAS SAID THE GRAVITON TRAP HERE WOULD WORK ON YOU, SO I HAD YOU STEAL IT FOR ME.
THEY TOTALLY HAVE YOU ON TAPE, TOO. LIED ABOUT THAT. SORRY.
HEY! NO SQUIRMING. BAD GUPPY FISH.
W WHAT'S GOING TO HAPPEN SET THE GRAVITON TRAP TO SPIN CYCLE, AND YOUR E FIELD THING BASICALLY OMES A COSMIC VACUUM CLEANER.
YOU OUGHT YOU'D THE BIG-SHOT UPER HERO.
INSTEAD, YOU GET TO BE THE INSTRUMENT WITH WHICH I GIVE MY REGARDS TO THE SCHOOL THAT YOU THINK IS SO IMPORTANT AND THAT I MISS OH SO MUCH.
AIN'T THAT A HOOT?

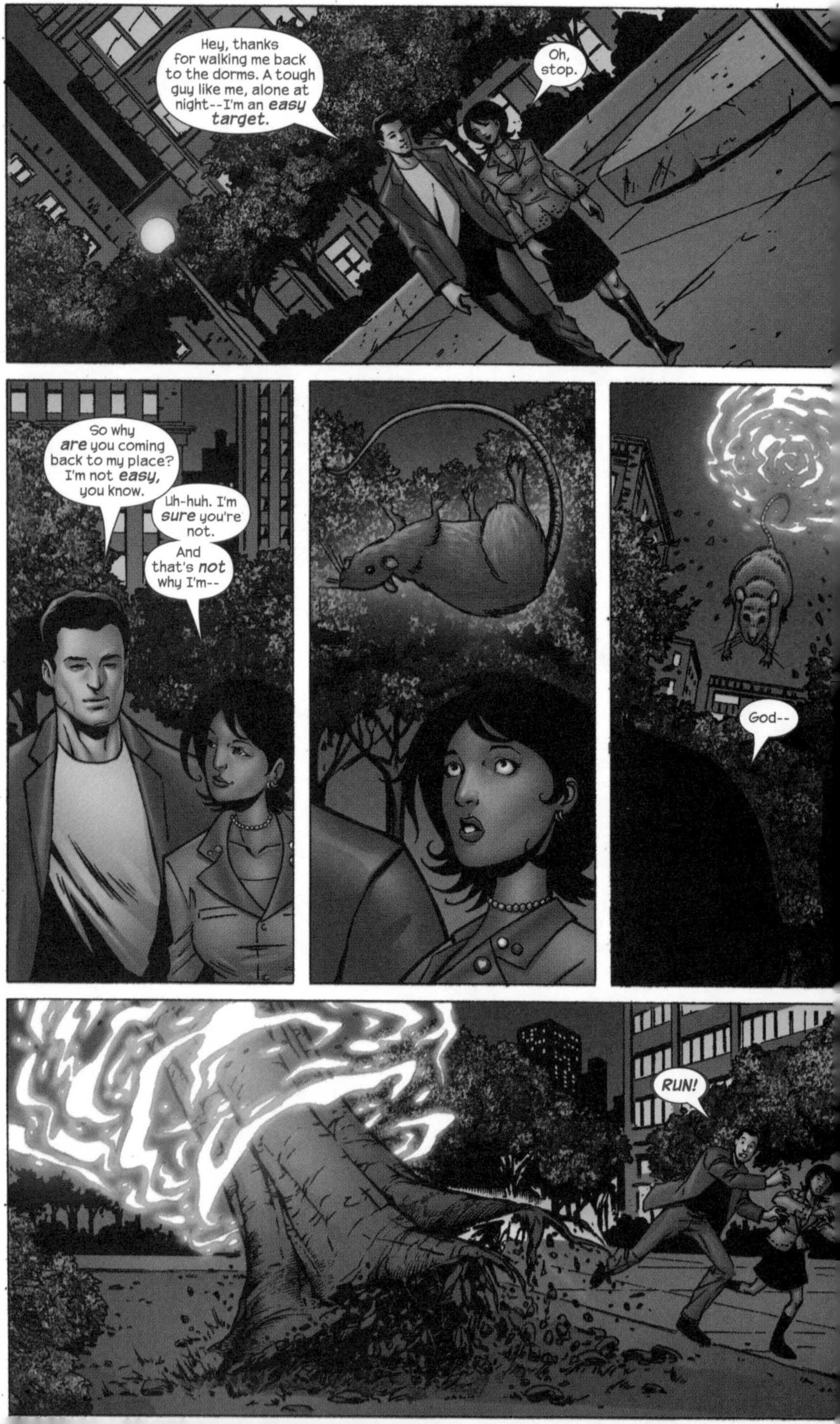
Hey, thanks for walking me back to the dorms. A tough guy like me, alone at night--I'm an *easy* *target.*
Oh, stop.
So why *are* you coming back to my place? I'm not *easy,* you know.
Uh-huh. I'm *sure* you're not.
And that's *not* why I'm--
God--
RUN!

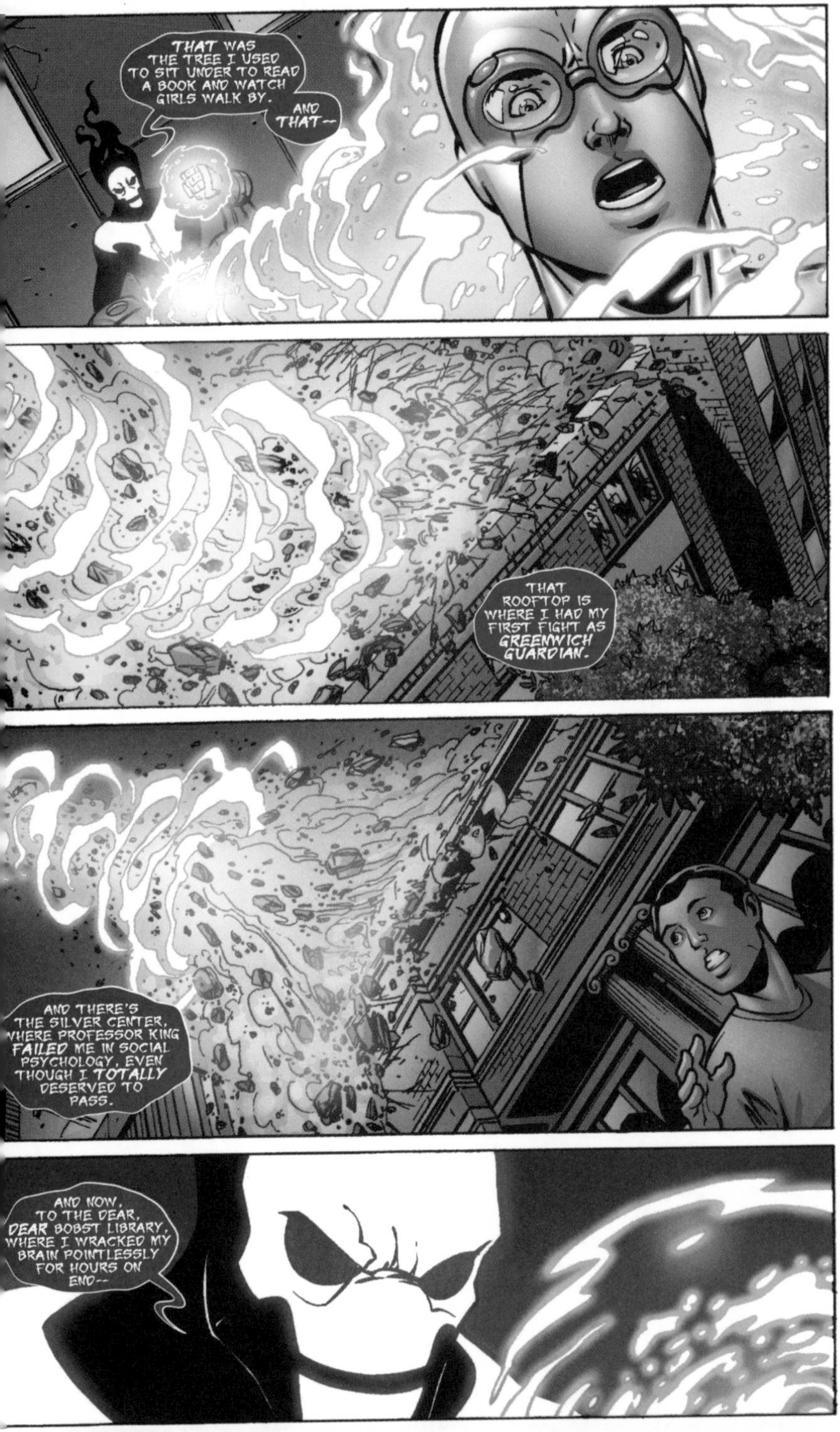
THAT WAS THE TREE I USED TO SIT UNDER TO READ A BOOK AND WATCH GIRLS WALK BY.
AND THAT--
THAT ROOFTOP IS WHERE I HAD MY FIRST FIGHT AS GREENWICH GUARDIAN.
AND THERE'S THE SILVER CENTER, WHERE PROFESSOR KING FAILED ME IN SOCIAL PSYCHOLOGY, EVEN THOUGH I TOTALLY DESERVED TO PASS.
AND NOW, TO THE DEAR, DEAR BOBST LIBRARY, WHERE I WRACKED MY BRAIN POINTLESSLY FOR HOURS ON END--

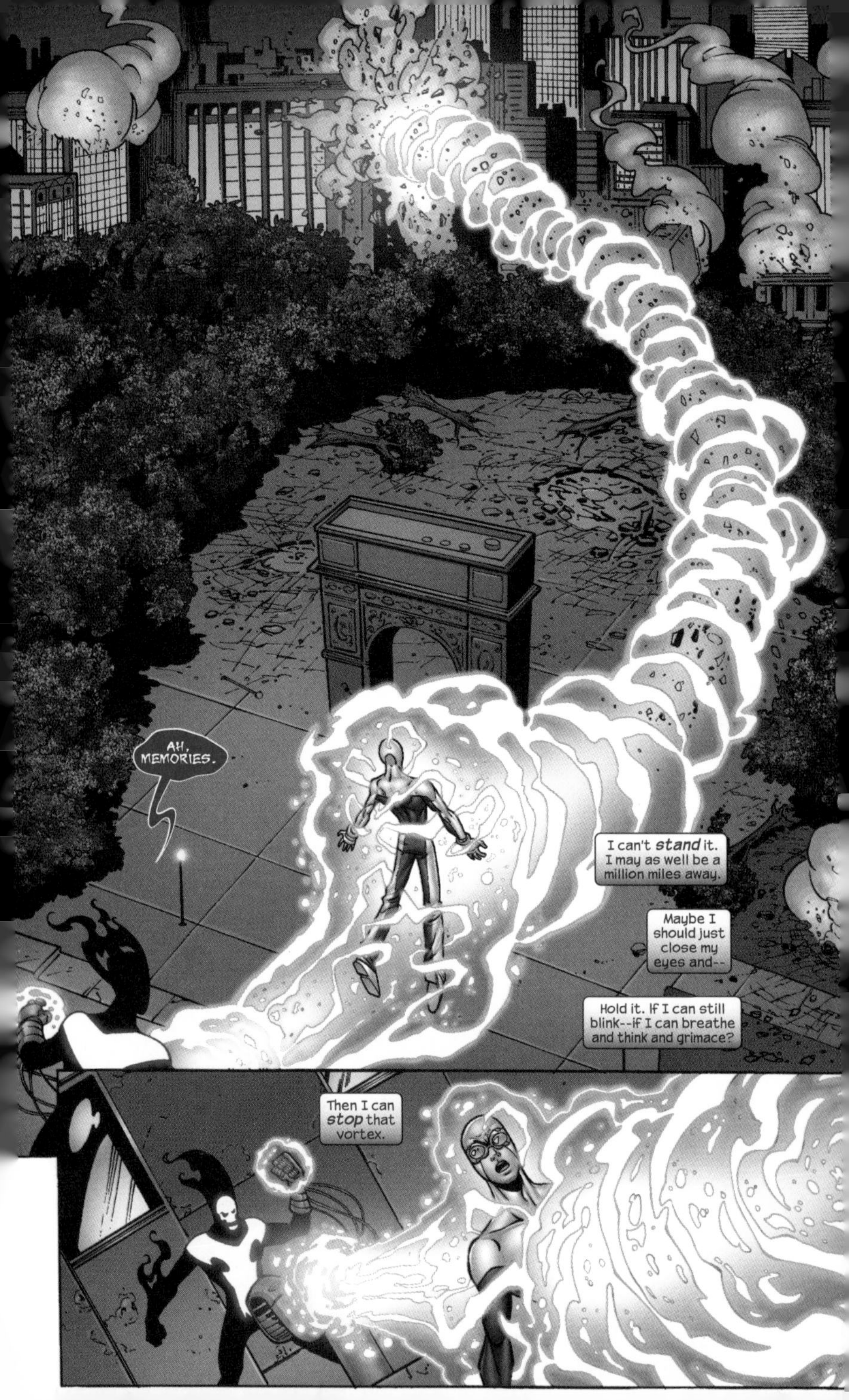
AH, MEMORIES.
I can't *stand* it. I may as well be a million miles away.
Maybe I should just close my eyes and--
Hold it. If I can still blink--if I can breathe and think and grimace?
Then I can *stop* that vortex.

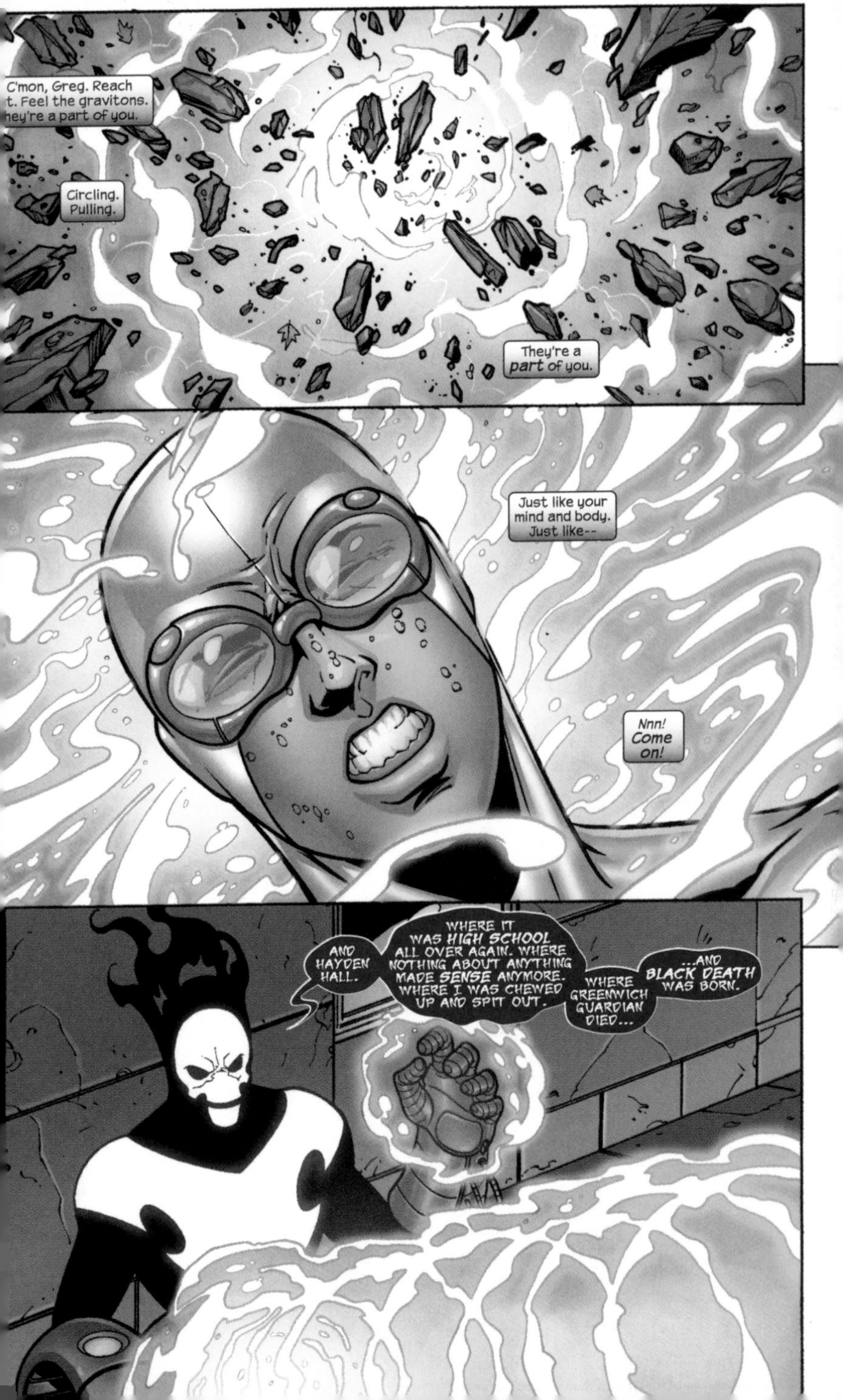
C'mon, Greg. Reach
t. Feel the gravitons.
hey're a part of you.
Circling. Pulling.
They're a part of you.
Just like your mind and body. Just like--
Nnn! Come on!
AND HAYDEN HALL.
WHERE IT WAS HIGH SCHOOL ALL OVER AGAIN. WHERE NOTHING ABOUT ANYTHING MADE SENSE ANYMORE. WHERE I WAS CHEWED UP AND SPIT OUT.
WHERE GREENWICH GUARDIAN DIED...
...AND BLACK DEATH WAS BORN.

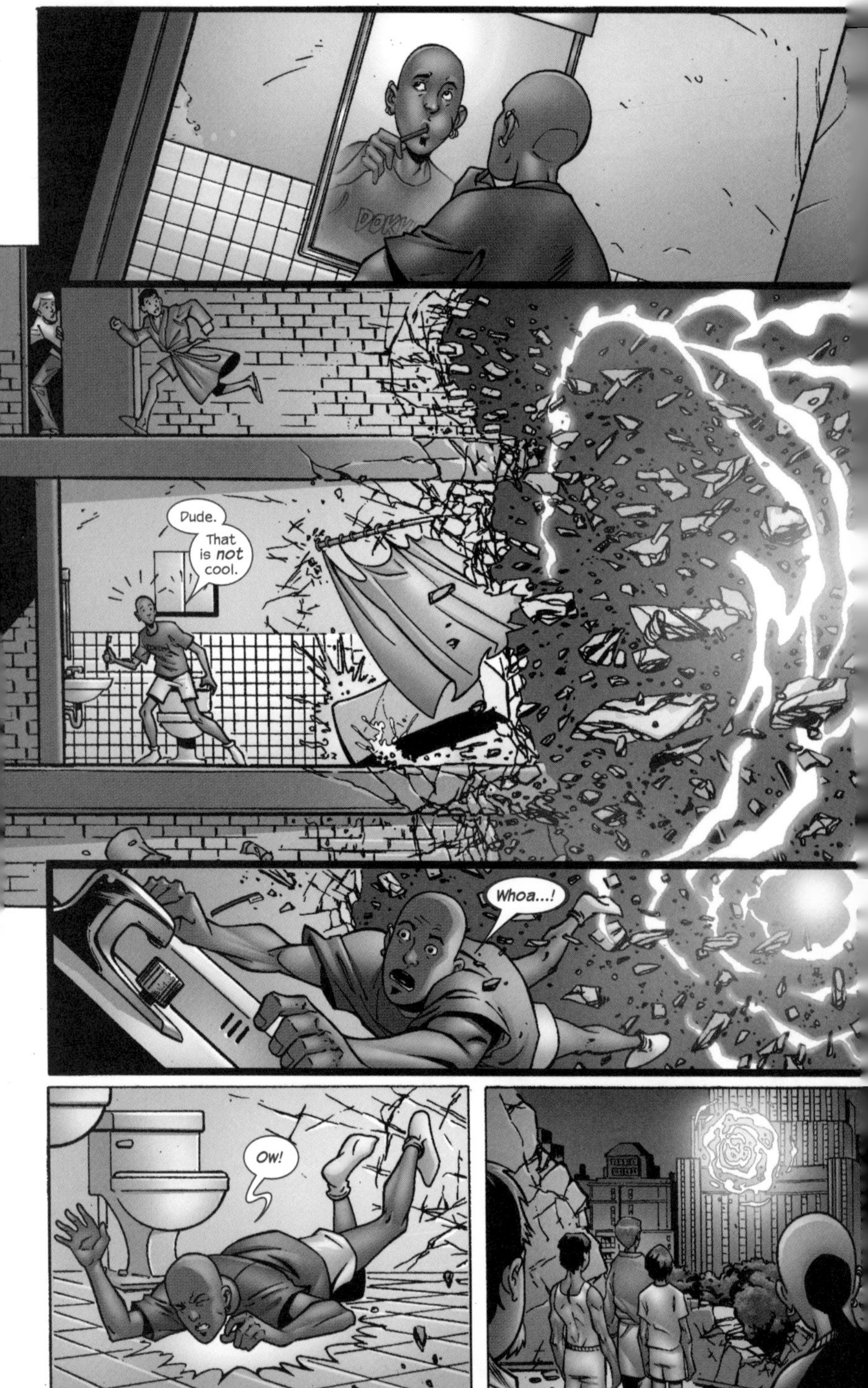
Dude.
That is **not** cool.
Whoa...!
Ow!

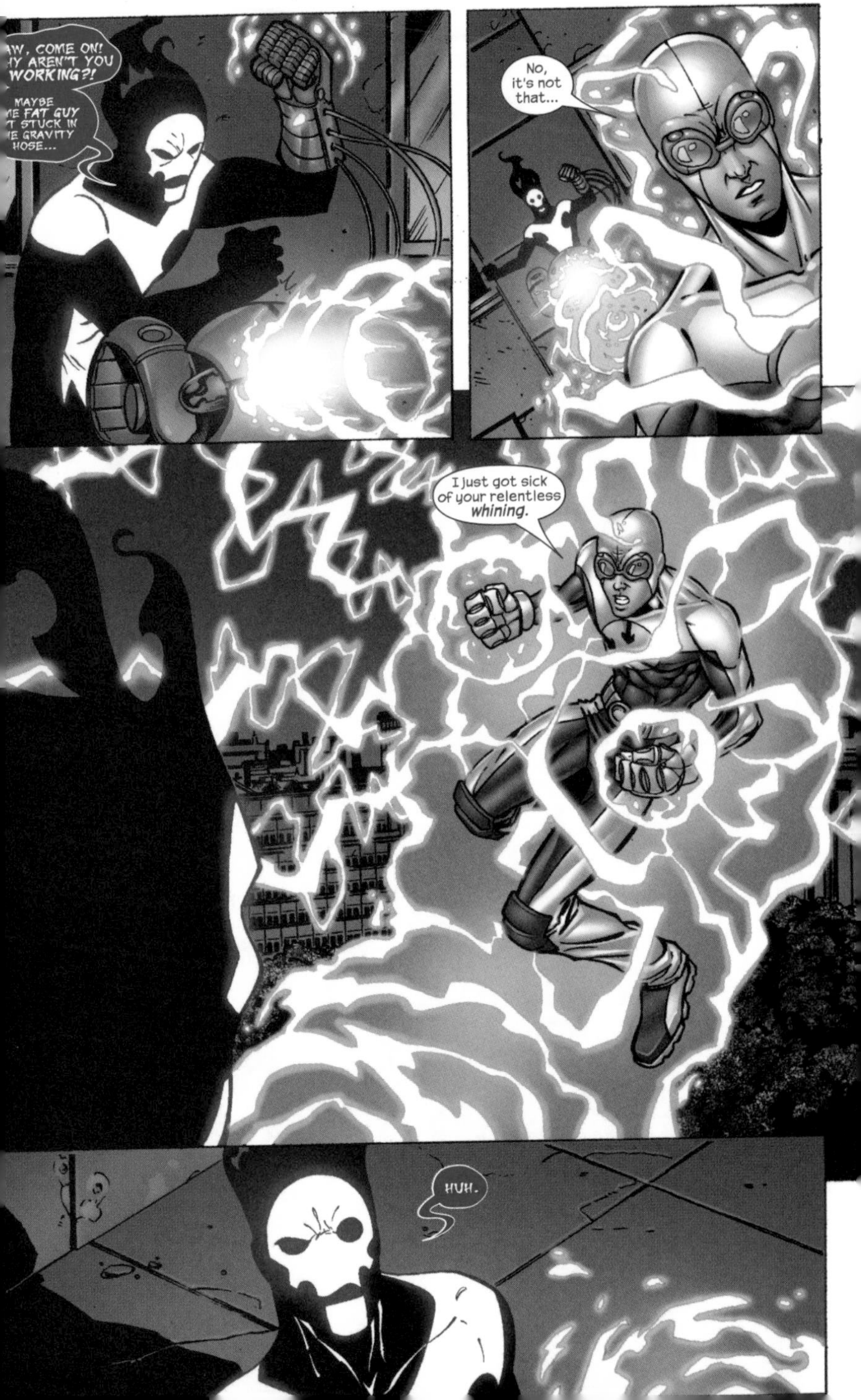
AW, COME ON!
HY AREN'T YOU
WORKING?!
MAYBE
E FAT GUY
T STUCK IN
E GRAVITY
HOSE...
No, it's not that...
I just got sick of your relentless *whining*.
HUH.

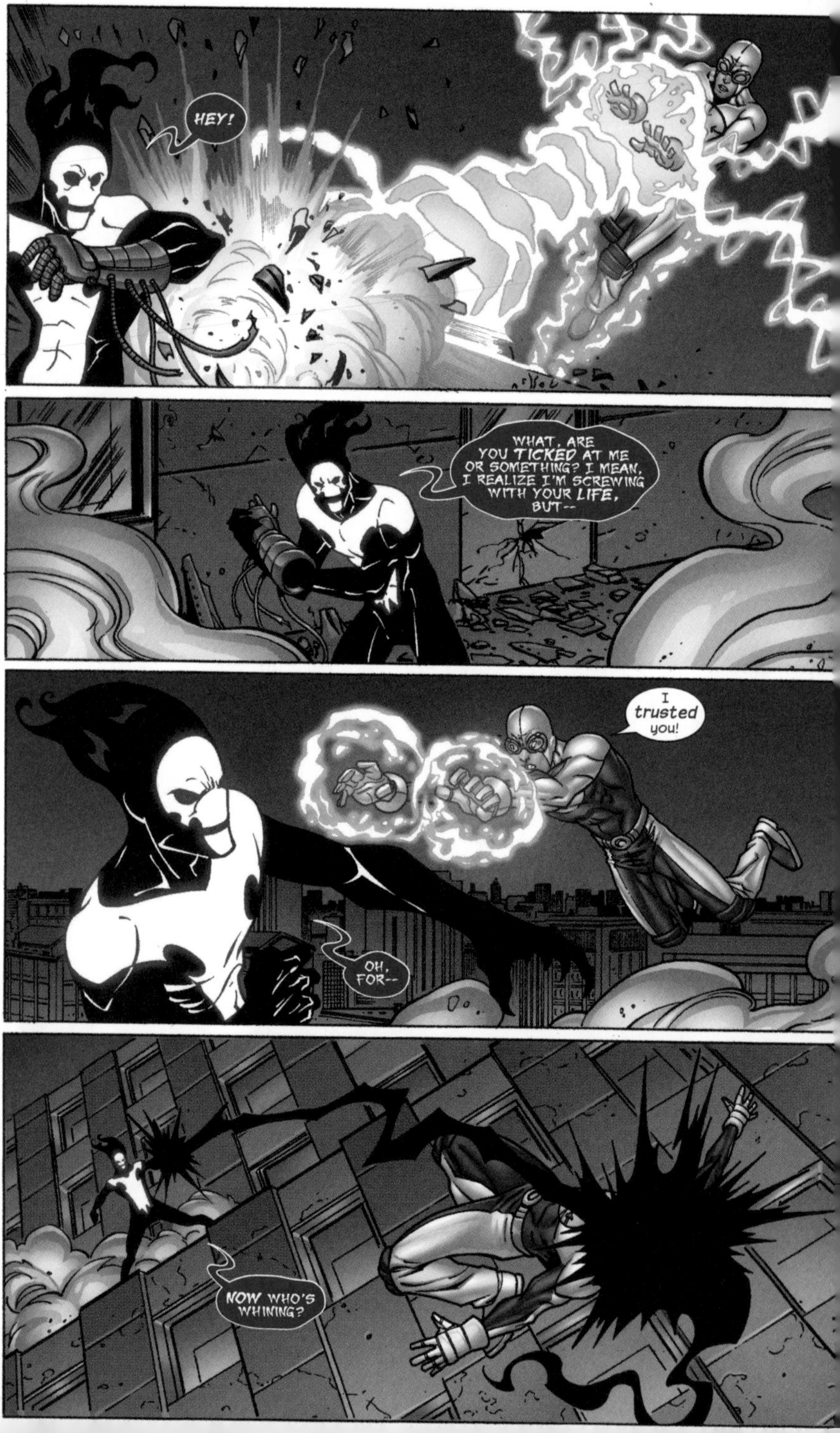
HEY!
WHAT, ARE YOU TICKED AT ME OR SOMETHING? I MEAN, I REALIZE I'M SCREWING WITH YOUR LIFE, BUT--
I trusted you!
OH, FOR--
NOW WHO'S WHINING?

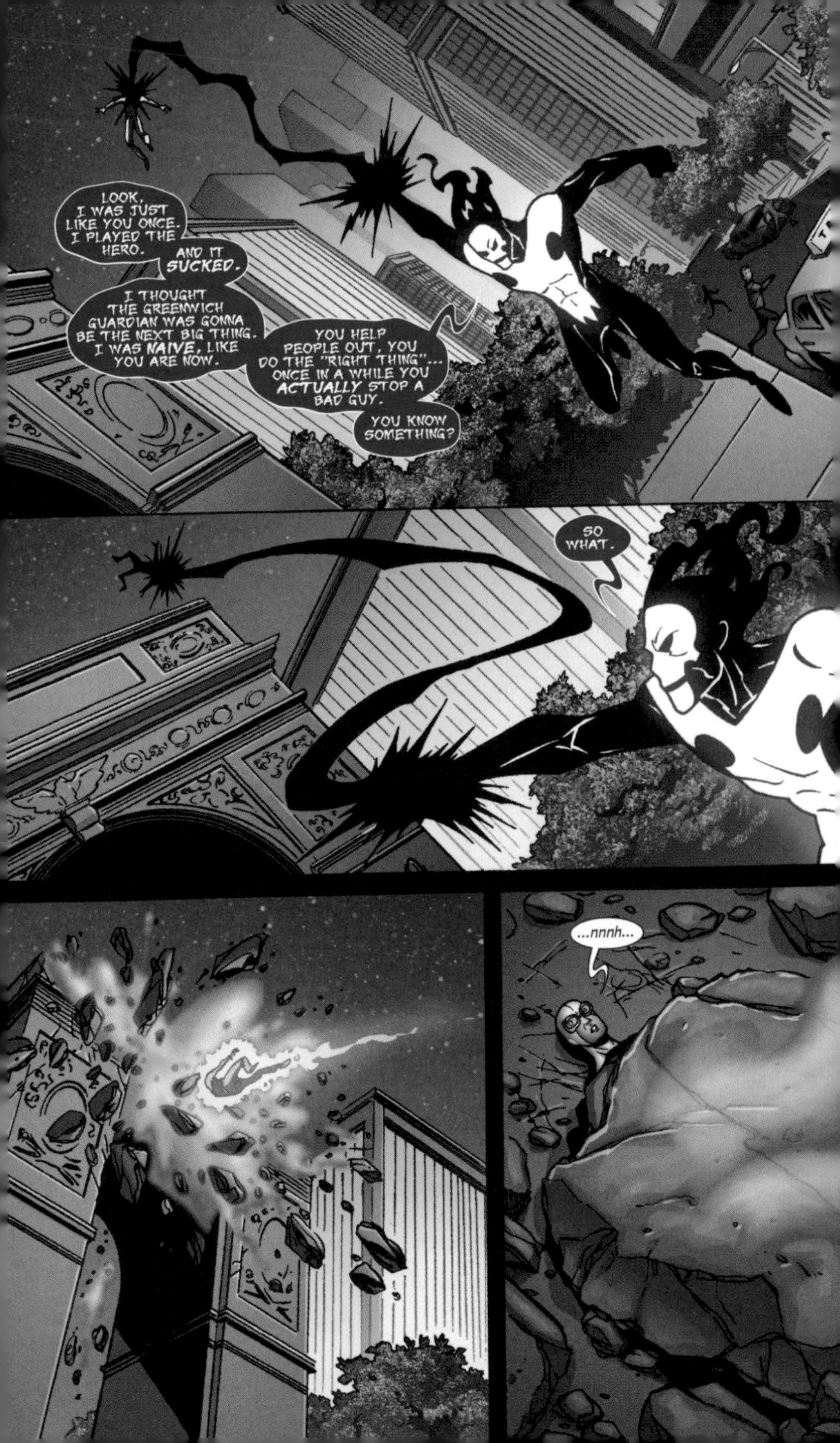
LOOK, I WAS JUST LIKE YOU ONCE. I PLAYED THE HERO.
AND IT SUCKED.
I THOUGHT THE GREENWICH GUARDIAN WAS GONNA BE THE NEXT BIG THING. I WAS NAIVE, LIKE YOU ARE NOW.
YOU HELP PEOPLE OUT, YOU DO THE "RIGHT THING"... ONCE IN A WHILE YOU ACTUALLY STOP A BAD GUY.
YOU KNOW SOMETHING?
SO WHAT.
...nnnh...

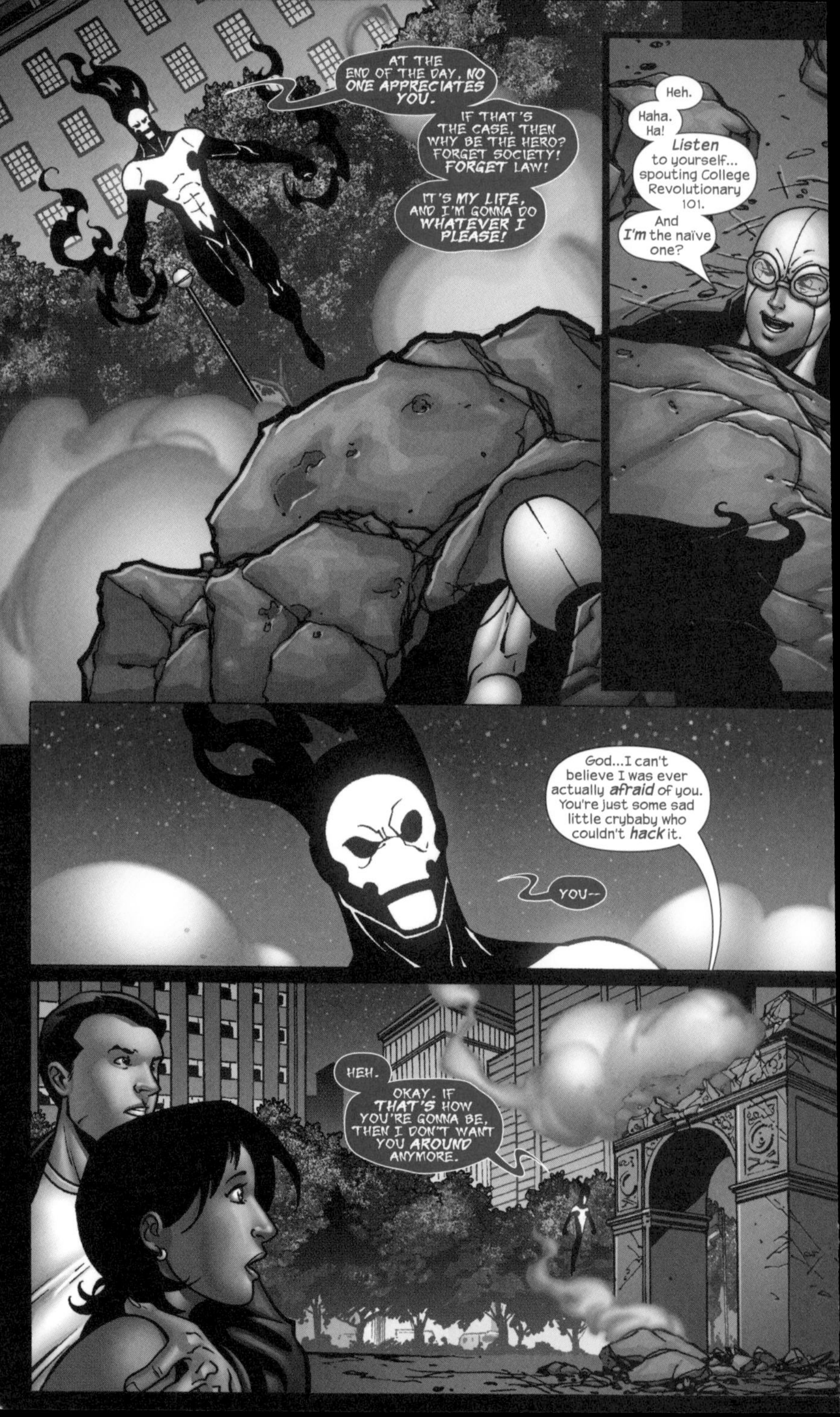
AT THE END OF THE DAY, NO ONE APPRECIATES YOU.
IF THAT'S THE CASE, THEN WHY BE THE HERO? FORGET SOCIETY! FORGET LAW!
IT'S MY LIFE, AND I'M GONNA DO WHATEVER I PLEASE!
Heh.
Haha. Ha!
Listen to yourself... spouting College Revolutionary 101.
And I'm the naïve one?
God...I can't believe I was ever actually afraid of you. You're just some sad little crybaby who couldn't hack it.
YOU--
HEH.
OKAY. IF THAT'S HOW YOU'RE GONNA BE, THEN I DON'T WANT YOU AROUND ANYMORE.

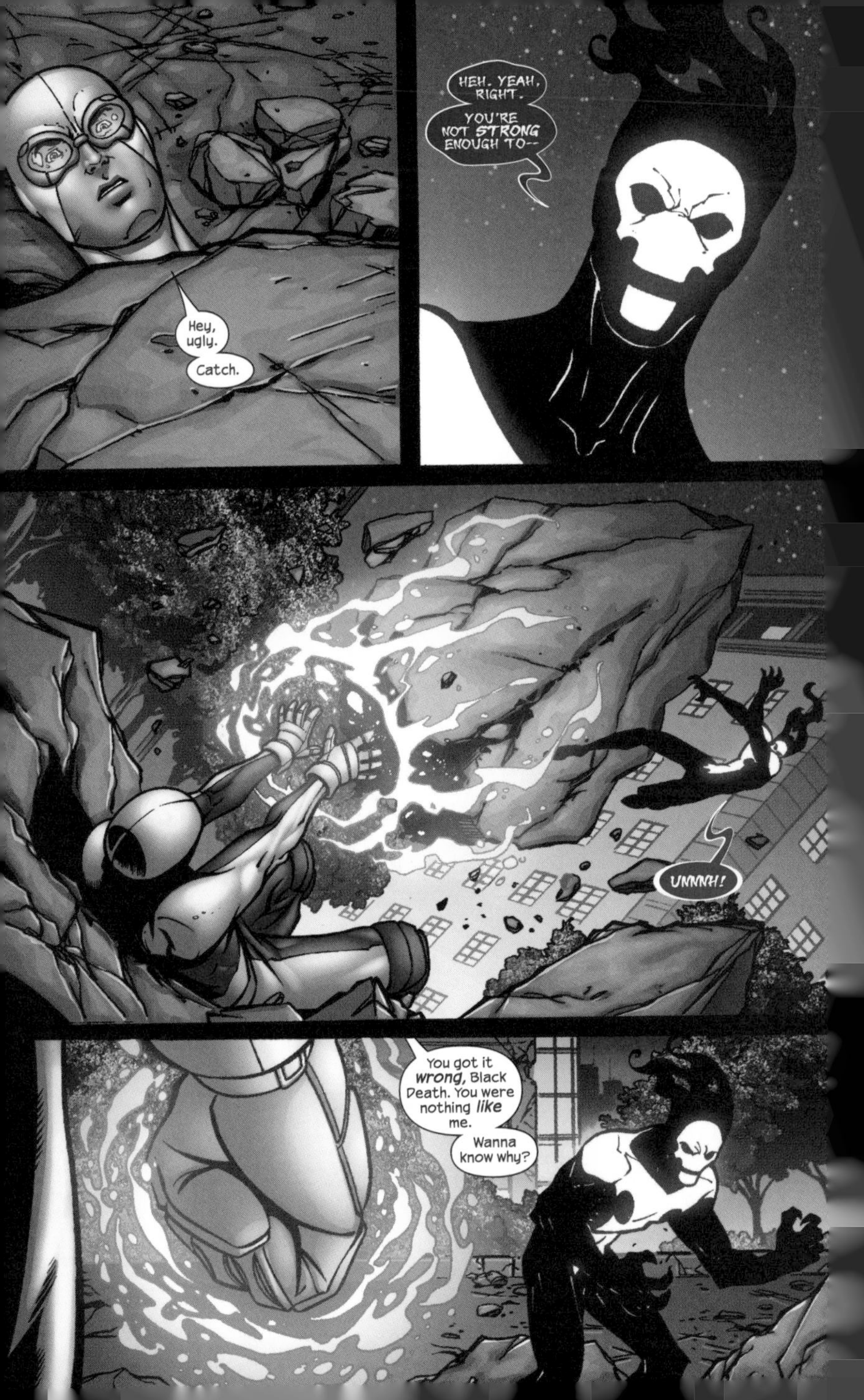
Hey, ugly.
Catch.
HEH. YEAH, RIGHT.
YOU'RE NOT STRONG ENOUGH TO--
UNNNH!
You got it wrong, Black Death. You were nothing like me.
Wanna know why?

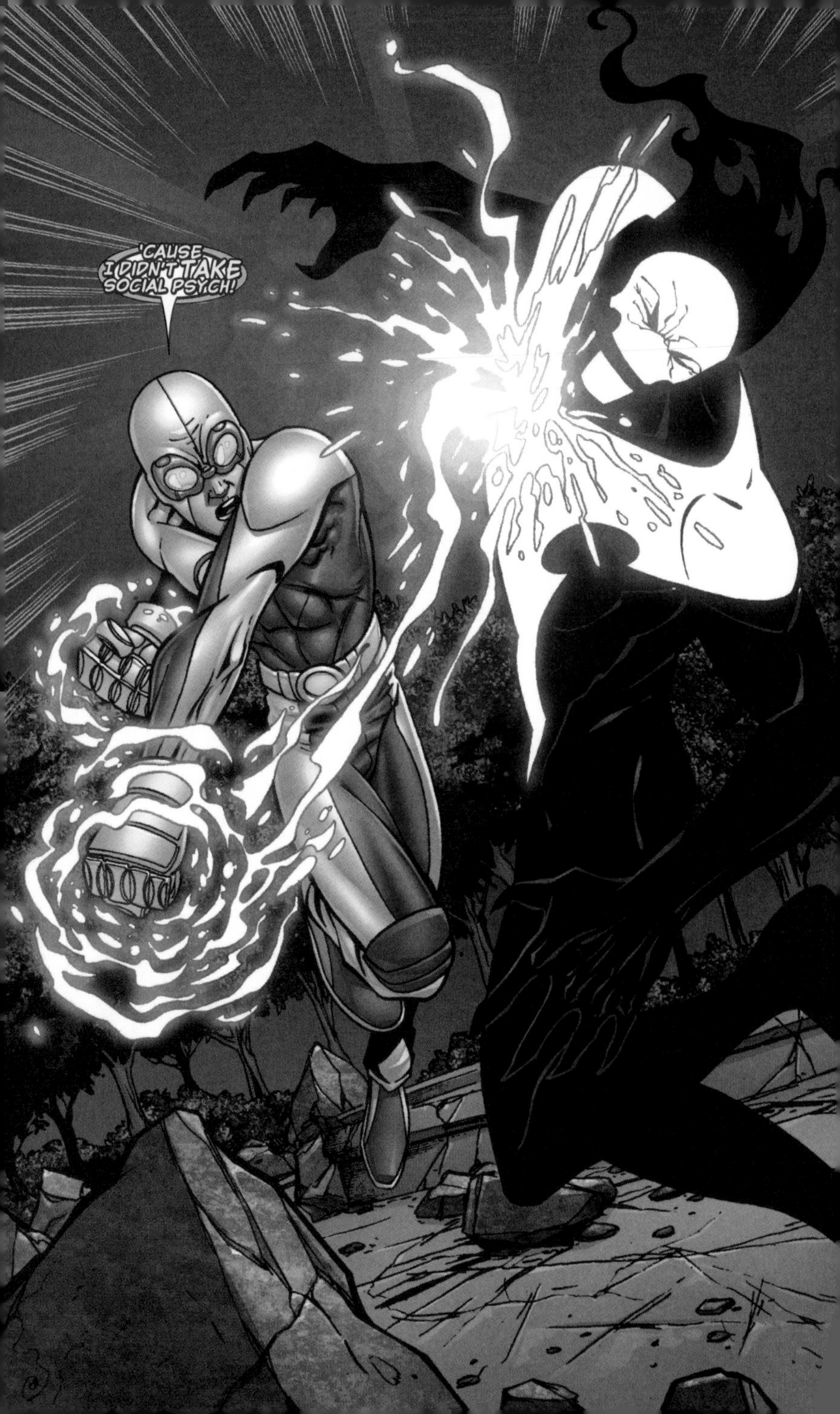
'CAUSE I DIDN'T TAKE SOCIAL PSYCH!

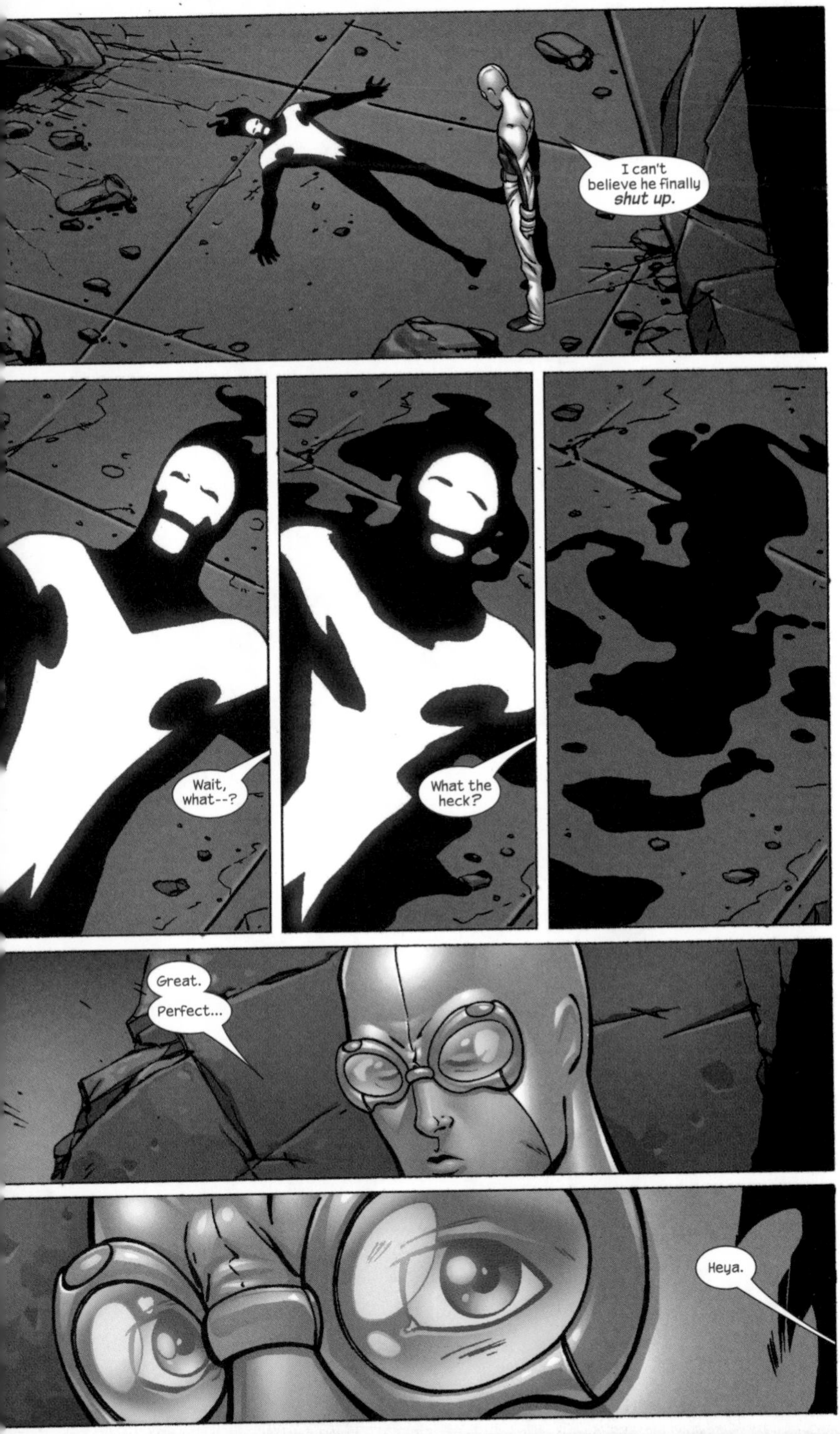
I can't believe he finally *shut up.*
Wait, what--?
What the heck?
Great.
Perfect...
Heya.

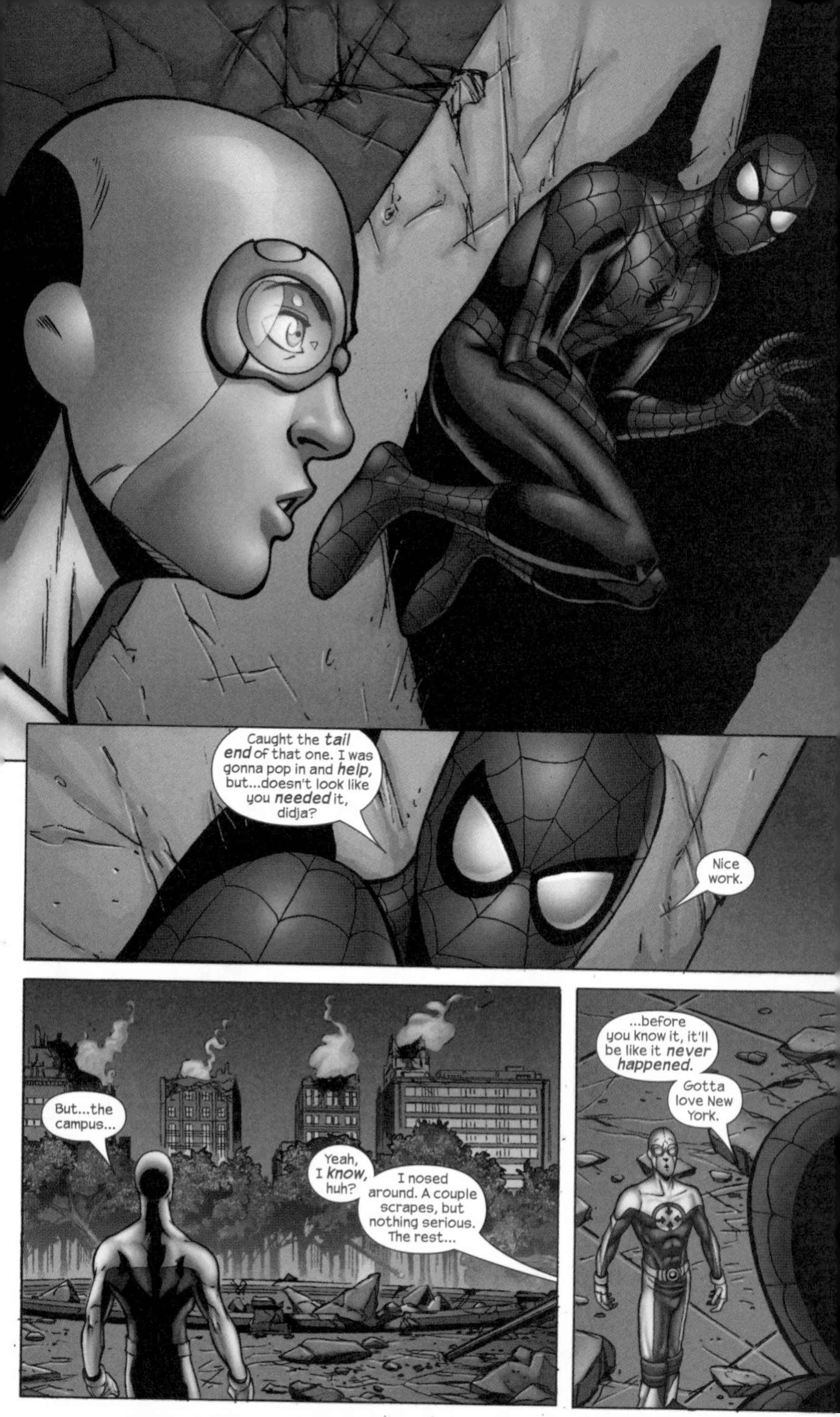
Caught the tail end of that one. I was gonna pop in and help, but...doesn't look like you needed it, didja?
Nice work.
But...the campus...
Yeah, I know, huh?
I nosed around. A couple scrapes, but nothing serious. The rest...
...before you know it, it'll be like it never happened.
Gotta love New York.

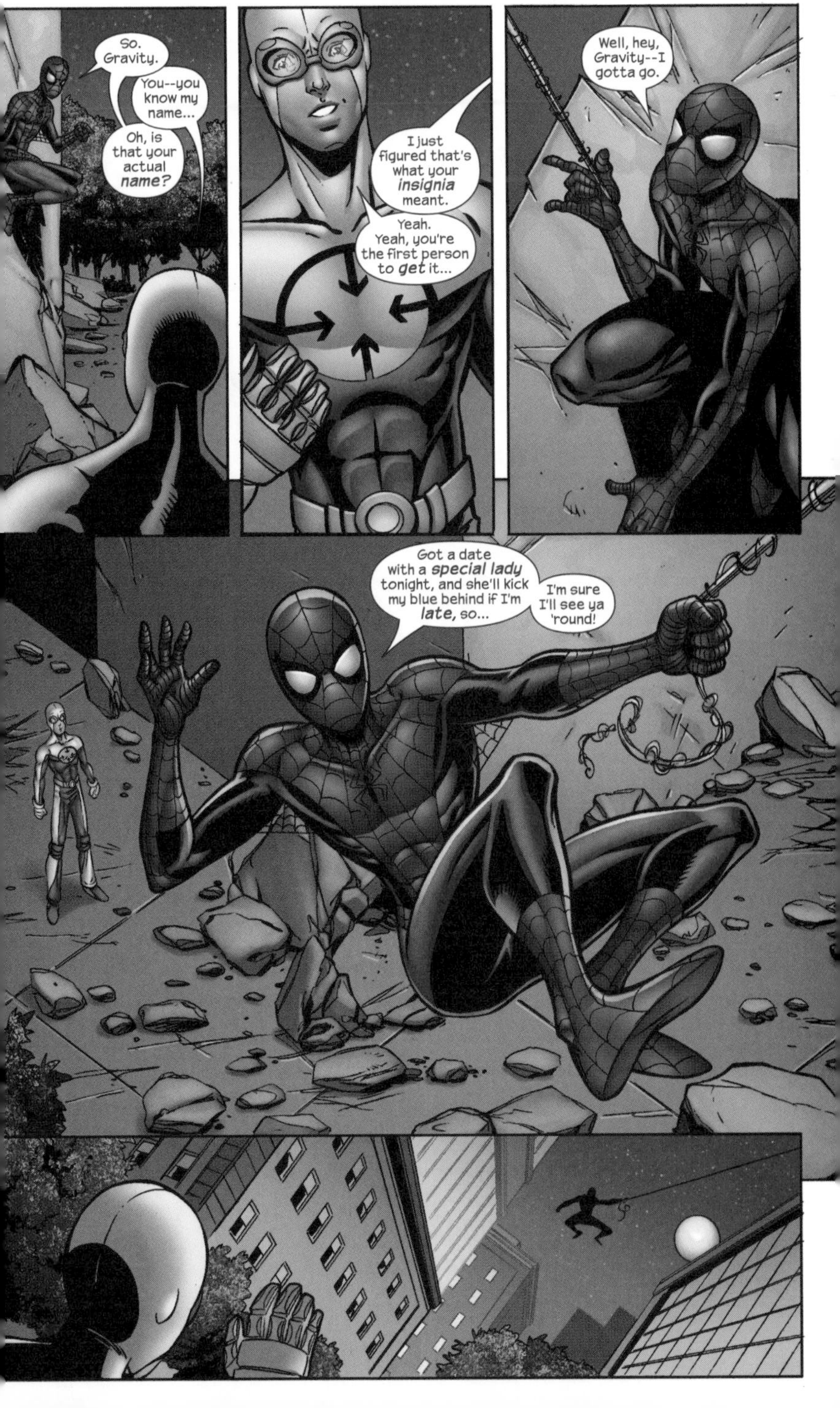
So. Gravity.
You--you know my name...
Oh, is that your actual *name?*
I just figured that's what your *insignia* meant.
Yeah. Yeah, you're the first person to *get* it...
Well, hey, Gravity--I gotta go.
Got a date with a *special lady* tonight, and she'll kick my blue behind if I'm *late*, so...
I'm sure I'll see ya 'round!

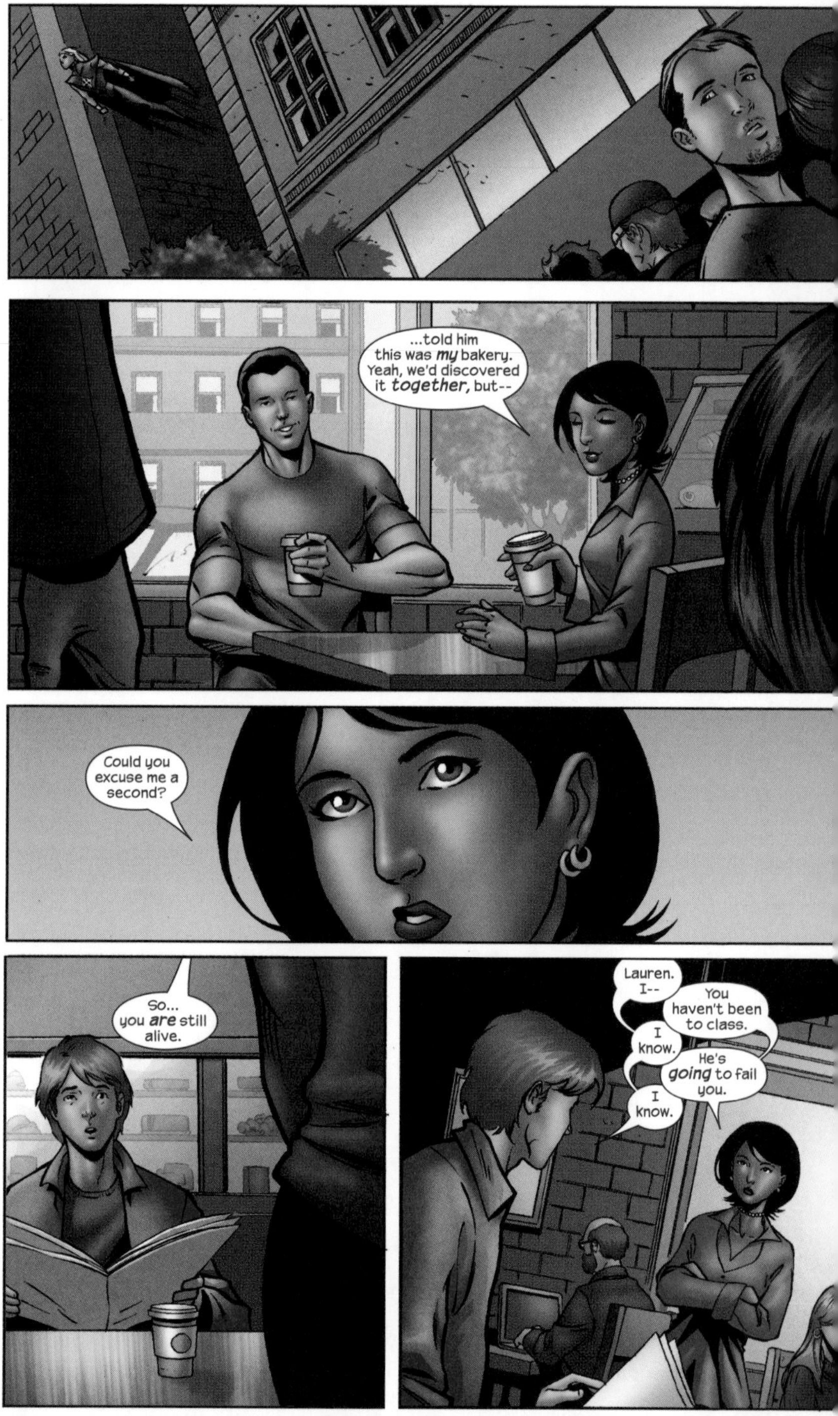
...told him this was *my* bakery. Yeah, we'd discovered it *together,* but--
Could you excuse me a second?
So... you *are* still alive.
Lauren. I--
You haven't been to class.
I know.
He's *going* to fail you.
I know.

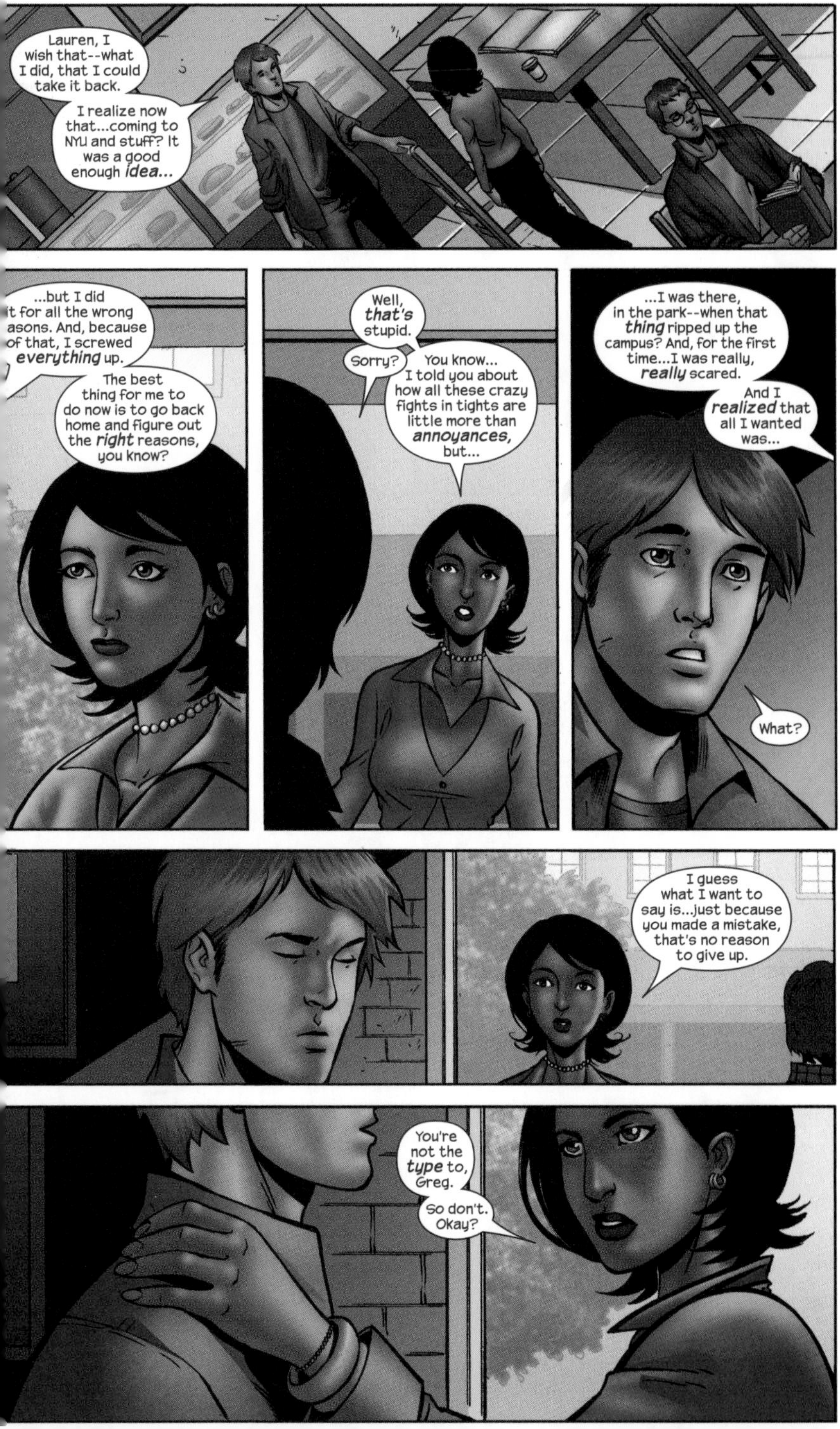
Lauren, I wish that--what I did, that I could take it back.
I realize now that...coming to NYU and stuff? It was a good enough *idea...*
...but I did it for all the wrong asons. And, because of that, I screwed *everything* up.
The best thing for me to do now is to go back home and figure out the *right* reasons, you know?
Well, *that's* stupid.
Sorry?
You know... I told you about how all these crazy fights in tights are little more than *annoyances,* but...
...I was there, in the park--when that *thing* ripped up the campus? And, for the first time...I was really, *really* scared.
And I *realized* that all I wanted was...
What?
I guess what I want to say is...just because you made a mistake, that's no reason to give up.
You're not the *type* to, Greg.
So don't. Okay?

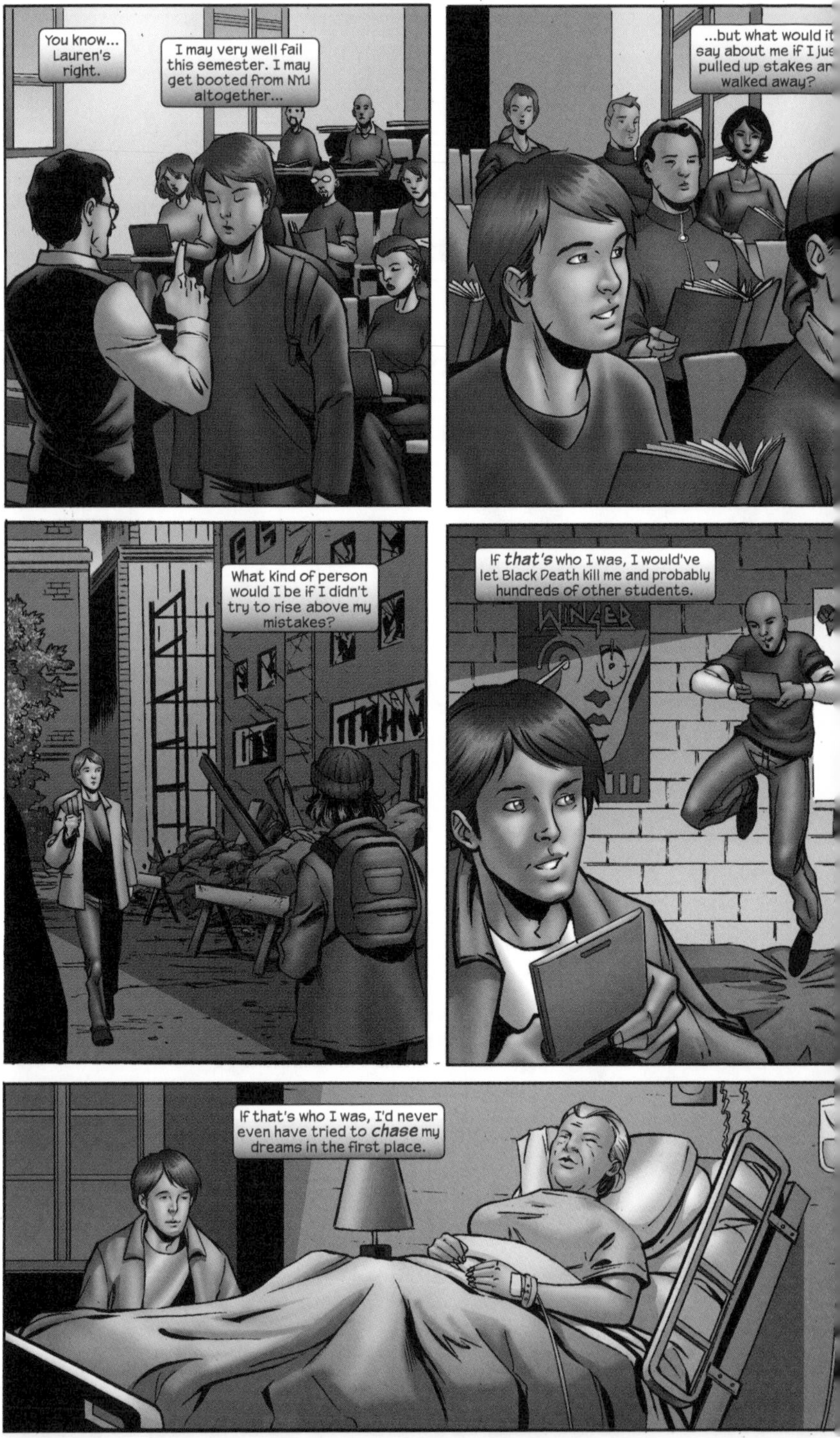

You know... Lauren's right.
I may very well fail this semester. I may get booted from NYU altogether...
...but what would it say about me if I jus pulled up stakes ar walked away?
What kind of person would I be if I didn't try to rise above my mistakes?
If *that's* who I was, I would've let Black Death kill me and probably hundreds of other students.
If that's who I was, I'd never even have tried to *chase* my dreams in the first place.

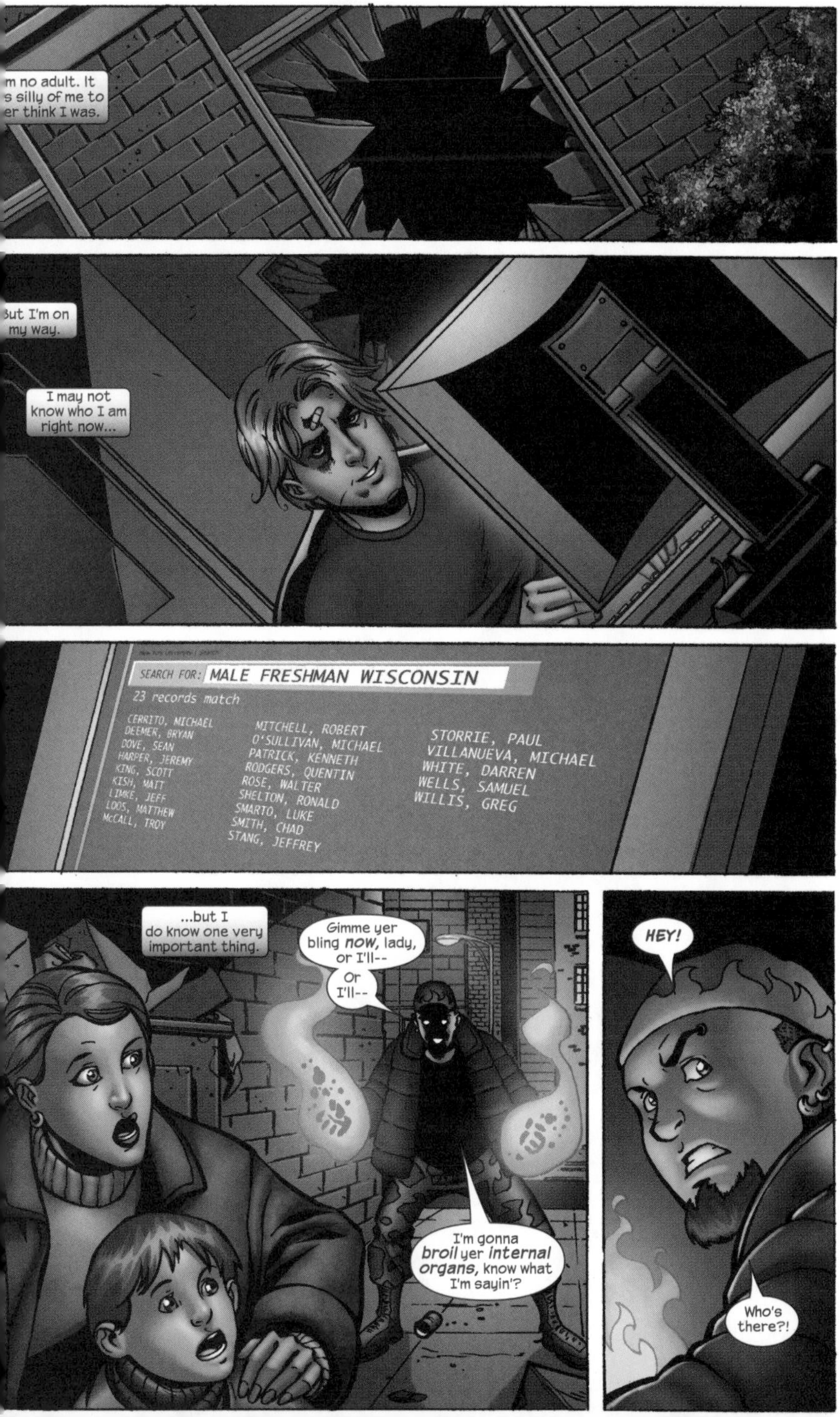
m no adult. It
s silly of me to
er think I was.
But I'm on my way.
I may not know who I am right now...
SEARCH FOR: MALE FRESHMAN WISCONSIN
23 records match
CERRITO, MICHAEL
DEEMER, BRYAN
DOVE, SEAN
HARPER, JEREMY
KING, SCOTT
KISH, MATT
LIMKE, JEFF
LOOS, MATTHEW
McCALL, TROY
MITCHELL, ROBERT
O'SULLIVAN, MICHAEL
PATRICK, KENNETH
RODGERS, QUENTIN
ROSE, WALTER
SHELTON, RONALD
SMARTO, LUKE
SMITH, CHAD
STANG, JEFFREY
STORRIE, PAUL
VILLANUEVA, MICHAEL
WHITE, DARREN
WELLS, SAMUEL
WILLIS, GREG
...but I do know one very important thing.
Gimme yer bling *now,* lady, or I'll--
Or I'll--
I'm gonna *broil* yer *internal organs,* know what I'm sayin'?
HEY!
Who's there?!

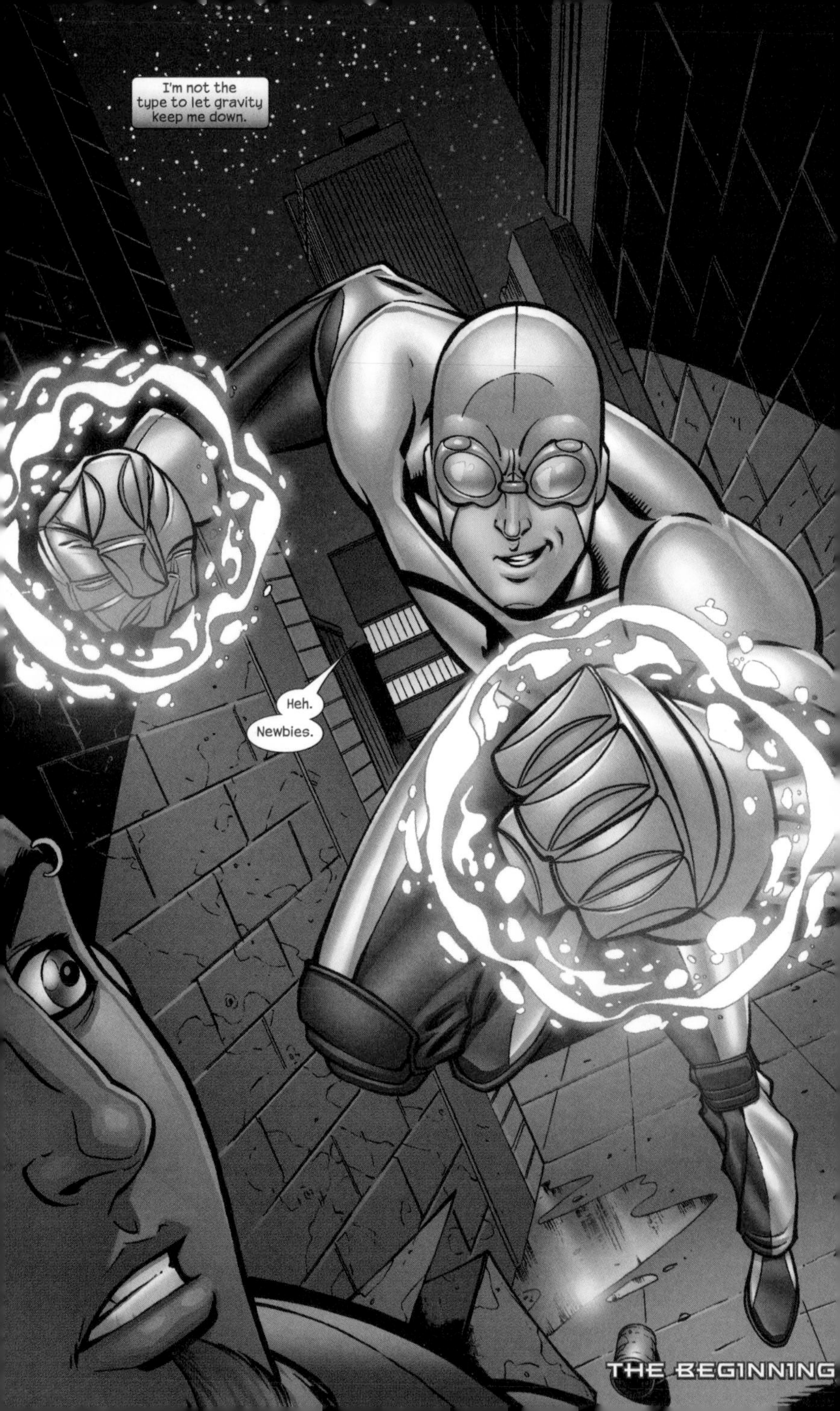
I'm not the type to let gravity keep me down.
Heh.
Newbies.
THE BEGINNING